Multimedia Security 2

SCIENCES

Image, Field Director – Laure Blanc-Feraud

Compression, Coding and Protection of Images and Videos,
Subject Head – Christine Guillemot

Multimedia Security 2

Biometrics, Video Surveillance and Multimedia Encryption

Coordinated by
William Puech

WILEY

First published 2022 in Great Britain and the United States by ISTE Ltd and John Wiley & Sons, Inc.

ISTE Ltd
27-37 St George's Road
London SW19 4EU
UK

www.iste.co.uk

John Wiley & Sons, Inc.
111 River Street
Hoboken, NJ 07030
USA

www.wiley.com

Any opinions, findings, and conclusions or recommendations expressed in this material are those of the author(s), contributor(s) or editor(s) and do not necessarily reflect the views of ISTE Group.

Library of Congress Control Number: 2022930820

British Library Cataloguing-in-Publication Data
A CIP record for this book is available from the British Library
ISBN 978-1-78945-027-9

ERC code:
PE6 Computer Science and Informatics
  PE6_5 Cryptology, security, privacy, quantum cryptography
  PE6_8 Computer graphics, computer vision, multi media, computer games

Contents

Chapter 6. Processing Encrypted Multimedia Data Using Homomorphic Encryption 173

Sébastien CANARD, Sergiu CARPOV, Caroline FONTAINE and Renaud SIRDEY

Chapter 7. Data Hiding in the Encrypted Domain 215

Pauline PUTEAUX and William PUECH

Foreword by Gildas Avoine

Gildas AVOINE
Director of the CNRS Computer Security Research Network, INSA Rennes,
Univ Rennes, IRISA, CNRS, France

French academic and industrial research in cybersecurity is at the forefront of the international scene. While France cannot claim to have sovereignty over cybersecurity technologies, it undeniably possesses a wealth of skills, as French expertise covers all areas of cybersecurity.

Research in cryptography illustrates French excellence, but it should not overshadow other domains where French influence is just as remarkable, including formal methods for security, protection of privacy, security of systems, software and networks, security of hardware systems and multimedia data security, according to the classification proposed by the CNRS Computer Security Research Network (GdR).

The security of multimedia data is covered in this book. The evolution of our society from the written word to sound and image, with the notable arrival of the mobile phone and the democratization of the Internet has brought about new security needs. These are only the beginning of the transformation of our society, and the recent deployment of videoconferencing shows that research into the security of multimedia data is constantly confronted with new scientific challenges.

The complexity of the subject and its multidisciplinary dimension, which primarily combines signal processing and cryptography, are perfectly illustrated by the variety of subjects detailed throughout this book. The chapters thus reveal the scientific obstacles to be dealt with by the community, by anchoring them in real scenarios, such as the fraudulent copying of films, the deception of artificial intelligence or the spreading of doctored images on social media.

This book, made up of two volumes, is thus promised to become a reference in the field of multimedia data security, an introduction that is both exhaustive and in-depth that students, engineers and researchers will be able to appreciate through more than 600 pages enriched with numerous references. Everyone can indulge in their favorite kind of reading, whether linear or random.

Finally, I would like to thank all of the authors for their commitment to supporting the scientific community, and I would particularly like to thank William Puech for editing this edition of the book. William, alongside Patrick Bas and then Caroline Fontaine, is responsible for the theme of multimedia data security within the Computer Security GdR, thus allowing the entire cybersecurity community to better understand this fascinating subject.

Happy reading!

Foreword by Cédric Richard

Cédric RICHARD
Director of the CNRS GdR ISIS, Côte d'Azur Observatory,
University of Côte d'Azur, Nice, France

With the relentless increase in bandwidth and storage space, as well as the proliferation of mobile devices and the development of new standards, multimedia data is affecting our societies by changing the way that we access data and information. It is also changing our relationship to culture, by transforming interactions between individuals and their relationships with organizations. Multimedia activities are present in all major sectors of activity (security, health, telecommunications, etc.) and have supported their successive developments because of the common backbone they build, from information support to the application and user.

In this context, by protecting confidentiality and copyright, verifying integrity, analyzing and authenticating content, tracing copies and controlling access, particularly critical questions about multimedia data security are being asked. For example, the protection strategies implemented must take into account the specific needs of multimedia while meeting the requirements of the means of communication, thus establishing a compromise. A wrong approach can indeed lead to excessive coding of the data, or the alteration of their perceptual quality, and thus failure in the targeted security objectives.

As an interface discipline, the art of multimedia security is difficult!

However, with this two-part book, William Puech and his co-authors take up the challenge brilliantly by painting an exhaustive and current panorama of multimedia security. They offer an in-depth analysis of authentication and hidden data embedding methods, biometric technologies and multimedia protection and encryption processes. Without giving in to an outdated formalism that could hinder the fluidity of their presentations, the authors captivate the reader by presenting the state of the art of each subject directly and in an illustrative way.

William Puech and the contributors to this book have provided considerable work to their French-speaking scientific communities of information, signal, image, vision and computer security, represented by the two appropriate French GdR groups of the CNRS. I would like to express all of my gratitude to them.

Preface

William PUECH

LIRMM, Université de Montpellier, CNRS, France

Nowadays, more than 80% of transmitted data on social media and archived in our computers, tablets, mobile phones or in the cloud is multimedia data. This multimedia data mainly includes images (photographs, computer-generated images), videos (films, animations) or sound (music, podcasts), but equally more and more three-dimensional (3D) data and scenes, for applications ranging from video games to medical data, passing through computer-aided design, video surveillance and biometrics. It is becoming necessary, urgent, not to say vital, to secure this multimedia data during its transmission or archiving, but also during its visualization. In fact, with everything digital, it is becoming increasingly easy to copy this multimedia data, to view it without rights, to appropriate it, but also to counterfeit it.

Over the last 30 years, we have observed an expansive development around multimedia security, both internationally and in France. In fact, at the French level, there are dozens of research teams in laboratories, but also a large number of industrials, who are focusing their activities on these aspects. This activity can also be found in several GdR (research groups) of the CNRS, but in particular the GdR ISIS (information, signal, image and vision) and the GdR computer security.

Multimedia security is a relatively new theme, as evidenced by the publication dates of the articles referenced in the various chapters of these two volumes. In fact, out of about 900 references, nearly 50% of them are less than 10 years old, and more than 35% are between 10 and 20 years old. Of course, let us not forget certain authors, such as Auguste Kerckhoffs (1835–1903) and Claude Shannon

(1916–2001), without whom our community would not have advanced in the same way. The history of multimedia security really begins at the end of the 1990s, with the beginning of watermarking, steganography, but in a very timid manner, this being motivated by the digitization of content and the protection of rights holders. In 2001, motivated by the attack of September 11, research in steganalysis hidden signal detection and statistical detection became the top priority. Between 2000 and 2010, there was an international explosion in watermarking security. There were also major contributions in steganography and steganalysis. During this same decade, research into securing multimedia data by specific encryption was born with the aspects of selective or partial encryption and crypto-compression, while guaranteeing the preservation of international formats and standards. From 2010, new facets of multimedia data security have emerged with *forensics* aspects, as well as statistical approaches. There has also been a strong development in signal processing in the encrypted domain, as well as the tracing of traitors. In 2020, research in forensics and steganalysis has been gaining momentum, in particular with the emergence of machine learning, and especially with the exploitation and development of deep convolutional neural networks. The recent advances in this field have varied greatly, from steganography (GAN), adversarial methods, methods by content generation, to the processing of encrypted content, including the links between learning and information leakage, applications in biometrics and "real-life" content analysis.

This project of works began more than two years ago and has really meant a lot to me. In fact, at the French level, we have a certain strength in this field, and numerous gems that we have brought to light. Nothing could have been achieved without the support of the GdR ISIS and GdR computer security. It is largely because of these GdR that we have succeeded in tracking research activities in the field of multimedia security from a French point of view. The towns represented in these two works illustrate the richness and national diversity (Caen, Grenoble, La Rochelle, Lille, Limoges, Lyon, Montpellier, Paris, Poitiers, Rennes, Saint-Étienne and Troyes), because some of these cities, as we will see during our reading, are represented by several laboratories and/or universities.

As we will be able to see throughout these two volumes, even if they are grouped around multimedia security, the research themes are very broad and the applications varied. In addition, the fields cover a broad spectrum, from signal processing to cryptography, including image processing, information theory, encoding and compression. Many of the topics in multimedia security are a game of cat and mouse, where the defender of rights must regularly transform into a counter-attacker in order to resist the attacker.

The first volume primarily focuses around the authentication of multimedia data, codes and the embedding of hidden data, from the side of the defender as well as the attacker. Concerning the embedding of hidden data, it also addresses the aspects of invisibility, color, tracing and 3D data, as well as the detection of hidden messages in images by steganalysis. The second volume mainly focuses on the biometrics, protection, integrity and encryption of multimedia data. It covers aspects such as image and video crypto-compression, homomorphic encryption, the embedding of hidden data in the encrypted domain, as well as the sharing of secrets. I invite the reader, whether they are a student, teacher, researcher or industrial to immerse themselves in these works, not necessarily by following the intended order, but going from one chapter to another, as well as from one volume to another.

These two volumes, even though they cover a broad spectrum in multimedia security, are not meant to be exhaustive. I think, and hope, that a third volume will complete these first two. In fact, I am thinking of sound (music and speech), video surveillance/video protection, camera authentication, privacy protection, as well as the attacks and counter-attacks that we see every day.

I would like to thank all of the authors, chapter managers, their co-authors, their collaborators and their teams for all of their hard work. I am very sorry that I have had to ask them many times to find the best compromises between timing, content and length of the chapters. Thank you to Jean-Michel, Laurent, Philippe ($\times 2$), Patrick ($\times 2$), Teddy, Sébastien ($\times 2$), Christophe, Iuliia, Petra, Vincent, Wassim, Caroline and Pauline! Thank you all for your openness and good humor! I would also thank the GdR ISIS and computer Security through Gildas and Cédric, but also Christine and Laure for their proofreading, as well as for establishing a connection with ISTE Ltd. I would also like to thank all of the close collaborators with whom I have worked for more than 25 years on the various themes that I have had the chance to address. PhD students, engineers, interns and colleagues, all of them will recognize themselves, whether they are in my research team (ICAR team) or in my research laboratory (LIRMM, Université de Montpellier, CNRS).

In particular, I would like to thank Vincent, Iuliia, Sébastien and Pauline for having accepted to embark on this adventure. Pauline, in addition to writing certain chapters, has been a tremendous collaborator for the advancement of this book. All of those responsible for the chapters have seen that, Pauline has been my shadow over the past two years, to ensure that these two works could see the light of day in 2021. Thank you Pauline! To conclude, I would like to warmly thank all of the members of my family, and in particular Magali and our three children, Carla, Loriane and Julian, whom I love very much and who have constantly supported me.

November 2021

1

Biometrics and Applications

**Christophe CHARRIER[1], Christophe ROSENBERGER[1]
and Amine NAIT-ALI[2]**

[1]*GREYC, Normandy University, University of Caen, ENSICAEN, CNRS, France*
[2]*LISSI, University of Paris-Est Créteil Val de Marne, France*

Biometrics is a technology that is now common in our daily lives. It is notably used to secure access to smartphones or computers. This chapter aims to provide readers with an overview of this technology, its history and the solutions provided by research on societal and scientific issues.

1.1. Introduction

There are three generic ways to verify or determine an individual's identity: (1) what we know (PIN, password, etc.); (2) what we have (badge, smart card, etc.); and (3) what we are (fingerprint, face, etc.) or what we know how to do (keystroke dynamics, gait, etc.). Biometrics is concerned with this last set of approaches. Biometrics, and more precisely security biometrics, consists of verifying or identifying the identity of an individual based on their morphological characteristics (such as fingerprints), behavioral characteristics (such as voice) or biological characteristics (such as DNA).

The biometric features by which an individual's identity can be verified are called biometric modalities. Examples of some biometric modalities are shown in Figure 1.1. These modalities are based on the analysis of individual data, and are

---

For a color version of all figures in this chapter, see www.iste.co.uk/puech/multimedia2.zip.

Multimedia Security 2,
coordinated by William PUECH. © ISTE Ltd 2022.

generally grouped into three categories: biological, behavioral and morphological biometrics. Biological biometrics is based on the analysis of biological data related to the individual (saliva, DNA, etc.). Behavioral biometrics concerns the analysis of an individual's behavior (gait, keyboard dynamics, etc.). Morphological biometrics relates to particular physical traits that are permanent and unique to any individual (fingerprints, face, etc.).

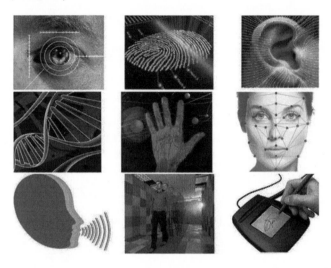

Figure 1.1. *Examples of biometric modalities used to verify or determine the identity of an individual*

Nowadays, the use of facial or fingerprint recognition has come to feel natural to many people, notably among the younger generations. Biometric technology is part of our everyday lives (used for border control, smartphones, e-payment, etc.). Figure 1.2 shows the spectacular evolution and market prospects of this technology. In an increasingly digital world, biometrics can be used to verify the identity of an individual using a digital service (social network or e-commerce). While fingerprints and facial or iris recognition are among the most well-known biometric modalities (notably due to their use in television series or movies), a very wide range of biometric data can be captured from an individual's body or from digital traces. An individual can be recognized in the physical and digital worlds using information from both spheres.

The use of this technology raises a number of questions: how new is this technology? How does a biometric system work? What are the main areas of current and future research? These questions will be addressed in the three main sections of this chapter: the history of biometrics (section 1.2), the technological foundations of biometrics (section 1.3) and the scientific issues and perspectives (section 1.4).

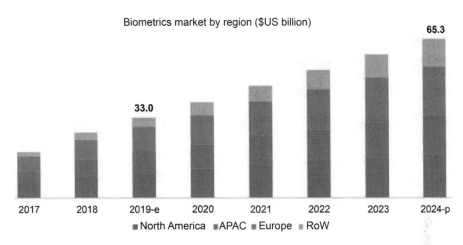

Figure 1.2. *Evolution and perspectives of the biometrics market (source: Biometric System Market, October 2019)*

1.2. History of biometrics

Biometrics may be as old as humanity itself. In essence, biometrics relates to a measurement that can be performed on living things, and in a security context, it refers to the recognition of individuals by their physical and/or behavioral characteristics. This property of recognition is primarily human based, and not dependent on technology. As humans, we recognize one another through aspects such as facial features, hands or gait; the human brain has the capacity to distinguish, compare and, consequently, recognize individuals. In reality, biometrics – as we now understand it – is simply a technological replication of what the human brain can do. Key aims include speed, reproducibility, precision and memorization of information for populations of theoretically infinite size (Nait-Ali and Fournier 2012).

From the literature, we find that biometrics began to be conceptualized several centuries BC, notably in the Babylonian civilization, where clay tablets used for trading purposes have been found to contain fingerprints. Similarly, fingerprinted seals appear to have been used in ancient China and ancient Egypt. It was not until the 14th century, however, that a Persian book, entitled *Jaamehol-Tawarikh*, mentioned the use of fingerprints for individual identification. Other later publications concerning the fingerprint and its characteristics include the work of G. Nehemiah (1684), M. Malpighi (1686), and a book published in 1788, in which the anatomist J. Mayer highlighted the unique nature of papillary traces.

It was only during the industrial revolution, notably in the mid-19th century, that the ability to clearly identify individuals became crucial, particularly due to an intensification of population mobility as a result of the development of commercial exchanges. The first true identification procedures were established in 1858, when William Herschel (working for the Indian Civil Service at the time) first used and included palm prints, then fingerprints, in the administrative files of employees (see Figure 1.3). Later, several medical scientists, anthropologists and statisticians, including Henry Faulds, Francis Galton and Juan Vucetich, developed their own studies of fingerprints. Vucetich was even responsible for the first instance of criminal identification using this technique, which took place in Argentina in 1892 (the Francisca Rojas case).

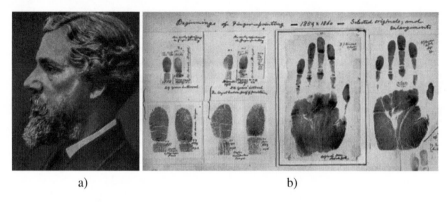

a)   b)

Figure 1.3. *a) William James Herschel (1833–1917), and b) example of palm and finger prints (source: public domain)*

A further turning point in biometrics occurred in the 1870s when Alphonse Bertillon, a French police officer, began to implement anthropometric techniques which came to be known as the Bertillon System, or "bertillonnage". Broadly speaking, this involved taking multiple measurements of the human body, including the face and hands. By combining these measurements with a photograph of the person and other physical descriptions (see Figure 1.4), Bertillon developed files which could be used to identify criminals and delinquents, even if they were disguised or using a false identity (see Figure 1.5). The first criminal identification using this technique in France occurred in 1902: Henri Léon Scheffer was identified by matching fingerprints taken from a crime scene with the information on his anthropological documents. At this time, the Bertillon system was used to a greater or lesser extent in many countries around the world.

Some 30 years later (1936), an ophthalmologist, Frank Burch, introduced the concept of identifying individuals by iris characteristics, although Burch did not develop this idea into an identification system. Biometrics as we now understand it began to take shape in the 1960s, drawing on technological advances in electronics, computing and data processing. The first semi-automatic facial recognition system was developed by the American Woodrow W. Bledsoe (Bledsoe and Chan 1965). The system consists of manually taking the coordinates of the characteristic points of the face from a photograph. These coordinates are then stored in a database and processed by computer by calculating distances with respect to reference points. In the same year, the first model of the acoustic speech signal was proposed by Gunnar Fan, in Sweden, laying the foundations for speech recognition. The first automatic biometric systems began to appear in the 1970s. Notable examples include a system for recognizing individuals by hand shape (1974), a system for extracting minutiae from fingerprints (FBI, 1975), a facial recognition system (Texas Instruments, 1976), a patent for a system for extracting signature characteristics for individual verification (1977), a patent for an individual verification system using 3D features of the hand (David Sidlauskas, 1985), a patent for the concept of recognizing individuals by the vascular network features at the back of the eye (Joseph Rice, 1995) and a patent for the concept of identifying individuals by characteristics of the iris (Leonard Flom and Aran Safir, 1986); the algorithm for this final system was later patented by John Daugman in 1994.

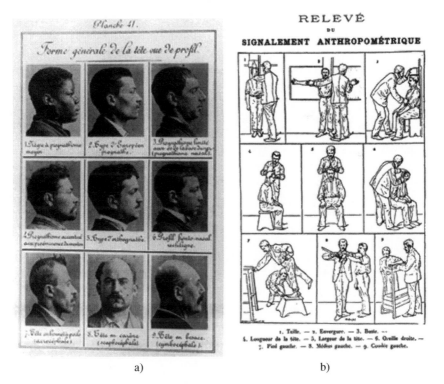

Figure 1.4. *Plate taken from the Identification Anthropométrique journal (1893). a) Criminal types. b) Anthropometric file*

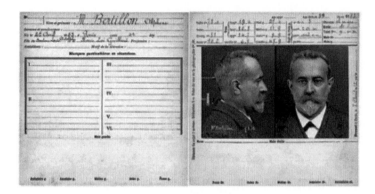

Figure 1.5. *Example of an anthropometric file*
using the Bertillon system
(source: public domain)

The 1980s–1990s also saw an upsurge in activity with respect to facial recognition, notably with the application of principal component analysis (PCA) techniques by Kirby and Sirovich in 1988 (Kirby and Sirovich 1990), then the introduction of Eigenfaces by Turk and Pentland (1991). Turk and Pentland's paper was well received by the biometrics community, and has been cited over 18,500 times at the time of writing (2020). The authors demonstrated facial recognition using a limited number of parameters (compared to the number of pixels in a digital image), permitting the use of real-time applications. The performance of this method was quickly surpassed in the 2000s by a wide range of new data-processing approaches, and thanks to developments in computer science and electronics, an accelerating factor in the design of biometric systems. Following on from early uses for security projects, including industrial, military and governmental applications, biometrics has gradually gained ground in the field of commercial products and services. For example, fingerprint authentication (e.g. Touch-ID) was first integrated into smartphones in 2013, followed by facial recognition (e.g. Face-ID) in 2017. Research and development in this area is currently booming, and biometrics research, applications and modalities continue to expand at a rapid pace. The socioeconomic implications of the technology are likely to prove decisive in the coming decades; the story of biometrics is far from over.

1.3. The foundations of biometrics

In this section, we shall present key foundational elements involved in biometrics and highlight the scientific issues at play in this domain.

1.3.1. *Uses of biometrics*

Before going into detail concerning the operation of biometrics, it is interesting to consider its applications. The first objective of biometrics is identity verification, that is, to provide proof to corroborate an assertion of the type "I am Mr X". A facial photograph or fingerprint acts in a similar way to a password; the system compares the image with a pre-recorded reference to ensure that the user is who they claim to be. The second application of biometrics concerns the identification of individuals in cases where their collaboration is not generally required (e.g. facial recognition based on video surveillance footage). Finally, biometrics is often used to secure access to places or tools (premises, smartphones and computers), for border control (automated border crossing systems), by police services (identity control) or for payment security (notably on smartphones), as shown in Figure 1.6.

Figure 1.6. *Some applications of biometrics*
(physical access control, social networks)

1.3.2. *Definitions*

In order to recognize or identify an individual k, reference information R_k must be collected for the individual during an initial enrollment phase. During the authentication/identification phase, a new sample is captured, denoted as E. A biometric system will compare sample E to R_k in an attempt to authenticate an individual k, or to multiple references in a biometric database in cases of identification. A decision is then made (is this the right person?) by comparing the comparison score (in this case, taken as a distance) to a pre-defined threshold T:

$$D = 1_{score(R_k,E)<T}$$

The threshold T is defined by the application. In the case of distance, the lower the threshold, the stricter the system is, because it requires a small distance between the sample and the individual's reference as proof of identity. A strict (high security) threshold will result in false rejections of legitimate users (measured by the FRR, false rejection rate). A looser threshold will result in an increased possibility of imposture (measured by the FAR, false acceptance rate). To set the threshold T for a given application, we consider the maximum permissible FAR for the system; the FRR results from this choice. As an example, consider a high security setting with an acceptable FAR rate of one in a million attempts. In this context, we expect an FRR of less than 2%. The equal error rate (EER) is the error obtained when the threshold is set so that the FRR is equal to the FAR. The EER is often used as an indicator of the performance of a biometric system, although using the associated threshold to parameterize a system is not of any particular practical use; it is simply easier to understand the performance of a system on the basis of a single EER value.

1.3.3. *Biometric modalities*

There are three main groups of biometric modalities (types of biometric information): morphology (part of the person's body, such as the face or the iris), behavior (an individual action, such as the voice or the way of signing) and physiology (such as DNA). The first two modalities are the most widespread in transactional contexts due to processing time limitations. These three categories of biometric modalities are illustrated below, represented by DNA, signature dynamics and fingerprints.

Figure 1.7. *Illustrations of the three categories of biometric modalities: DNA, signature dynamics and fingerprints*

Almost any morphological or behavioral characteristic may be considered as a biometric characteristic, as long as it satisfies the following properties (Prabhakar *et al.* 2003):

– universality: all people to be identified must possess the characteristic;

– uniqueness: the information should be as different as possible from one person to the next;

– permanence: the collected information must remain present throughout the individual's lifetime;

– collectability: it must be possible to collect and measure the information in order to permit comparison;

– acceptability: the system must respect certain criteria (ease of acquisition, rapidity, etc.) in order to permit use.

Criterion \ Modality	U	N	P	C	A	E
DNA	Yes	Yes	Yes	Low	Low	*****
Blood	Yes	No	Yes	Low	No	*
Gait	Yes	No	Low	Yes	Yes	***
Typing dynamics	Yes	Yes	Low	Yes	Yes	****
Voice	Yes	Yes	Faible	Yes	Yes	****
Iris	Yes	Yes	Yes	Yes	Low	*****
Retina	Yes	Yes	Yes	Yes	Low	*****
Face	Yes	No	Low	Yes	Yes	****
Hand geometry	Yes	No	Yes	Yes	Yes	****
Veins on hand	Yes	Yes	Yes	Yes	Yes	*****
Ear	Yes	Yes	Yes	Yes	Yes	*****
Fingerprint	Yes	Yes	Yes	Yes	Yes	****

Table 1.1. *Comparison of biometric modalities based on the following properties: (U) universality, (N) uniqueness, (P) permanence, (C) collectability, (A) acceptability and (E) performance. For performance, the number of stars is linked to the value of the equal error rate (EER) obtained in the state of the art source: Mahier* et al. *(2008)*

Not all biometric features have these properties, or they may have them, but to different degrees. Table 1.1, taken from Mahier *et al.* (2008), compares the main biometric modalities according to the properties listed above. As we see from this table, no characteristic is ideal; different modalities may be more or less suitable to particular applications. For example, DNA-based analysis is one of the most effective techniques for verifying an individual's identity or for identification (Stolovitzky *et al.* 2002). However, it cannot be used for logical or physical access control, both due to the computation time and the fact that nobody would be willing to provide a sample of their blood for verification purposes. The choice of modality is thus based on a compromise between some or all of these properties according to the needs of each application. Note that the choice of the biometric modality may also depend on local cultures. In Asia, methods requiring physical contact, such as fingerprints, are not widely accepted for hygiene reasons; contactless methods are more widespread, and more readily accepted, in this setting.

1.4. Scientific issues

Biometrics is a rapidly evolving field as new operational applications emerge in our daily lives (e.g. unlocking smartphones via facial recognition). Several scientific issues relating to biometrics, resulting from the new needs of this technology, are discussed below.

1.4.1. *Presentation attacks*

There are many ways of attacking a biometric system (Ratha *et al.* 2001). An attacker may alter the storage of biometric credentials (e.g. replace a user's biometric credentials in order to spoof the system), or replace a sub-module, such as the decision module, so that it returns a positive response to any attempt. In this section, we shall focus on presentation attacks, which consist of presenting the capture subsystem with biometric data intended to alter the operation of the biometric system. This type of attack can be quite easy to perform, for example by presenting a photo of the user's face printed on paper. Impostors may also present biometric systems with falsified biometric data (e.g. a gelatin fingerprint), with or without the participation of the individual concerned. One particularly active area of research concerns the development of hardware or software mechanisms to detect this type of attack (Galbally *et al.* 2019).

The most common attack of this type is carried out on facial recognition systems. Facial recognition technology has come on in leaps and bounds since its invention in the 1970s, and is now the most "natural" of all biometric measures. By the same token, it has become a major focus for hackers. For example, Grigory Bakunov has developed a solution that can confuse facial recognition devices, by designing an algorithm that creates specific makeup arrangements to fool facial recognition software (see Figure 1.8(a)).

In late 2017, a Vietnamese company successfully bypassed the Face ID facial recognition feature of Apple's iPhone X using a mask (see Figure 1.8(b)).

At the same time, researchers at a German company developed an attack technique to bypass Windows 10 Hello facial authentication. A key element of the attack appears to be taking a picture of the authenticated user with a near-infrared (IR) camera, since Windows Hello uses infrared imaging to unlock Windows devices (see Figure 1.8(c)).

In May 2018, *Forbes* magazine reported that researchers at the University of Toronto (Canada) had developed an algorithm (privacy filter) that confuses facial recognition software. The software changes the value of specific pixels in the image posted online. These changes, imperceptible to the human visual system (HVS), confuse the recognition algorithms.

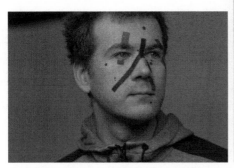

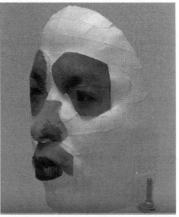

a) Special makeup designed to hack facial
recognition systems

b) Mask used to hack the Face ID
facial recognition function on Apple's
iPhone X

c) Photo used to hack the Hello facial
recognition function on Windows 10

Figure 1.8. *Examples of techniques used
to hack facial recognition systems*

One response to these types of attack is to use video rather than still images (Matta and Dugelay 2009). Some operators use interviews, via video conferencing software, to authenticate a person. Unfortunately, new attacks have already been developed for video authentication, and we can expect these attacks to become more sophisticated in the years to come. Video streams can now be manipulated in real time to show the facial reactivity of a counterfeiter on top of another person's face (Thies *et al*. 2016), or through face swapping (Bitouk *et al*. 2008).

Numerous works have been published on this subject, mostly by researchers in the Image Forensics community (Redi *et al.* 2011; Yeap *et al.* 2018; Roy *et al.* 2020); the main approach involves looking for abnormalities in images or flows to identify locations where manipulations have occurred. Modifications are detected on the basis of inconsistencies or estimated abnormalities on image points, inconsistencies in sensor noise, recompressions, internal or external recopies and inconsistencies in terms of illumination or contours. Several technological challenges have been launched by DARPA, IEEE and NIST in the United States and by the DGA in France (including a DEFALS with participation from EURECO, UTT and SURYS) to measure the effectiveness of this type of method. It should be noted that significant progress has recently been made because of deep learning techniques. Passive detection can also draw on knowledge of the particularities of attacks, such as what is known to happen during morphing between two images (Raghavendra *et al.* 2016), or on the history of operations on the images in question (Ramachandra and Busch 2017).

However, the effectiveness of these countermeasures is beginning to be undermined by advances in inpainting technologies using deep learning, which create highly credible computer-generated images, produced in real time, using just a few photos of the person whose identity is being spoofed and a video stream of the spoofer responding (potentially) to all of the requests of the preceding tests. However, face spoofing can be detected in video streams by focusing on known features of the processed images, such as specific 3D characteristics of a face (Galbally *et al.* 2014). Evidently, more work is urgently needed in this area.

1.4.2. *Acquisition of new biometric data or hidden biometrics*

The objective here is to collect known biometric data by new capture methods (3D, multi-spectral (Venkatesh *et al.* 2019) and motion (Buriro *et al.* 2019)), or capture new biometric information (for example, the electrical signal from an individual's body (Khorshid *et al.* 2020)). The goal is to propose new information which offers improved individual recognition, or which has a greater capacity to detect presentation attacks.

Elsewhere, considerable efforts have been made in recent years in exploring a specific form of biometrics, known as hidden biometrics. The principle consists of identifying or verifying people on the basis of physical characteristics, which are not accessible by traditional techniques, or which are not directly observable or perceivable by humans. This property makes systems particularly robust to attacks.

Hidden biometrics also concerns features that vary over time, that cannot be quantified at a given moment, and which can only be predicted (e.g. variations resulting from aging) or recovered (e.g. by rejuvenation). In this case, we speak of forward or backward prediction.

Certain modalities used in hidden biometrics rely on technologies developed in the fields of medicine or forensic science, particularly for data acquisition. Examples include the use of electrocardiograms (ECG), electroencephalograms (EEG) or electromyographs (EMG), involving a variety of imaging techniques (infrared, thermal, ultrasound, etc.) (Nait-Ali 2019a, 2019b).

In this section, we shall focus on three modalities used in hidden biometrics, namely human brain biometrics, hand biometrics and digital facial aging/rejuvenation.

In 2011, researchers showed that a biological signature, the "Braincode", can be obtained from the human brain and used to distinguish between individuals. Both 2D and 3D processing approaches have been explored, using images obtained by magnetic resonance imaging (MRI). In the 2D approach, one idea is to extract biometric features from a single specific axial slice, as shown in Figure 1.9. Defining a region of interest (ROI) in the form of a crown, using an algorithm similar to the one used in iris biometrics, a recognition rate of around 98.25% can be achieved. In the 3D approach, the whole volume of the image obtained via the MRI scan is used in order to obtain a Braincode. The idea is to explore the whole volume image obtained by MRI to extract the Braincode. In an article published in Aloui *et al.* (2018), the envelope of the brain was estimated, highlighting the structure of convolutions, as shown in Figure 1.10.

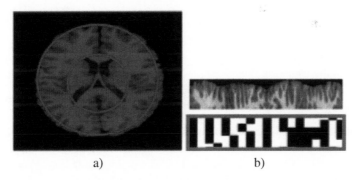

a)   b)

Figure 1.9. *Brain biometry via MRI. a) Determination of a region of interest (ROI) from an axial slice. b) Extraction of "brainprint" characteristics using a similar approach to iris biometrics*

While this modality cannot currently be used for practical applications, notably due to its technical complexity, cost and low level of user acceptability, future uses are not to be excluded.

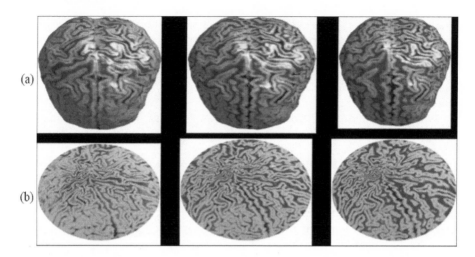

Figure 1.10. *Hidden brain biometrics: extraction of a brainprint from MRI images of the brain. a) Curvilinear envelopes, estimated using one brain at three different depths (10 voxels-1 cm). b) 2D projection of the estimated envelopes*

Palm biometrics in the visible or infrared range (vein biometrics) are potentially vulnerable to attack. One reason for this relates to the superficiality of features extracted from the region of interest.

Technically, this risk can be considerably reduced by using a modality based on X-ray imaging. In this context, experiments have been carried out on many samples; researchers have shown that a biometric signature can be extracted by modeling the phalanges of the hand (see Figure 1.11 (Kabbara *et al.* 2013, 2015; Nait-Ali 2019a)).

In the algorithm in question, the image is segmented in order to highlight all of the phalanges. Each phalanx is then modeled using a number of parameters, which are then concatenated to create a biometric signature. Evidently, this approach raises questions concerning the impact of X-rays on user health. The study in question took the recommendations of the National Council on Radiation Protection and Measurements (NCRP) into account, limiting the radiation dose of the systems to 0.1 μSv/scan to ensure user safety.

1.4.3. *Quality of biometric data*

The quality of biometric data is not always easy to estimate. While quality metrics have been established for morphological modalities such as fingerprints (Yao *et al.* 2016b), much work is still needed in the case of behavioral modalities.

Work carried out in recent years has highlighted the importance of sample quality for recognition systems or comparison algorithms. The performance of a biometric system depends, to a great extent, on the quality of the sample image. Over the last decade, many research works have focused on defining biometric data quality metrics for the face (Nasrollahi and Moeslund 2008; Wasnik *et al.* 2017), vein networks (Qin and El Yacoubi 2017) and, especially, fingerprints (Tabassi *et al.* 2011; Yao *et al.* 2015a; Liu *et al.* 2016).

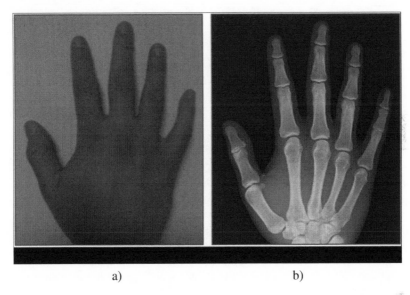

a)   b)

Figure 1.11. *Hidden palmar biometrics. a) Imaging in the visible domain. b) X-ray imaging is more robust against attacks. Once the phalanges have been modeled, the biometric signature can be extracted*

The development of a quality measurement for biometric data centers on an objective demonstration of the superiority of one indicator over others. In the case of image quality, the aim is to develop an algorithm that assigns quality ratings that correlate perfectly with human judgment; in biometrics, a quality measurement must combine elements of image quality with elements relating to the quality of the extracted biometric characteristics, ensuring that a system will perform well. In this case, the working framework is different and the real-world situation is not fully known, and this can prove problematic.

Yao *et al.* (2015a) have proposed a methodology for quantifying the performance of a quality metric for biometric data. Their approach is generic, and can be applied to any modality. The method estimates the proximity of a metric to an optimal judgment.

1.4.3.1. *Relevance of a quality metric*

The principle of the proposed method consists of evaluating the relevance of a metric for a user enrollment task using a database of biometric samples from several users. In this case, a heuristic is needed to designate the user's reference sample. Once this choice has been made, all legitimate scores in the database are calculated by comparing the samples with the reference of each user. The same is done for imposture scores, by comparing a reference with the samples of all other individuals in the database. These scores are used to compute the FRR and FAR for different values of the decision threshold. These values are then used to calculate the DET curve (evolution of the quantity of false rejections as a function of false acceptances), the EER and the area under the DET curve (AUC).

Two co-existing strategies may be used to choose the reference sample for a user:

1) *choice of the first sample* as the point of reference for an individual. This approach is widespread, and is considered as the default option (see Figure 1.12(a));

2) *choice of a reference based on a heuristic* (see Figure 1.12(b)).

The heuristic may be based on a measurement of sample quality. In this case, the sample with the highest quality is selected as the reference sample for the user.

Another option is to use a heuristic based on the minimum AUC value. This comes down to determining the optimal choice of a reference sample with respect to the performance of the biometric system in question (lowest AUC).

A further alternative is to choose the sample which results in the highest value of the AUC.

Figure 1.13 shows the performances obtained on a biometric database for different reference choice heuristics. The DET curve using the worst sample as a reference is shown in black, and the DET curve using the best sample is shown in green. We see that the choice of reference results in system performances with an AUC of between 0.0352 and 0.2338. Using two metrics, we obtain performances of 0.0991 (blue) and 0.0788 (red). Metric 1 (blue curve) is considered less efficient than metric 2 (red curve). This demonstrates the possibility for improvement in sample quality measurements.

1.4.3.2. *Metric behavior*

Twelve biometric databases from the FVC competition (Maltoni *et al.* 2009) were used to study the behavior of metrics: FVC 2000 (DB1, DB2, DB3, DB4), FVC 2002 (DB1, DB2, DB3, DB4) and FVC 2004 (DB1, DB2, DB3, DB4). Five additional synthetic fingerprint databases of different qualities were also generated using SFINGE (Cappelli *et al.* 2004): SFINGE0 (containing fingerprints of varying quality), SFINGEA (excellent quality), SFINGEB (good quality), SFINGEC (average quality) and SFINGED (poor quality).

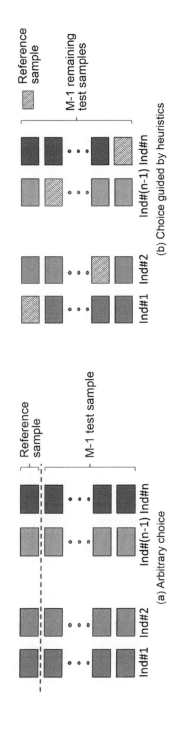

Figure 1.12. *Examples of methods used in selecting enrollment samples*

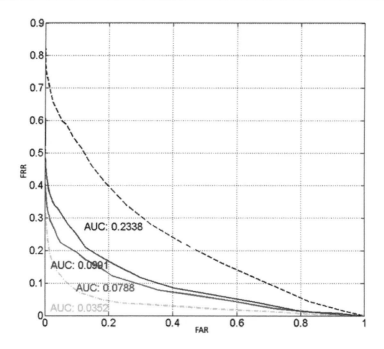

Figure 1.13. *Representation of performance as a function of reference choice: worst choice (black), best choice (green), choice using metric 1 (blue) and choice using metric 2 (red)*

Seven current fingerprint quality metrics were tested:

1) *NFIQ*: this metric classifies fingerprint images by five quality levels, based on a neural network (Tabassi *et al.* 2011). This metric has served as the industry standard for the past 15 years, and is included in all commercial biometric systems.

2) *NFIQ 2.0*: Olsen *et al.* (2013) trained a two-layer self-organizing map (SOM neural network) to obtain a SOM unit activation histogram. The trained characteristic is then input into a random forest in order to estimate genuine matching scores. NFIQ 2.0 is the new ISO standard for measuring fingerprint quality.

3) *OCL*: Lim *et al.* (2002) developed a quality measure based on a weighted combination of local and global quality scores, estimated as a function of several characteristics, such as the orientation certainty level.

4) *QMF*: this metric is calculated by considering several different aspects, such as (1) the fingerprint image itself (using blind image quality evaluation and texture functions) and (2) the associated minutia model (Yao *et al.* 2015a). The quality metric is implemented via a linear combination of quality characteristics.

5) *NBIS*: this quality indicator is a simple measure, based on the quality of minutia extracted by the NIST NBIS program (Ko 2007). The metric corresponds to the mean value of the quality of the minutia in the model.

6) *MSEG*: this measure is based on cutting out the pixels from the foreground of a poor-quality image (Yao *et al.* 2016a).

7) *MQF*: an original metric that calculates a quality score based on a minutia model (Yao *et al.* 2015b). Metrics of this type present a significant advantage for biometric systems integrated into chips or smart objects, where computation and storage constraints in the secure part of the chip mean that only the minutia model is available.

Table 1.2 shows the quality score obtained from the metrics tested on the first sample of four datasets. Note that, for NFIQ, a low value corresponds to high fingerprint quality, while for all other metrics a high score indicates good performance. The evaluation results seem to be effective. For example, almost all metrics identify a fingerprint from the SFINGEA (high quality) database as being of the best quality. We also note significant differences in scores between the metrics, especially between the image from the FVC2002DB3 database and the SFINGED database. However, since the metrics have values in very different ranges, these results are not directly comparable.

Dataset	NFIQ	NFIQ2	OCL	QMF	NBIS	MSEG	MQF
FVC2000DB1	2	65	0.73	83.81	14.16	0.44	59 802
FVC2000DB3	4	40	0.71	28.06	15.11	0.18	29 804
SFINGEA	1	69	0.90	76.09	57.46	0.83	55 720
SFINGED	3	28	0.47	91.19	10	0.006	43 546

Table 1.2. *Examples of values obtained for the first samples from different databases using different quality indicators*

Many further avenues remain to be explored in order to develop better quality metrics for fingerprint samples.

1.4.4. *Efficient representation of biometric data*

Once biometric data has been collected and authenticated, the best possible representation must be extracted in order to make comparisons. For many years, the search for relevant parameters to characterize biometric data focused on signal attributes and images (Wu *et al.* 2019). Recently, however, the use of convolutional neural networks has revolutionized the field, and statistical learning approaches are becoming increasingly widespread (Parkhi *et al.* 2015). Current research aims to generalize this type of approach to all biometric modalities, even in cases where large databases are not available.

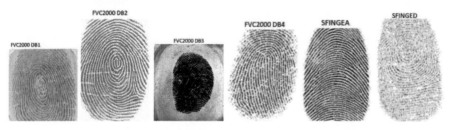

Figure 1.14. *Examples of fingerprints from the different image databases*

The performance of biometric systems has progressively improved since the 2000s because of advancements in electronics (more powerful sensors), computing (more powerful computers) and algorithmics (more sophisticated data processing techniques). These three components are closely linked within the classical architecture of a biometric system; in other words, the failure of one of these three essential components can seriously compromise the overall performance of the system. Considering the algorithmic aspect, the last few years have seen significant changes due to the success of deep learning methods in various image processing and data analysis applications. The generic structure of biometric systems has been modified to include the parameter extraction phase within a multi-layered neural architecture, such as that shown in Figure 1.15. This architecture has resulted in considerable improvements in the performance of biometric systems, reliant on access to powerful computers equipped with GPU, for example, and on the availability of large databases for learning purposes. Learning mechanisms result in the creation of robust models that are easy to use in the test phase.

In this context, deep learning has been successfully applied to a range of biometric modalities:

1) *Facial recognition* (performance $\sim$99%): DeepFace (AlexNet model), DeepID, DeepID2, DeepID3 (Modèle VGGNet-10), VGGface (VGGNet-16 model), FaceNet (googLeNet model).

2) *Fingerprint recognition* (performance $\sim$95% to $\sim$98%): FingerNet, DeepCNN.

3) *Palmprint recognition* (performance $>$ 99%): Deep Scatering, MobileNetV2 + SVM, Deform-invariant.

4) *Iris recognition* (performance $\sim$99%): DeepCNN, Deep Scatering, Deep Features.

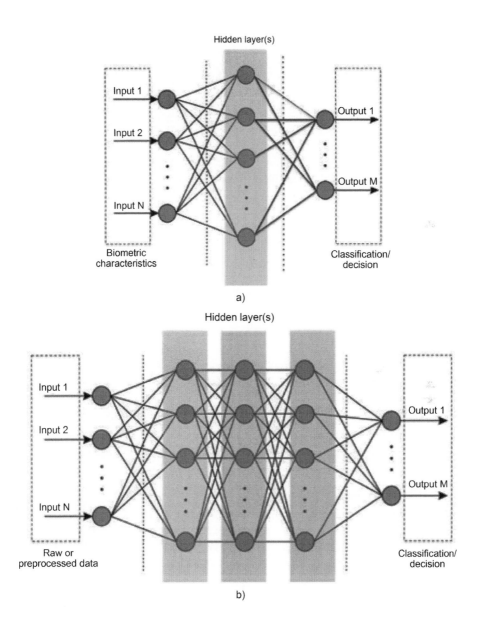

Figure 1.15. *Generic diagram of a neural architecture. a) Single-layer architecture using biometric characteristics as input. b) Multi-layer architecture (used in deep learning), in which biometric characteristics may be estimated in the hidden layers*

5) *Signature recognition* (performance 81–93%): Embending, SIGAN.

6) *Gait recognition* (performance 68–95%) : Yan *et al.*, Li *et al.*, Zhang *et al.*

More details may be found in published "survey" articles, such as in Minaee *et al.* (2019).

1.4.5. *Protecting biometric data*

Biometric data are, by definition, personal data. The General Data Protection Regulation (GDPR) of 2018 reinforces the obligation to protect individual privacy (Voigt and Von dem Bussche 2017), and, evidently, covers biometric data. These data must be protected for both security and user privacy reasons. Solutions are therefore needed, both in terms of protection (Atighehchi *et al.* 2019) and for evaluating attack resistance (Gomez-Barrero and Galbally 2020).

1.4.5.1. *State of the art*

There are several possible approaches to protecting biometric data:

– *Classic encryption*: classic approaches to encrypting biometric data usually rely on symmetric (e.g. AES) and asymmetric (e.g. RSA) cryptosystems. This approach has the disadvantage of needing to decrypt the biometric reference for comparison with a capture, making it vulnerable during this time. This approach is necessary (especially for storage in a biometric database) but not sufficient, considering the lifetime of a biometric data element (an algorithm which is secure at present may be broken during an individual's lifetime). This is the minimum that is expected of a biometric system.

– *Storage in a secure element*: this approach consists of storing clear or, preferably, encrypted biometric data in a hardware enclave such as a microcircuit chip (Wang *et al.* 2018). This method is classically used in smartphones, for example, where a micro-circuit chip may be linked to a fingerprint sensor. This chip stores the biometric reference and carries out the comparison with a new capture (see Figure 1.16). A hardware enclave guarantees very high resistance to physical and logical attacks (Maciej *et al.* 2019; Im *et al.* 2020). This type of approach also allows the individual to remain in possession of their own biometric data (in a smartphone or passport).

– *Cancelable biometrics*: one major criticism of biometrics is the intrinsic non-revocability of biometric data. For instance, a fingerprint cannot be changed in the same way as a password. The aim of cancelable biometrics is to regenerate a biometric signature for an individual, even in cases of interception by an attacker, without impinging on their privacy. The general principle is to apply a non-invertible transformation of the biometric data, parameterized by a secret key (represented by a random number or a password (Lacharme and Plateaux 2011)), as illustrated in Figure 1.17. This type of approach is similar to two-factor authentication (combining biometrics and secret information). Note that knowledge of the secret information alone is not sufficient for an attacker to retrieve the initial biometric data, but may be sufficient to permit an attack (e.g. imposture) in certain cases (Lacharme *et al.* 2013). The verification step is relatively simple, requiring comparison with a distance (notably Hamming). Diversifying keys allows one individual to possess several biometric signatures using the same biometric data, preventing an attacker from accessing multiple digital services using the same individual identity.

– *Secure computation*: this approach aims to offer protection for secure storage of biometric data (particularly in the Cloud) and permit identity verification without having to decrypt an individual's biometric reference. Homomorphic encryption (Barrier 2016) is one possible approach used here. However, while biometric data elements are often small in size (such as a fingerprint, which may require less than 200 bytes), homomorphic encryption results in much larger signatures (several megabytes), and this limits its use for practical applications.

a)   b)

Figure 1.16. *Hardware storage of biometric data in a) a biometric physical access control system and b) a biometric passport*

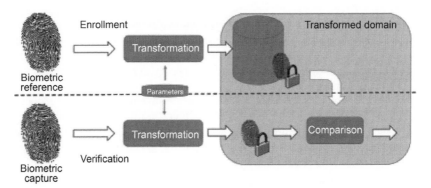

Figure 1.17. *Operation of a cancelable biometric system based on a transformation*

1.4.5.2. *Discussion*

Biometric data is a particularly sensitive kind of personal data (due to its irrevocable nature and inherent connection to an individual). The protection of these data is therefore crucial, and unprotected storage of biometric data elements is, evidently, unthinkable. Conventional encryption offers a standard default approach, but is not sufficient. Hardware-based protection is a good approach, but is limited to objects in an individual's possession (such as smartphones, smart watches, smart cards and flash drives). The current trend in biometric authentication is to adopt a centralized, cloud-based approach. Cancelable biometrics is another promising avenue, and the small size of protected biometric signatures is an advantage in terms of implementation; this approach is also more secure than classic encryption. Secure computation is an interesting prospect, but the biometric signatures used must be compatible with fast, Internet-based transmission. Other approaches using secret information or cryptographic keys must include a clear separation between the holder of the cryptographic keys and the service used to store the signatures, in order to avoid any breach of privacy (as decryption is generally possible).

Research into the protection of biometric data is unfortunately lacking. Many researchers aim to develop increasingly powerful and precise systems in terms of recognition errors, but the practical adoption of these systems is essentially dependent on security and privacy protection criteria. As we saw in the previous section, the use of deep learning techniques for biometrics may provide further answers in this area. Architectures of this type may include biometric data protection mechanisms, as recent articles have pointed out (Jami *et al.* 2019; Walia *et al.* 2020).

1.4.6. *Aging biometric data*

Biometric data do not always remain constant over the course of time. While fingerprints change little, an individual face can vary considerably. Behavioral biometric data are also subject to intrinsic intraclass variation that is difficult to manage in terms of recognition. This raises the need for new biometric systems with the capacity to manage data aging, in order to ensure consistently high performance, in terms of recognition, over the course of time (Pisani *et al.* 2019).

Despite the remarkable progress made in deep-learning based facial recognition approaches in recent years, in terms of both verification and identification performance, the neural architecture still has limitations. These limitations relate to the database used in the learning phase. If the selected database does not contain enough instances, the result may be systematically affected. For example, the performance of a facial biometric system may decrease if the person to be verified or identified was enrolled over 10 years ago. In adult individuals, aging results in changes to the texture of the face, notably with the appearance of wrinkles and skin sagging due to a loss of elasticity. These changes may be accentuated by weight gain or loss. In cases where enrollment is performed on a young child, verification/identification of the same individual's identity during adolescence or even adulthood using a static or "invariant" facial recognition system may fail. To counteract this problem, researchers have developed models for facial aging or digital rejuvenation, and work in this area is still ongoing. Both GAN (Generative Adversarial Network) and statistical models have produced impressive results in terms of perception. Digital rejuvenation or aging is used to compensate for the differences in facial characteristics, which appear over a given time period. This feature can be incorporated into facial recognition systems in order to improve their performance.

Figure 1.18 shows virtual faces at different stages of adult life. Figure 1.19 shows changes in appearance from childhood through adolescence and into adulthood. As Farazdaghi and Nait-Ali (2017) have indicated, the appearance of a face at different times can be predicted using specific mathematical models, which combine a statistical element with a parametric model, of which the parameters are estimated using geometric transformations based on anthropometric measurements. The model can be extended to process 3D digitized faces, as shown in Figure 1.20. Initial results for applications in a facial verification context can be found in Heravi *et al.* (2019).

| 21-30 | 31-40 | 41-50 | 51-60 | 61-70 | 71-80 |

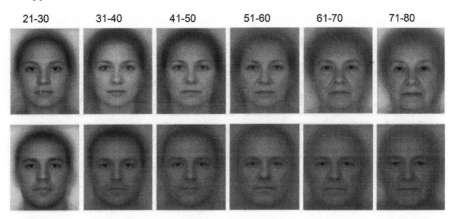

Figure 1.18. *2D digital aging and rejuvenation of an adult face. Models are shown across several age ranges: 21–30, 31–40, 41–50, 51–60, 61–70 and 71–80 years old*

1.5. Conclusion

In this chapter, we aimed to provide a synthetic overview of key aspects of security biometrics at the time of writing. The broad outlines given here are intended to provide readers with a framework from which to explore the subject further, based on their own interests, aims and priorities. This chapter is intended for a wide audience, from beginners to experts; certain technical details were voluntarily omitted, and readers are encouraged to consult further works on the subject as required. Biometrics is a flourishing area of both research and application. Only time will tell what the future holds.

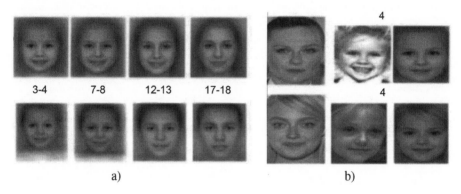

a)   b)

Figure 1.19. *2D digital aging and rejuvenation of a child's face. a) Models of faces for several age ranges: 3–4, 7–8, 12–13 and 17–18 years old. b) Digital rejuvenation of a face based on a reference photo (adult) and comparison of the "artificial" face with a real photograph (child at age 4)*

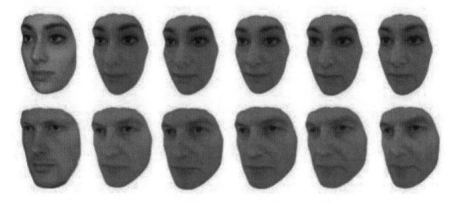

Figure 1.20. *3D aging and rejuvenation: male and female examples*

1.6. References

Aloui, K., Nait-Ali, A., Naceur, M.S. (2018). Using brain prints as new biometric feature for human recognition. *Pattern Recognition Letters*, 113, 38–45.

Atighehchi, K., Ghammam, L., Barbier, M., Rosenberger, C. (2019). GREYC-hashing: Combining biometrics and secret for enhancing the security of protected templates. *Future Generation Computer Systems*, 101, 819–830.

Barrier, J. (2016). Chiffrement homomorphe appliqué au retrait d'information privé. PhD Thesis, INSA, Toulouse.

Bitouk, D., Kumar, N., Dhillon, S., Belhumeur, P., Nayar, S.K. (2008). Face swapping: Automatically replacing faces in photographs. *ACM Trans. Graph.*, 27(3), 1–8.

Bledsoe, W.W. and Chan, H. (1965). A man-machine facial recognition system – Some preliminary results. Technical report, Panoramic Research, Inc., Palo Alto.

Buriro, A., Crispo, B., Conti, M. (2019). Answerauth: A bimodal behavioral biometric-based user authentication scheme for smartphones. *Journal of Information Security and Applications*, 44, 89–103.

Cappelli, R., Maio, D., Maltoni, D. (2004). Sfinge: An approach to synthetic fingerprint generation. In *International Workshop on Biometric Technologies Proceedings*. BT, Calgary, 147–154.

Farazdaghi, E. and Nait-Ali, A. (2017). Backward face ageing model (b-fam) for digital face image rejuvenation. *IET Biometrics*, 6(6), 478–486.

Galbally, J., Marcel, S., Fierrez, J. (2014). Biometric antispoofing methods: A survey in face recognition. *IEEE Access*, 2, 1530–1552.

Galbally, J., Fierrez, J., Cappelli, R. (2019). An introduction to fingerprint presentation attack detection. In *Handbook of Biometric Anti-Spoofing*, Marcel, S., Nixon, M.S., Fierrez, J., Evans, N. (eds). Springer, Berlin/Heidelberg.

Gomez-Barrero, M. and Galbally, J. (2020). Reversing the irreversible: A survey on inverse biometrics. *Computers & Security*, 90, 101700.

Heravi, F.M.Z., Farazdaghi, E., Fournier, R., Nait-Ali, A. (2019). Impact of aging on three-dimensional facial verification. *Electronics*, 8(10), 1170.

Im, J.-H., Jeon, S.-Y., Lee, M.-K. (2020). Practical privacy-preserving face authentication for smartphones secure against malicious clients. *IEEE Transactions on Information Forensics and Security*, 15, 2386–2401.

Jami, S.K., Chalamala, S.R., Jindal, A.K. (2019). Biometric template protection through adversarial learning. In *International Conference on Consumer Electronics*. IEEE, Las Vegas.

Kabbara, Y., Shahin, A., Nait-Ali, A., Khalil, M. (2013). An automatic algorithm for human identification using hand X-ray images. In *2nd International Conference on Advances in Biomedical Engineering*. IEEE, Tripoli.

Kabbara, Y., Naït-Ali, A., Shahin, A., Khalil, M. (2015). Hidden biometrie identification/authentication based on phalanx selection from hand X-ray images with safety considerations. In *International Conference on Image Processing Theory, Tools and Applications*. IEEE, Orléans.

Khorshid, A.E., Alquaydheb, I.N., Kurdahi, F., Jover, R.P., Eltawil, A. (2020). Biometric identity based on intra-body communication channel characteristics and machine learning. *Sensors*, 20(5), 1421.

Kirby, M. and Sirovich, L. (1990). Application of the Karhunen-Loeve procedure for the characterization of human faces. *IEEE Transactions on Pattern Analysis and Machine Intelligence*, 12(1), 103–108.

Ko, K. (2007). User's guide to Nist biometric image software (NBIS). Report, NIST Interagency/Internal Report (NISTIR), 7392.

Lacharme, P. and Plateaux, A. (2011). PIN-based cancelable biometrics. *International Journal of Automated Identification Technology (IJAIT)*, 3(2), 75–79 [Online]. Available at: https://hal.archives-ouvertes.fr/hal-00984027/file/IJAIT2.pdf.

Lacharme, P., Cherrier, E., Rosenberger, C. (2013). Preimage attack on biohashing. In *International Conference on Security and Cryptography (SECRYPT)*. IEEE, Reykjavik.

Lim, E., Jiang, X., Yau, W. (2002). Fingerprint quality and validity analysis. In *International Conference on Image Processing*. IEEE, Rochester.

Liu, X., Pedersen, M., Charrier, C., Bours, P., Busch, C. (2016). The influence of fingerprint image degradations on the performance of biometric system and quality assessment. In *International Conference of the Biometrics Special Interest Group (BIOSIG)*. IEEE, Darmstadt.

Maciej, B., Imed, E.F., Kurkowski, M. (2019). Multifactor authentication protocol in a mobile environment. *IEEE Access*, 7, 157185–157199.

Mahier, J., Pasquet, M., Rosenberger, C., Cuozzo, F. (2008). Biometric authentication. In *Encyclopedia of Information Science and Technology*, Khosrow-Pour, M. (ed.). IGI, Hershey.

Maltoni, D., Maio, D., Jain, A.K., Prabhakar, S. (2009). *Handbook of Fingerprint Recognition*, 2nd edition. Springer, London.

Matta, F. and Dugelay, J.-L. (2009). Person recognition using facial video information: A state of the art. *Journal of Visual Languages & Computing*, 20, 180–187.

Minaee, S., Abdolrashidi, A., Su, H., Bennamoun, M., Zhang, D. (2019). Biometric recognition using deep learning: A survey. arXiv preprint, arXiv:1912.00271.

Nait-Ali, A. (2019a). *Hidden Biometrics: When Biometric Security Meets Biomedical Engineering*. Springer Nature, Singapore.

Nait-Ali, A. (2019b). *Biometrics under Biomedical Considerations*. Springer, Singapore.

Nait-Ali, A. and Fournier, R. (2012). *Signal and Image Processing for Biometrics*. ISTE Ltd, London, and John Wiley & Sons, New York.

Nasrollahi, K. and Moeslund, T.B. (2008). Face quality assessment system in video sequences. In *European Workshop on Biometrics and Identity Management*. BioID, Roskilde.

Olsen, A.M., Tabassi, E., Makarov, A., Busch, C. (2013). Self-organizing maps for fingerprint image quality assessment. In *Conference on Computer Vision and Pattern Recognition Workshops*. IEEE, Portland.

Parkhi, O., Vedaldi, A., Zisserman, A. (2015). Deep face recognition. In *British Machine Vision Conference*. BVMC, Swansea.

Pisani, P.H., Mhenni, A., Giot, R., Cherrier, E., Poh, N., Ferreira de Carvalho, A.C.P.D.L., Rosenberger, C., Amara, N.E.B. (2019). Adaptive biometric systems: Review and perspectives. *ACM Computing Surveys (CSUR)*, 52(5), 1–38.

Prabhakar, S., Pankanti, S., Jain, A.K. (2003). Biometric recognition: Security and privacy concerns. *IEEE Security Privacy*, 1(2), 33–42.

Qin, H. and El Yacoubi, M.A. (2017). Deep representation for finger-vein image quality assessment. *IEEE Transactions on Circuits and Systems for Video Technology*, 28(8), 1677–1693.

Raghavendra, R., Raja, K.B., Busch, C. (2016). Detecting morphed face images. In *8th International Conference on Biometrics Theory, Applications and Systems*. IEEE, Niagara Falls.

Ramachandra, R. and Busch, C. (2017). Presentation attack detection methods for face recognition systems: A comprehensive survey. *ACM Computing Surveys (CSUR)*, 50(1), 1–37.

Ratha, N.K., Connell, J.H., Bolle, R.M. (2001). Enhancing security and privacy in biometrics-based authentication systems. *IBM Systems Journal*, 40(3), 614–634.

Redi, J., Taktak, W., Dugelay, J.-L. (2011). Digital image forensics: A booklet for beginners. *Multimedia Tools Appl.*, 51, 133–162.

Roy, A., Dixit, R., Naskar, R., Chakraborty, R.S. (eds). (2020). Copy-move forgery detection exploiting statistical image features. In *Digital Image Forensics*. Springer, Singapore.

Stolovitzky, G., Rudin, N., Inman, K., Rigoutsos, I. (2002). DNA based identification. In *Biometrics: Personal Identification in Networked Society*, Jain, A.K., Bolle, R., Pankanti, S. (eds). Kluwer Academic Publishers, Norwell.

Tabassi, E., Wilson, C., Watson, C. (2011). Fingerprint Image Quality (NFIQ). Report, NISTIR.

Thies, J., Zollhöfer, M., Stamminger, M., Theobalt, C., Nießner, M. (2016). Face2Face: Real-time face capture and reenactment of RGB videos. In *Conference on Computer Vision and Pattern Recognition*. IEEE, Las Vegas.

Turk, M. and Pentland, A. (1991). Eigenfaces for recognition. *Journal of Cognitive Neuroscience*, 3(1), 71–86.

Venkatesh, S., Ramachandra, R., Raja, K., Busch, C. (2019). A new multi-spectral iris acquisition sensor for biometric verification and presentation attack detection. In *Winter Applications of Computer Vision Workshops*. IEEE, Waikoloa Village.

Voigt, P. and Von dem Bussche, A. (2017). *The EU General Data Protection Regulation (GDPR): A Practical Guide*, 1st edition. Springer International Publishing, New York.

Walia, G.S., Aggarwal, K., Singh, K., Singh, K. (2020). Design and analysis of adaptive graph based cancelable multi-biometrics approach. *IEEE Transactions on Dependable and Secure Computing*, 19, 54–66.

Wang, D., Shen, J., Liu, J.K., Choo, K.-K.R. (2018). Rethinking authentication on smart mobile devices. *Wireless Communications and Mobile Computing*, 1–4.

Wasnik, P., Raja, K.B., Ramachandra, R., Busch, C. (2017). Assessing face image quality for smartphone based face recognition system. In *5th International Workshop on Biometrics and Forensics*. IEEE, Coventry.

Wu, W., Elliott, S.J., Lin, S., Sun, S., Tang, Y. (2019). Review of palm vein recognition. *IET Biometrics*, 9(1), 1–10.

Yao, Z., Le Bars, J.-M., Charrier, C., Rosenberger, C. (2015a). Fingerprint quality assessment combining blind image quality, texture and minutiae features. In *International Conference on Information Systems Security and Privacy*. IEEE, Angers.

Yao, Z., Le Bars, J.-M., Charrier, C., Rosenberger, C. (2015b). Quality assessment of fingerprints with minutiae delaunay triangulation. In *International Conference on Information Systems Security and Privacy*. IEEE, Angers.

Yao, Z., Charrier, C., Rosenberger, C. (2016a). Pixel pruning for fingerprint quality assessment. In *International Biometric Performance Testing Conference (IBPC)*. NIST, Gaithersburg.

Yao, Z., Le Bars, J.-M., Charrier, C., Rosenberger, C. (2016b). Literature review of fingerprint quality assessment and its evaluation. *IET Biometrics*, 5(3), 243–251.

Yeap, Y.Y., Sheikh, U., Ab Rahman, A.A.-H. (2018). Image forensic for digital image copy move forgery detection. In *14th International Colloquium on Signal Processing and Its Applications*. IEEE, Penang.

2

Protecting Documents Using Printed Anticopy Elements

Iuliia TKACHENKO[1], Alain TREMEAU[2] and Thierry FOURNEL[2]

[1] LIRIS, Université Lumière Lyon 2, CNRS, France
[2] LaHC, University of Lyon, University of Saint-Étienne, CNRS, France

The fight against counterfeiting of printed documents, such as identity documents or packaging, is more relevant than ever. The availability of increasingly efficient printing devices has contributed to an increase in the number of counterfeit documents being produced each year. In this chapter, we provide a brief overview of the different approaches to document authentication, before focusing on the different approaches to protection using elements sensitive to the variability inherent in copying systems. A range of state-of-the-art copying solutions, including protection elements and the associated authentication processes, will be presented.

2.1. Introduction

Printed documents form an integral part of our daily lives, whether as packaging on manufactured products such as medicines or, more generally, in the form of printed papers, the origin and contents of which are often indicated by the issuer by means of distinctive design elements. Examples include official documents such as passports, tax stamps, notarial deeds, certificates and show tickets. Individualization gives meaning to the notion of an authentic copy which, in legal terms, means a physical copy with the same probative force as an original.

For a color version of all figures in this chapter, see www.iste.co.uk/puech/multimedia2.zip.

Multimedia Security 2,
coordinated by William PUECH. © ISTE Ltd 2022.

Improvements in the performance and availability of document printing and scanning systems have contributed to an upsurge in counterfeit document production. According to the Association for Packaging and Processing Technology, the number of counterfeits is increasing 3% per year worldwide[1]. For official organizations, this increase represents a significant threat. For companies, it may result in significant financial losses and in damage to brand image and reputation. For consumers, this increase betrays a shortfall in compliance checks, and it is a potential source of danger in the health, food, energy and transport sectors. Industrialized countries have begun to work on developing their legal arsenals in response to the increase in counterfeiting. In France, new measures were brought in in 2014 to strengthen the existing 2007 laws against counterfeiting. In terms of research and development, the authentication of printed documents has become a research and development topic in its own right, in the same way as biometric authentication (see Chapter 1).

One of the first countermeasures to reduce counterfeiting, used by print media manufacturers and printing companies, involves the use of special substrates and/or special inks. Proposed solutions include gonio-apparent approaches (Van Renesse 2005), such as optical variable devices (OVDs), featuring holograms, kinegrams and relief prints, and optical variable inks (OVIs). However, these production-contingent approaches are all reliant on undisclosed proprietary processes.

Today, anti-counterfeiting solutions need to respond to a number of requirements: (1) low cost; (2) a high level of global protection; (3) a fast registration phase that is easy to integrate and, where marking is involved, uses standard components; and (4) a simple and reliable verification phase, using a standard acquisition system, such as a (flat) scan of the object plane or direct image capture using a smartphone camera. These requirements may be satisfied by an authentication approach that does not rely on specific manufacturing processes and exclusive hardware specifications, but instead is based on the variabilities inherent in production. Three groups of approaches are presented in the literature, corresponding to different processes in the production chain:

– the *substrate approach* relates to the process used in producing the substrate to which print is applied;

– the *forensic approach* concerns the mechanisms involved in the printing process itself;

– the *anti-copy approach*, the focus of this chapter, relates to the interactions between the printing system and the substrate.

Section 2.2 provides a broad overview of different document authentication approaches, whereas section 2.3 is devoted to different printing test forms. Section 2.4 is focused on copy-sensitive graphical codes (CSGCs). Our conclusions are presented in section 2.5.

2.2. Document authentication approaches: an overview

Printed document authentication processes rely on an initial registration step, carried out when the document is printed, before any verification can be carried out. In this initial stage, the document is printed and production-specific characteristics may be acquired and saved as necessary. In the case of the substrate approach, acquisition is required for each record, either through print-free online registration (in the case of connection to a registration base), or printed offline registration involving digital protection. Printed documents can then be verified by comparing their characteristics with the record in the database. In forensic approaches, verification is carried out by calibrating the printing system; in this case, acquisition at the registration stage is not directly relevant. In anti-copy approaches, protection elements may be constructed in a way that limits acquisition constraints, and verification is based on an evaluation of print quality.

Since the work of Goldman (1983) on the use of paper fibers and ink spots as non-cloneable physical characteristics, different types of fingerprints or patterns have been identified to permit document authentication from a substrate. These include robust hashing, digitally signed by the legal authority before printing on the document; random signatures (Boutant *et al.* 2005), which self-encrypt the digital signature of data (Fournel *et al.* 2007), if necessary with dedicated holographic encoding (Fournel 2009); or one-way physical functions (Pappu *et al.* 2002) implemented as covering (Skoric *et al.* 2007), producing figures of speckle. In practice, use of these figures requires extremely precise angular positioning of the reading device. Use of a focused laser with photodetector signal acquisition from four different angles permits 1D marker extraction to within two degrees. Another option is photo-inscription of the figures on documents, covered with a reconfigurable photo-chromic layer (Fournel *et al.* 2008; Crespo-Monteiro *et al.* 2012). This option, which is compatible with data updates and different authentication protocols, is sufficient for verification under standard conditions. This criterion corresponds to a proven need, in particular for smartphone-based mobile authentication, which has acted as a driving force for a range of different developments (Wong and Wu 2015, 2017; Schraml *et al.* 2018).

The forensic group of approaches aims to identify traces left by a printer, or the profile of the printing/reading chain. Oliver and Chen (2002) suggest using image quality analysis in order to identify the digital printing technology used, differentiating between different models produced by the same brand. For example, the presence of non-controlled strips may be exploited for printer type recognition (Mikkilineni *et al.* 2005). Kee and Farid have taken a different approach, based on the occurrence of letters in text: the printer profile is then determined through principal component analysis (PCA) (Kee and Farid 2008). Analyzing letters in text offers a means of identifying a printer or printers. Chiang *et al.* (2010) propose an identification of the full chain, including both the printer and the scanner. Recurring features are extracted from printed characters via a variety of descriptors, such as a grayscale covariance matrix (Mikkilineni *et al.* 2010, 2011), noise energy, contour sinuosity or grayscale gradients (Shang *et al.* 2014). Different classification methods, such as support vector machine (SVM), linear discriminant analysis (LDA), and so on have been used with these descriptors to carry out classification and identify printers. Scanners may be identified using the recurring component of sensor noise (Khanna and Delp 2009; Khanna *et al.* 2009). Navarro *et al.* (2018) present a classification based on decision trees (random decision forest), with extensions that can be interpreted by human experts in order to qualify the results. More recently, deep learning techniques have also been applied to forensic analysis (Ferreira *et al.* 2017).

In anti-copy approaches, documents are protected by printing an element designed to indicate duplication on a new medium. Depending on the printing technology used, different types of noise may occur, altering the printed version (Mayer *et al.* 2018). The non-deterministic interaction between ink and substrate, combined with the irregularities of the printer's mechanisms, are then exploited through the printing of a copy protection element selected or designed for its sensitivity to printing noise under fixed conditions. Thus, unidentified degradation or the loss of too much information would indicate that the document is not original.

The first category of anti-copy features (ACFs) corresponds to identifying the degradation or deformation of a print test shape (PTS). On registration, a copy of the print is extracted and saved in a database (hosted by a trusted third party) or printed after signature and digital security (by the legal authority), in the same way as for a substrate approach. Various different types of PTS, such as geometric shapes, glyphs and guilloches, will be presented in section 2.3.

For the second category of ACFs, we seek to gauge the extent and normality of information loss suffered by a CSGC. Duplication detection can thus be performed without having to explicitly register a marker via an episode (Wirnitzer 2003). An episode is defined as the difference between a printed form and an initial form, where data are encoded as a binary grid (*datagrid*). This code has been the subject of various studies and developments (Wirnitzer *et al.* 2007; Bonev and Wirnitzer 2008). It is suitable for use in offset printing, where common traces can be found within episodes printed from the same portion of the offset plate. When used at the module (symbol) level of a data grid, in a version called a *nanogrid*, this approach can prevent duplication. The subject of CSGCs is discussed in more detail in section 2.4, focusing on different graphical codes that can be implemented without the need to record an image at the registration stage (Picard 2004); the binary code to be printed is used directly as a reference. These include copy-detection patterns (Picard 2004), two-level QR codes (Tkachenko *et al.* 2016a) and watermarked QR codes (Nguyen *et al.* 2018).

2.3. Print test shapes

A PTS is a continuous element considered to be a binary object for analysis, containing the discriminating characteristics of a print. It consists of a single region or multiple related regions with continuous or piecewise continuous underlying contours or generating curves, and its shape or (gray) level is uniquely modulated during printing.

The contour(s) and generating curve(s) of a PTS thus have a geometric or radiometric characteristic that, after digitization, can act as a print marker. During verification, the marker of the document to authenticate is extracted and compared, by means of an appropriate metric, with the registered print(s). Forgeries in principle, can be detected on the basis of a metric value in excess of a statistically fixed threshold.

Shape modulation focuses on a specific predefined mark, such as a set of discs, or the occurrence of a character of a given size in a given font. In the latter case, the test shape is included in the data to be printed and protected. The generating curves, contours and/or skeleton that are deformed in the printing process are measured using an ad hoc shape descriptor. This descriptor gives the marker.

Glyphs and guilloches can also be characterized via the modification of grayscale levels. The level along a generating curve, such as the skeleton, which is subject to the variability of the print-scan chain, can then be used as a marker. Figure 2.1 illustrates the average grayscale match between digital input and output after printing and scanning (Print and Scan, P&S) using a laser printer and flatbed scanner. It shows the nonlinearity and non-constant variability of the output level as a function of the input level.

There are various reasons why the P&S behaves in this way, beginning with the transformation of the digital image to print into halftone. On the printing side, the technology used to transfer the ink onto the substrate, the physicochemical properties of the inks and the mechanical properties of the substrate all influence the distribution of the ink. The optical properties of the print itself and the digitization carried out by the acquisition device also have an impact on the image produced.

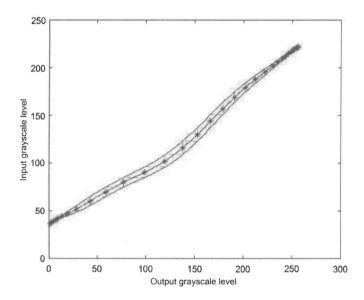

Figure 2.1. *Grayscale response curve of a chain consisting of an HP LaserJet P3005dn printer and an EPSON Perfection V700 photo scanner, following model fitting (Villán et al. 2006). Considering a margin fixed at 40% of the standard deviation value, only 32 gray levels can be determined in a stable manner*

PTS are made up of geometric figures, typographical symbols and guilloche marks of variable shape, linking them to CSGC codes. Print markers are extracted from these continuous shapes, for example based on the printer profile, and the distance between these markers and the original records forms the basis for authenticity assessments. Different approaches will be described below, focusing, respectively, on PTS and their print signatures, glyphs and patterns based on print profiles, and guilloches and radiometric modulation markers.

2.3.1. *Print test signatures*

The non-reproducible aspects of a print may be observed directly by looking at a printed character under a microscope. At this scale, a portion of a character does not produce exactly the same pattern when reprinted (Figure 2.2). This is even more evident in cases where the image of the original print is reprinted.

In this case, elementary printed dots, or disks which are sufficiently small for their contour to be entirely affected by ink alignment discrepancies, may be considered as test shapes.

a)   b)   c)   d)

Figure 2.2. *Comparison of the upper part of the character "a": a) digital image; b) and c) two versions that have been printed then scanned at 600 dpi; d) copy of b) (re-printed then scanned) in 600 dpi. Images b)–d) were obtained using a ZEISS microscope with 5x magnification*

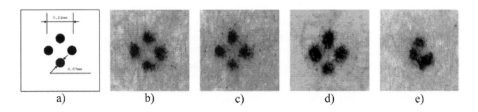

a)   b)   c)   d)   e)

Figure 2.3. *Print signature pattern proposed by Zhu* et al. *(2003): a) digital original; b) and c) versions printed using an HP LaserJet 8100 printer at 600 dpi; d) version printed using an HP LaserJet 4050 printer at 1,200 dpi; e) photocopy of image b) made using a 600 × 600 dpi Minolta Di152 digital copier*

Zhu *et al.* (2003) analyzed the variability of toner powder deposits produced by a laser printer with a resolution of 600 dpi (dots per inch) using a pattern of dots with a diameter of 70 μm, based on images examined under a microscope with 200x magnification. We clearly see that the dots and their contours are all altered in different ways (Figure 2.3). The normalized polar radius, measured from the center of gravity of a deformed dot, acts as a signature (to be concatenated with those of the other dots).

The shape of a dot at microscopic level is another characteristic of the printing technology used. Nguyen *et al.* (2014) highlighted this notion, showing that each printer, and each brand, is characterized by a different printed dot shape. Based on an experimental study, the digital image of a dot was modeled as a set of random pixels distributed according to an inverse link function, depending on the center, pixel darkness, spreading area and shape (Nguyen *et al.* 2014). Taking account of interactions with neighboring pixels by means of a Markov chain increased the level of differentiation between printers of different types (Nguyen *et al.* 2018). During the verification step, feature extraction is performed again and the resulting print signature, F, is compared with a stored signature, F_{ref}, using a hypothesis test:

$$d(F, F_{ref}) \underset{H_0}{\overset{H_1}{\gtrless}} \tau_0$$

where the null hypothesis (H_0) is eliminated in favor of hypothesis H_1 if and only if the Euclidean distance $d(F, F_{ref})$ between characteristics is greater than the value τ_0, deduced from a predefined confidence threshold corresponding to the desired strictness of the authentication strategy.

For a PTS consisting of a single disk and a false negative rate set at 0.5%, for regular sampling from 72 (respectively, 8) angles, the false positive rate given by Zhu et al. (2003) was less than 10^{-33} (respectively, 10^{-3}). This shows the robustness of this method to counterfeiting using re-printing or scanning/re-printing techniques.

This authentication method may be extended to other types of printers, such as offset or inkjet printers, and to test non-star shapes (Idrissa et al. 2010). However, at such magnifications and under certain P&S conditions (depending on the properties of the substrates, ink, illumination, scan, etc.), image segmentation prior to print extraction may result in optical dot gain, resulting in variability and outlying points (Figure 2.4). Downstream filtering, for example to improve robustness to contour convexification (Coltuc et al. 2012), may be applied but similar false positive rates to those obtained previously were only achieved through outlier filtering.

2.3.2. *Glyphs*

Drawing on work by Zhu et al. (2003), a number of authors (Pollard et al. 2010a, 2010b; Simske and Adams 2010; Adams et al. 2011) have proposed the use of model-based signature profiles (MBSP), that is, a glyph-based approach. MBSP signatures resulting from two different captures of the same printable figure are shown in Figures 2.5(g) and (h). MBSP extraction relies on a predefined model of a glyph as a set of N uniformly distributed points and the associated normal unit vectors. The model is then fitted to any occurrence of the glyph in a document image via a homogeneous transformation. The image of the occurrence is then rectified using standard interpolation. The locations of the control points are shown in yellow and red in the image before rectification (Figure 2.5(e)) and after rectification (Figure 2.5(f)). The signature of the analyzed character is extracted from image profiles using a grayscale contour metric (for more details, see Pollard et al. (2010b)). Signatures are compared using a modified Hamming distance, known as the shape distortion encoding distance (SDED).

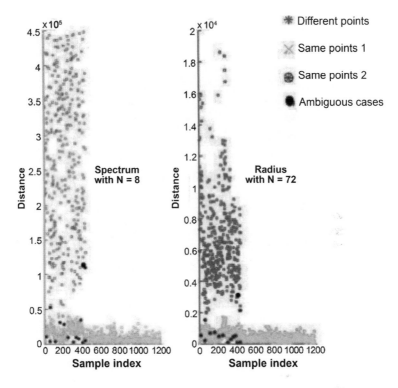

Figure 2.4. *Euclidean distances obtained using contour sampling from 8 and 72 angles between print signatures extracted from 4-dot PTS. Results for identical PTS are shown in green, with results between different PTS in read. Note the presence of a number of outlying points (black). Adopted from Idrissa et al. (2010)*

The performance of MBSPs has been tested using several different HP inkjet printers and a line scan camera. A specially-designed small form factor relay lens with integrated illumination was used (Adams 2010). This Dyson Relay lens imaging device has an effective resolution of 3.5 μm, which is sufficient for high-resolution glyph analysis; MBSPs cannot be extracted using standard scanners due to their limited resolution, set at 1,200 spi (sample per inch) or 2,400 spi.

2.3.3. *Guilloches*

Guilloches are a type of PTS used to personalize documents by simple randomization or encoding of information. Such additional lines were originally used by goldsmiths as smooth aesthetic lines offering some visual protection against falsification based on the continuity and the quality of the lines. Today, guilloches are used as a (visible) means of watermarking an image that forms an integral part of the data to be protected, such as a background design or a passport photograph.

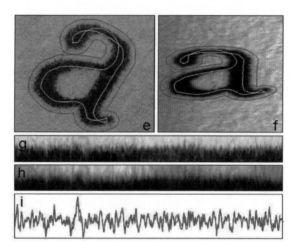

Figure 2.5. *Extraction of an MBSP for the same printed letter using different mechanisms (Pollard et al. 2010b)*

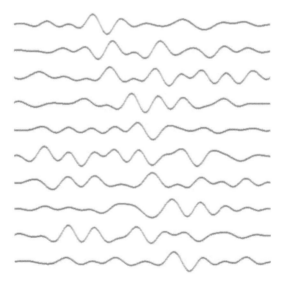

Figure 2.6. *Guilloche encoding 16 bits per line*

Different methods have been proposed for closed curve encoding, including shifts of a same closed curve and/or variations in the line thickness (Kiuchi and Matsumoto 2011), which can take the form of rosettes (Simske *et al.* 2012), or deformations with connections at fixed points (Fan *et al.* 2010). Encoding can also be carried out within continuous curves following a chosen direction, using a 2D virtual array of strong and weak attracting elements (Rhoads and Rodriguez 2009), of irregular control points (Coltuc and Fournel 2011) or by spread spectrum modulation (Fournel 2015). Leibenguth *et al.* (2017) proposed a solution in which each guilloche holds a codeword, for example after keyed cryptographic hashing. The bits in the codeword may thus determine the position of the guilloche's control points or define its coefficients in a frequency domain, as shown in Figure 2.6. If more than 160 bits of information are stored in this way, it is possible to make use of error correcting code without negatively affecting visual admissibility (in the case of a visible insertion). Blind extraction of guilloches is tricky, but reconstructing the hash at verification level enables robust automatic detection based on an evaluation of local contrast, taking account of the insertion. The gray level along the extracted lines can be used to identify the printed image in which the the guilloches are inserted. A biometric version of variable guilloches has also been proposed in Fournel (2012) and Leibenguth *et al.* (2017): in this case the carrier lines are the fingerprint of the document holder.

2.4. Copy-sensitive graphical codes

CSGCs are discret elements that are designed to be difficult to duplicate from an authentic print. These elements, which consist of an unpredictable graphical code, are printed using a low number of ink dots per pixel (dpi/ppi, pixels per inch) at a noisy print resolution, which inexorably alters the quality of the code.

A quality index can be used to measure the alteration of a printed code after reading (grayscale image $\tilde{I}$). A measure of similarity, noted φ, often a correlation coefficient, is evaluated with respect to a numerical CSGC I used as a reference: $\varphi(\tilde{I}, I)$. For a pixel with coordinates (j, k), the P&S chain generates a distribution of the output gray levels given the value i of the input bit (Figure 2.7). These distributions generally behave like a conditional probability density $p(\tilde{I}_{jk}|I_{jk} = i)$ described by a mean value and a dispersion parameter (a log-normal distribution in the case of laser printing) (Baras and Cayre 2012).

The unpredictability of a CSGC, generally constructed from useful data and a key, means that counterfeiters have no choice but to scan it in an attempt to estimate it, then re-print it to duplicate the document. This re-print introduces further degradations that reduce the quality of the print and the degree of similarity. On principle, the copy will then be detected as the similarity measure $\varphi(\tilde{I}, I)$ is below a predetermined threshold τ_0.

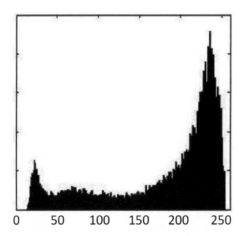

Figure 2.7. *Histogram of an 8-bit acquisition of a uniform rasterized image (overlap rate of less than 50% in this case) printed at 600 dpi (figure taken from Coltuc et al. (2012))*

P&S noise may theoretically be corrected by averaging images of samples printed using the same CSGC; for example, Baras and Cayre (2012, 2013) used around a dozen codes. In reality, however, each CSGC is only printed once, by definition, and it would not be possible to estimate an average in this way.

Three types of CSGC are described below: maximum entropy CDPs, 2LQR codes using two-level matrix bar codes and W-QR codes, using watermarked matrix patterns.

2.4.1. *Copy detection pattern*

The copy detection pattern (CDP) is a form of CSGC that is totally unpredictable. It is with maximum entropy, printed at an optimal resolution (Picard 2004; Picard and Zhao 2011) so that the distribution $p(\tilde{I}|I)$ will be significantly affected by duplication. Adjusting the resolution of a calibrated print is a practical means of adjusting the standard deviation of its noise. Printing with a large number of dots for each bit of the CDP code would result in a code, which is easy to reproduce without error; conversely, printing with a low dpi/ppi ratio results in prints of authentic documents that are as noisy as those of counterfeits. The model presented in Phan Ho *et al.* (2014b), which assumes that the moduli of an 8-bit scan (as a ratio of the number of scan samples per pixel of the code, spi/ppi > 1) of a code printed using laser-type printing are independent and identically distributed, indicates that a standard deviation of a few tens of gray levels is optimal. The estimated false positive rate in this case is around 10^{-30} for a false negative rate of 10^{-6}.

The coverage rate of a CDP is typically $50 \pm 5\%$, printed on paper at 1,200 dpi and scanned at 2,400 dpi. An example of a CDP and its printed-scanned (i.e. degraded) version is shown in Figure 2.8.

a)

b)

Figure 2.8. *a) Example of a CDP and b) printed-scanned copy*[2]

The impact of the P&S process is considered a non-reproducible characteristic due to the physical errors that are introduced and their stochastic nature.

The authentication test, based on a comparison of the P&S version with the original digital CDP, can be performed in the spatial domain using a correlation coefficient, the *Mediasec Quality Index* (Picard 2004), and a pre-defined decision threshold. As the P&S process induces high-frequency filtering, the test can also be carried out in the frequency domain by considering the cosine transform (DCT) coefficients on the basis of a correlation or a distance. This allows the detector to take account of significant frequencies of the CDP in a weighted manner. It is also possible to combine comparisons in the spatial and frequency domains. Several alternative metrics have recently been proposed to perform this comparison (Dirik and Haas 2012): the 4-point autocorrelation metric, an entropy metric, a Fourier domain sharpness metric, a wavelet domain sharpness metric and a prediction error metric. Experimental results, obtained using a 300 ppi resolution printer and scanner, reveal that the entropy and prediction error metrics perform best in terms of copy detection.

The authentication test may be formulated as a statistical hypothesis test (Phan Ho *et al.* 2014b) based on observations of the read code and a model of the P&S channel of the pixel in the digital code:

2 Samples from the image base are available at: https://www.univ-st-etienne.fr/graphical-code-estimation.

$$\mathcal{L} = log \frac{p_{\tilde{I}|I}^{(H_0)}}{p_{\tilde{I}|I}^{(H_1)}} \underset{H_0}{\overset{H_1}{\gtrless}} \tau_1$$

where $\mathcal{L}$ and τ_1 denote the log-likelihood function and decision threshold, respectively.

A CDP can be embedded into an image, as suggested in Picard (2004). It may be incorporated into a 1D barcode or logo, or a logo can be inserted in the low frequencies of a CDP (Zhao *et al.* 2010). It can also be merged with an invisible mark. Each black module of a DataMatrix can be replaced by a CDP (Picard *et al.* 2014) so as to prevent copying of the conventional 2D barcode, which encodes the data of a document. A CSGC of this type is shown in Figure 2.9.

a)   b)

Figure 2.9. *Examples of barcodes with anti-copy protection (Picard* et al. *2014): a) DataMatrix with the black modules replaced by CDPs; b) close up view of the models in the DataMatrix*

Picard and Landry (2017) embed a CDP in a QR code to guarantee authenticity, sacrificing part of the backup (redundant) information encoded in this space. The CDP is split into regions with different coverage rates; for an average of $50 \pm 5\%$, as in Figure 2.10, one region may present a rate of 60% while another may be 40%.

2.4.2. *Two-level barcodes*

The 2LQR code is another type of CSGC, featuring two levels of storage. The second level, which is only accessible to authorized users, is intended to prevent duplication of the first level code, which can be accessed by standard reading. A

2LQR code increases the amount of information stored in a given area of print while providing copy protection for the first level barcode. An example of a 2LQR code is shown in Figure 2.11.

Figure 2.10. *QR code including both primary and secondary information (Picard and Landry 2017)*

a)   b)

Figure 2.11. *a) Example of the original digital 2LQR code and b) image of the (degraded) version obtained after P&S*

The second (private) level is constructed by replacing the black modules in the QR code with textured patterns, chosen for their sensitivity to the P&S process (Tkachenko *et al.* 2015).

Experimental results were obtained using a printer resolution of 600 dpi (or 1,200 dpi) and a scanner resolution of 600 spi. At first glance, the 2LQR code looks like the CSGC shown in Figure 2.9. However, there are two points of difference between the two CSGCs:

– the textured motifs in the 2LQR code form an alphabet of dimension q, which may be used to code information stored on the second level via q-ary error correction codes. These motifs are also used for identification. Note that the second level of a CDP code, such as the DataMatrix shown in Figure 2.9, is only used for authentication, in the same way as a classic CDP. Although certain information may, on principle, be stored in a CDP, to the best of our knowledge there are no indications in the literature concerning the amount of information that could be stored in this way; furthermore, this would result in part of the CDP being unavailable for identification purposes;

– the smallest element of the 2LQR code is a textured pattern of $p \times p$ black or white pixels, while the smallest element of the CDP is a square of $u \times u$ pixels that are either all black or all white.

The smallest elements of both types of CSGC are shown in Figure 2.12, which also gives an example of the degradations occurring as a result of the P&S process. For more details concerning this difference between CDP and 2LQR, see Tkachenko and Destruel (2018).

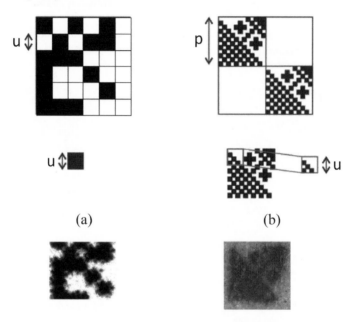

Figure 2.12. *Comparison of the smallest elements of a) a CDP code and b) a 2LQR code, showing the effect of the P&S process on the CSGC*

Patterns on the second level are read by correlation with the alphabet and the decision of a hypothesis test formulated on its mean:

$$E[\rho(\tilde{P}_i^j, P_i)] \underset{H_0}{\overset{H_1}{\gtrless}} \tau_2$$

where $\rho(\tilde{P}_i^{\,j}, P_i)$ denotes the correlation between the binary pattern P_i of the alphabet and the jth printed and scanned pattern $\tilde{P}_i^{\,j}$ out of the N_i patterns in the 2LQR code corresponding to P_i, and τ_2 denotes a predefined validation threshold, determined experimentally.

A variety of correlation coefficients (Pearson, Kendall, Spearman and weighted Kendall) have been tested; the Spearman coefficient appears to offer the best performance in this context (Tkachenko *et al.* 2017).

Another proposition for improving the quality of 2LQRs after P&S and increasing the gap between the correlation values of authentic printed codes and of duplicated codes involves the use of a super-resolution technique (Tkachenko *et al.* 2018). Naive attacks, such as duplication using a standard copier (Tkachenko *et al.* 2016b) or the use of low-level image processing tools such as histogram equalization or sharpness enhancement (Tkachenko *et al.* 2017), can be detected by correlation. However, the use of predetermined patterns to construct 2LQRs means that an attack based on an estimation of these patterns, drawing on printed examples, may be possible. Experiments with a 600 dpi laser printer and a 600 spi scanner have shown that patterns can be classified into several classes, but low-level binarization methods – using statistical thresholding, majority voting after duplication, a P&S at 1,200 spi and 1,200 dpi and four connected pixels – did not effectively estimate the initial structure of the textured patterns after P&S (Tkachenko and Destruel 2018). Another possibility to consider involves the use of neural networks, which will be discussed in section 2.4.4.

2.4.3. *Watermarked barcodes*

Conventional 2D barcodes such as QR codes may be protected using copy-sensitive watermarking (Nguyen *et al.* 2017). The white background of the barcode, in this case the graphical code containing the copy-sensitive pattern, can be replaced by a specifically generated texture using appropriate parameters. The generated texture is a clipped Gaussian noise (any value lower than 0 is set to 0, any value higher than 1 is set to 1) with parameters μ and σ, denoting the mean and standard deviation of the Gaussian. The CSGC obtained in this way is known as a W-QR code (Watermarked QR code). Duplication of the pattern causes a degradation of the texture and a modification of its statistical characteristics. This modification can be detected by means of a statistical test on the $\Gamma(a, b)$ distribution of the local variance of the noise after calibration of the a and b parameters from images of authentic textures:

$$\mathcal{H}_0 : X \sim \Gamma(a, b), \qquad \mathcal{H}_1 : X \not\sim \Gamma(a, b)$$

Figure 2.13 shows the digital version of the W-QR code alongside authentic and duplicated printed versions.

a)   b)   c)

Figure 2.13. *Example of a copy-sensitive graphical W-QR code: a) electronic copy; b) original paper copy; c) non-original paper copy created by a scan and reprint attack (Nguyen et al. 2017)*

Experimental results obtained with a resolution of 600 dpi and image capture using a Samsung Galaxy S6 smartphone at its highest resolution indicate good resistance to duplication. However, it is important to ensure that a sufficient number of gray levels can be reliably recovered after P&S. In practice, we cannot count on the P&S of over 100 gray levels with a digital print-scan on 8 bits (Villán *et al.* 2005), due to the compromise between printing resolution and number of halftones, and the joint digitization of the scanner (with automatic tone correction in some cases). Only a limited number of levels, around 10–12 gray levels, are generally detectable after P&S (Villán *et al.* 2006). An adjustment such as that shown in Figure 2.14 highlights the best range(s) to use for gray levels to ensure correct detection after P&S.

W-QR code protection is based on the secret parameters of a Gaussian texture, which a counterfeiter may attempt to estimate or approximate in order to fool the authentication test. The security of these CSGCs is still a matter for further research.

2.4.4. *Performance of CSGC authentication*

The security aspects of CSGC have not yet been studied exhaustively, in theoretical or experimental terms, notably with respect to portable systems available to the general public; the performance of these systems is constantly increasing, notably in terms of optical resolution.

Forms of CSGC differ in terms of construction and the associated authentication methods. A summary of different specificities of CDPs, 2LQR and W-QR, along with usage values, is shown in Table 2.1.

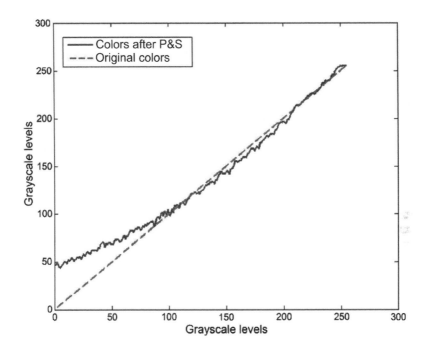

Figure 2.14. *Example of changing gray levels*
(Tkachenko et al. *2014) in the P&S process.*
Red line: original gray level; blue line: gray level after P&S

	CDP	2LQR	W-QR
Print resolution	1,200 dpi	600 dpi	600 dpi
Acquisition device	Scanner	Scanner	Smartphone
Scan resolution	1,200/2,400 dpi	600 dpi	Highest resolution
Storage capacity	No	Yes	Yes
Decodable by barcode reader	No	Yes (1st level)	Yes

Table 2.1. *Characteristics and usage values of CDP, 2LQR and W-QR CSGCs*

In terms of verification, Phan Ho *et al.* (2013, 2014a) propose using the P&S channel model for authentication. In this context, authentication is possible when the verifier can observe a set of false codes in order to estimate the parameters of a model of their distribution. On the counterfeiter's side, digital printing is now the hardest aspect: the estimation (i.e. the binarization of the printed code) required for a re-print (and thus duplication) is of crucial importance. A theoretical study (Phan Ho *et al.*

2014b) has shown, in the context of independent observations with equal variances of the black and white pixels of the original CDP, that making a hypothesis test fuzzy at verification, given a false negative rate, may be considered an optimization of the false positive rate. When the counterfeiter is active (i.e. adjusting their own P&S channel to deceive the system), an attack can be formalized as a minimax game with the authentication center. It is in the authentication center's best interest to adjust their P&S channel to minimize the false positive rate, but a counterfeiter will seek to maximize their own channel within a margin that appears to be limited. The worst case is that of a passive counterfeiter with access to the P&S channel of the legal printer. In this type of internal attack, the only unknown is the initial graphical code. The only actor involved in this optimization problem is the authentication center, which may minimize the false positive rate by adjusting the printing resolution; after calibration of the P&S channel, this amounts to adjusting the noise of this channel. If the dpi/ppi ratio is too high, the initial graphic code will be too easy to read, whereas if the ratio is too low, an authentic (printed and scanned) graphical code will be noisy and difficult to distinguish from a forgery.

Binarization itself has been approached from different perspectives. In Dirik and Haas (2012), an adversary attempts to estimate an inverse model of the P&S. In Diong et al. (2012), the authors tested different preselected characteristics of the image (statistical moments, PCA and PLS) and different classifiers (SVM, LDA, etc.) for decoding a CDP. Methods based on convolutional neural networks, in which the image and classifier features are learned simultaneously, were first introduced in 2019. The classifier output provides a binarized image by simply thresholding the histogram. Using databases of different resolutions, Taran el al. and Yadav et al. showed that such networks are able to create falsified documents with the capacity to fool the verification system (Taran et al. 2019; Yadav et al. 2019b). The most time-consuming step in this process is database construction. Yadav et al. (2019b), however, showed that a data augmentation with only five printed and scanned image codes can be enough to correctly binarize a CDP. Thus, the BN DNN network (Taran et al. 2019), the SAE autoencoder (Yadav et al. 2019b) and the srGANb architecture (Yadav et al. 2019a) may be used to attack a CDP by estimation. The BN DNN, unlike the other cited mechanisms, contains fully connected layers of neurons. The SAE network relies on bit-by-bit decoding, while the srGANb network operates through regeneration.

Using a database constructed for comparison purposes[3], the srGANb generator (Figure 2.15) produced the best binarization of printed CDP with a resolution of 600 dpi and a dpi/ppi scale of 1, with less than 10% of erroneous bits and an average verification correlation score of only 1% lower than that measured for an authentic print. During the learning process for counterfeit production, the srGANb

---

3 Data available at: https//www.univ-st-etienne.fr/graphical-code-estimation.

implements a generator network (the counterfeiter) and a discriminator network (to simulate the verifier).

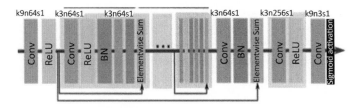

Figure 2.15. *srGANb convolutive neural network (Yadav* et al. *2019a)*

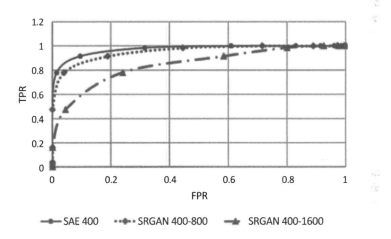

Figure 2.16. *ROC curves showing the performance of the SAE and SRGANb architectures in estimations presented in Yadav* et al. *(2019a)*

The experimental tests presented in Yadav *et al.* (2019a) resulted in Receiver Operating Characteristic (ROC) curves illustrated in Figure 2.16. We see that, for a true positive rate of 5%, an SAE can cause a standard verification system – based on thresholding to minimize intraclass variance – to accept 20% of false positives. This figure rises to 70% for an SRGANb architecture, which is identical to srGANb but in super-resolution mode, that is, including an additional layer for × 2 oversampling. These results give a glimpse of the potential of convolutive neural networks for estimating different types of CSGCs, such as those presented in this chapter.

Including neural-based binarization in the verification system makes the authentication system more robust (Figure 2.17). The inclusion of a × 2 SRGANb increases the mean correlation score of an authentic print from 48% to 82%. At the same time, estimation-based attacks become more difficult, with a verification based on correlation that increases on average from 3% to 15%.

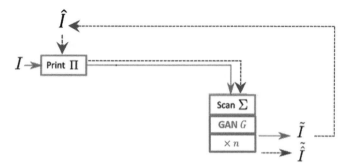

Figure 2.17. *Improvement of the verification system using a neural network at the end of the automatic learning process*

2.5. Conclusion

The performance of any document protection system based on the use of anti-copy elements, whether in the form of a PTS or CSGC, is dependent on in-depth knowledge of the print-scan chain involved.

CSGCs remove the need for acquisition recording and, consequently, for reference management. However, they are now threatened by improvements in the performance of deep-learning based code estimation algorithms used by counterfeiters. The application of algorithms of this type, post-learning, as part of the verification process offers a means of limiting the impact of these attacks. The use of color (Simske *et al.* 2009), which, in principle, would not limit smartphone compatibility (Maleshliyski and Garcia 2009), is one pathway to explore in order to improve protection. The evaluation of this protection is also a subject for further research. The security level of printed documents can also be increased by the addition of integrity checks: these form the subject of the following chapter.

2.6. References

Adams, G. (2010). Hand held Dyson relay lens for anti-counterfeiting. *Proceedings of the International Conference on Imaging Systems and Techniques (IST)*. IEEE, Thessaloniki, Greece.

Adams, G., Pollard, S., Simske, S. (2011). A study of the interaction of paper substrates on printed forensic imaging. *Proceedings of the 11th ACM Symposium on Document Engineering*. ACM, Mountain View, USA.

Baras, C. and Cayre, F. (2012). 2D bar-codes for authentication: A security approach. *Proceedings of the 20th European Signal Processing Conference (EUSIPCO).* EURASIP, Bucharest, Romania.

Baras, C. and Cayre, F. (2013). Towards a realistic channel model for security analysis of authentication using graphical codes. *Proceedings of the International Workshop on Information Forensics and Security (WIFS).* IEEE, Canton, China.

Bonev, S. and Wirnitzer, B. (2008). Security printing for product packaging in industrial printing applications. *Proceedings of the 35th International Research Conference of IARIGAI.* IARIGAI, Valencia, Spain.

Boutant, Y., Fournel, T., Becker, J.-M. (2005). Method for extracting random signatures from a material element and method for generating a decomposition base to implement the extraction method. Patent, FR28955431.

Buchanan, J.D., Cowburn, R.P., Jausovec, A.-V., Petit, D., Seem, P., Xiong, G., Atkinson, D., Fenton, K., Allwood, D.A., Bryan, M.T. (2005). "Fingerprinting" documents and packaging. *Nature*, 436(7050), 475–475.

Chiang, P.-J., Khanna, N., Mikkilineni, A.K., Segovia, M.V.O., Allebach, J.P., Chiu, G.T., Delp, E.J. (2010). Printer and scanner forensics: Models and methods. In *Intelligent Multimedia Analysis for Security Applications*, Sencar, H.T., Velastin, S., Nikolaidis, N., Lian, S. (eds). Springer, Berlin/Heidelberg.

Coltuc, D. and Fournel, T. (2011). The binary Guilloché patterns generator developed in the frame of project COSEC-ID. Report, Euripidès Project COSEC-ID.

Coltuc, D., Petrovici, M., Idrissa, A., Fournel, T. (2012). Print signatures after convex shaping for reliable document authentication. *Proceedings of the 11th Euro-American Workshop on Information Optics (WIO).* IEEE, Quebec, Canada.

Crespo-Monteiro, N., Destouches, N., Fournel, T. (2012). Updatable random texturing of Ag/TiO2 films for goods authentication. *Applied Physics Express*, 5(7), 075803.

Diong, M.L., Bas, P., Pelle, C., Sawaya, W. (2012). Document authentication using 2D codes: Maximizing the decoding performance using statistical inference. *Proceedings of the International Conference on Communications and Multimedia Security.* IFIP, Canterbury, UK.

Dirik, A.E. and Haas, B. (2012). Copy detection pattern-based document protection for variable media. *IET Image Processing*, 6(8), 1102–1113.

Fan, Z., Eschbach, R., Stinehour, J.E. (2010). Font printing system having embedded security information comprising variable data periodic line patterns. Patent, 7,787,154.

Ferreira, A., Bondi, L., Baroffio, L., Bestagini, P., Huang, J., dos Santos, J.A., Tubaro, S., Rocha, A. (2017). Data-driven feature characterization techniques for laser printer attribution. *IEEE Transactions on Information Forensics and Security*, 12(8), 1860–1873.

Fournel, T. (2009). Holographic codes and object authentication. In *Three Dimensional Imaging, Visualization and Display*, Javidi, B., Son, J.-Y., Martinez-Corral, M., Okano, F., Osten, W. (eds). International Society for Optics and Photonics, Bellingham, USA.

Fournel, T. (2012). "Biometric guilloches" for visual or automatic authentication. Report, Euripidès Project COSEC-ID.

Fournel, T. (2015). Generator of spread-spectrum based guilloches. Report, Euripidès Project COSEC-ID.

Fournel, T., Becker, J.-M., Boutant, Y. (2007). Self-encryption for paper document authentication. *Journal of Physics*, 77, 012007.

Fournel, T., Boutant, Y., Bois, L., Destouches-Castagna, N. (2008). Method for reconfigurable random texturing of a photochromatic component and security and/or authentication method implementing same. Patent, EP2359317A1.

Goldman, R.N. (1983). Non-counterfeitable document system. Patent, 4,423,415.

Idrissa, A., Fournel, T., Aubert, A. (2010). Secure embedded verification of print signatures. *Journal of Physics*, 206, 012036.

Kee, E. and Farid, H. (2008). Printer profiling for forensics and ballistics. *Proceedings of the 10th ACM Workshop on Multimedia and Security*. ACM, Oxford, UK.

Khanna, N. and Delp, E.J. (2009). Source scanner identification for scanned documents. *Proceedings of the First IEEE International Workshop on Information Forensics and Security*. IEEE, London, UK.

Khanna, N., Mikkilineni, A.K., Delp, E.J. (2009). Scanner identification using feature-based processing and analysis. *IEEE Transactions on Information Forensics and Security*, 4(1), 123–139.

Kiuchi, M. and Matsumoto, Y. (2011). Printed product, printed product detection method and detection apparatus, and authentication method and authentication apparatus. Patent, 8,055,064.

Leibenguth, J., Fournel, T., Coltuc, D. (2017). Procédé de génération de motifs de guilloches variables, dispositif de mise en oeuvre et document d'identification comprenant de tels motifs. Patent, WO2019064286.

Maleshliyski, S. and Garcia, F. (2009). Integration of anti-counterfeiting features into conventional 2D barcodes for mobile tagging. *Proceedings of the TAGA 61st Annual Technical Conference*. Technical Association of the Graphic Arts, Pittsburgh, USA.

Mayer, J., Borges, P.V., Simske, S.J. (2018). *Fundamentals and Applications of Hardcopy Communication: Conveying Side Information by Printed Media*. Springer, Cham, Switzerland.

Mikkilineni, A.K., Chiang, P.-J., Ali, G.N., Chiu, G.T., Allebach, J.P., Delp, E.J. (2005). Printer identification based on graylevel co-occurrence features for security and forensic applications. In *Security, Steganography, and Watermarking of Multimedia Contents VII*, Delp III., E.J., Wong, P.W. (eds). International Society for Optics and Photonics, Bellingham, USA.

Mikkilineni, A.K., Khanna, N., Delp, E.J. (2010). Texture based attacks on intrinsic signature based printer identification. In *Media Forensics and Security II*, Memon, N.D. (ed.). International Society for Optics and Photonics, Bellingham, USA.

Mikkilineni, A.K., Khanna, N., Delp, E.J. (2011). Forensic printer detection using intrinsic signatures. In *Media Watermarking, Security, and Forensics III*, Memon, N.D. (ed.). International Society for Optics and Photonics, Bellingham, USA.

Navarro, L.C., Navarro, A.K., Rocha, A., Dahab, R. (2018). Connecting the dots: Toward accountable machine-learning printer attribution methods. *Journal of Visual Communication and Image Representation*, 53, 257–272.

Nguyen, Q.-T., Delignon, Y., Chagas, L., Septier, F. (2014). Printer technology authentication from micrometric scan of a single printed dot. *Proceedings of the IS&T/SPIE-Electronic Imaging*. International Society for Optics and Photonics, San Francisco, USA.

Nguyen, H.P., Delahaies, A., Retraint, F., Nguyen, D.H., Pic, M., Morain-Nicolier, F. (2017). A watermarking technique to secure printed QR codes using a statistical test. *Proceedings of the Global Conference on Signal and Information Processing (GlobalSIP)*. IEEE, Montreal, Canada.

Nguyen, Q.-T., Delignon, Y., Septier, F., Phan Ho, A.-T. (2018). Probabilistic modelling of printed dots at the microscopic scale. *Signal Processing: Image Communication*, 62, 129–138.

Oliver, J. and Chen, J. (2002). Use of signature analysis to discriminate digital printing technologies. *Proceedings of the NIP & Digital Fabrication Conference*. Society for Imaging Science and Technology, San Diego, USA.

Pappu, R., Recht, B., Taylor, J., Gershenfeld, N. (2002). Physical one-way functions. *Science*, 297(5589), 2026–2030.

Phan Ho, A.-T., Mai Hoang, B.-A., Sawaya, W., Bas, P. (2013). Document authentication using graphical codes: Impacts of the channel model. *Proceedings of the First ACM Workshop on Information Hiding and Multimedia Security*. ACM, Montpellier, France.

Phan Ho, A.-T., Mai Hoang, B-A., Sawaya, W., Bas, P. (2014a). Authentication using graphical codes: Optimisation of the print and scan channels. *Proceedings of the 22nd European Signal Processing Conference (EUSIPCO)*. IEEE, Lisbon, Portugal.

Phan Ho, A.-T., Mai Hoang, B.-A., Sawaya, W., Bas, P. (2014b). Document authentication using graphical codes: Reliable performance analysis and channel optimization. *EURASIP Journal on Information Security*, 2014(1), 9.

Picard, J. (2004). Digital authentication with copy-detection patterns. *Proceedings of SPIE-Electronic Imaging*. International Society for Optics and Photonics, San Jose, USA.

Picard, J. and Landry, P. (2017). Two dimensional barcode and method of authentication of such barcode. Patent, 9,594,993.

Picard, J. and Zhao, J. (2011). Techniques for detecting, analyzing, and using visible authentication patterns. Patent, 7,937,588.

Picard, J., Sagan, Z., Foucou, A., Massicot, J.-P. (2014). Method and device for authenticating geometrical codes. Patent, 8,727,222.

Pollard, S.B., Adams, G.B., Simske, S.J. (2010a). Resolving distortion between linear and area sensors for forensic print inspection. *Proceedings of the International Conference on Image Processing (ICIP)*. IEEE, Hong Kong, China.

Pollard, S.B., Simske, S.J., Adams, G.B. (2010b). Model based print signature profile extraction for forensic analysis of individual text glyphs. *Proceedings of the International Workshop on Information Forensics and Security (WIFS)*. IEEE, Seattle, USA.

Rhoads, G.B. and Rodriguez, T.F. (2009). Secure documents with hidden signals, and related methods and systems. Patent, 7,555,139.

Schraml, R., Debiasi, L., Uhl, A. (2018). Real or fake: Mobile device drug packaging authentication. *Proceedings of the 6th ACM Workshop on Information Hiding and Multimedia Security*. ACM, Innsbruck, Austria.

Shang, S., Memon, N., Kong, X. (2014). Detecting documents forged by printing and copying. *EURASIP Journal on Advances in Signal Processing*, 1, 140.

Simske, S.J. and Adams, G. (2010). High-resolution glyph-inspection based security system. *Proceedings of the International Conference on Acoustics Speech and Signal Processing (ICASSP)*. IEEE, Dallas, USA.

Simske, S.J., Sturgill, M., Aronoff, J.S. (2009). Effect of copying and restoration on color barcode payload density. *Proceedings of the 9th ACM Symposium on Document Engineering*. ACM, Munich, Germany.

Simske, S.J., Sang, H., Mucher, P. (2012). Variable guilloche and method. Patent, 8,289,579.

Skoric, B., Schrijen, G.-J., Ophey, W., Wolters, R., Verhaegh, N., van Geloven, J. (2007). Experimental hardware for coating PUFs and optical PUFs. In *Security with Noisy Data*, Tuyls, P., Skoric, B., Kevenaar, T. (eds). Springer, London.

Smith, J.R. and Sutherland, A.V. (1999). Microstructure based indicia. *Proceedings of the Second Workshop on Automatic Identification Advanced Technologies*. IEEE, Morristown, USA.

Taran, O., Bonev, S., Voloshynovskiy, S. (2019). Clonability of anti-counterfeiting printable graphical codes: A machine learning approach. *Proceedings of the International Conference on Acoustics, Speech and Signal Processing (ICASSP)*. IEEE, Brighton, UK.

Tkachenko, I. and Destruel, C. (2018). Exploitation of redundancy for pattern estimation of copy-sensitive two level QR code. *Proceedings of the Workshop on Information Forensics and Security (WIFS)*. IEEE, Hong Kong, China.

Tkachenko, I., Puech, W., Strauss, O., Gaudin, J.-M., Destruel, C., Guichard, C. (2014). Fighting against forged documents by using textured image. *Proceedings of the 22nd European Signal Processing Conference*. EUSIPCO, Lisbon, Portugal.

Tkachenko, I., Puech, W., Strauss, O., Destruel, C., Gaudin, J.-M., Guichard, C. (2015). Rich QR code for multimedia management applications. *Proceedings of the 18th International Conference on Image Analysis and Processing*. ICIAP, Genoa, Italy.

Tkachenko, I., Puech, W., Destruel, C., Strauss, O., Gaudin, J.-M., Guichard, C. (2016a). Two-level QR code for private message sharing and document authentication. *IEEE Transactions on Information Forensics and Security*, 11(3), 571–583.

Tkachenko, I., Puech, W., Strauss, O., Destruel, C., Gaudin, J.-M. (2016b). Printed document authentication using two level QR code. *Proceedings of the International Conference on Acoustics, Speech and Signal Processing (ICASSP)*. IEEE, Shanghai, China.

Tkachenko, I., Destruel, C., Strauss, O., Puech, W. (2017). Sensitivity of different correlation measures to print-and-scan process. *Electronic Imaging*, 7, 121–127.

Tkachenko, I., Kucharczak, F., Destruel, C., Strauss, O., Puech, W. (2018). Copy sensitive graphical code quality improvement using a super-resolution technique. *Proceedings of the Image Processing Conference (ICIP)*. IEEE, Athens, Greece.

Van Renesse, R.L. (2005). *Optical Document Security*, 3rd edition. Artech House, Boston, USA, London, UK.

Villán, R., Voloshynovskiy, S., Koval, O., Pun, T. (2005). Multilevel 2D bar codes: Towards high capacity storage modules for multimedia security and management. *Proceedings of SPIE – Electronic Imaging*. SPIE IS&T, San Jose, USA.

Villán, R., Voloshynovskiy, S., Koval, O., Pun, T. (2006). Multilevel 2D bar codes: Towards high capacity storage modules for multimedia security and management. *IEEE Transactions on Information Forensics and Security*, 1(4), 405–420.

Wirnitzer, B. (2003). Copies with copy protection and method for generating a security code. Patent, DE10345669.

Wirnitzer, B., Gebhardt, R., Maleshliyski, S. (2007). Method for generating a security code for a matrix printing data memory. Patent, WO2009071673.

Wong, C.-W. and Wu, M. (2015). Counterfeit detection using paper PUF and mobile cameras. *Proceedings of the International Workshop on Information Forensics and Security (WIFS)*. IEEE, Rome, Italy.

Wong, C.-W. and Wu, M. (2017). Counterfeit detection based on unclonable feature of paper using mobile camera. *IEEE Transactions on Information Forensics and Security*, 12(8), 1885–1899.

Yadav, R., Tkachenko, I., Trémeau, A., Fournel, T. (2019a). Copy sensitive graphical code estimation: Physical vs numerical resolution. *Proceedings of the Workshop on Information Forensics and Security (WIFS)*. IEEE, Delft, Netherlands.

Yadav, R., Tkachenko, I., Trémeau, A., Fournel, T. (2019b). Estimation of copy-sensitive codes using a neuronal approach. *Proceedings of the Workshop on Information Hiding and Multimedia Security*. ACM, Paris, France.

Zhao, J., Picard, J., Thorwirth, N. (2010). Visible authentication patterns for printed document. Patent, 7,809,152.

Zhu, B., Wu, J., Kankanhalli, M.S. (2003). Print signatures for document authentication. *Proceedings of the 10th ACM Conference on Computer and Communications Security*. ACM, Washington D.C., USA.

3

Verifying Document Integrity

Petra GOMEZ-KRÄMER
L3i, La Rochelle University, France

An ever-increasing number of documents are dematerialized and processed every day, forming large streams of document images in companies, banks and administrative bodies. These documents may be original digital documents or scans of printed documents. Modern image editing software is easy to use and offers a simple way to modify the content of these images, for example by altering a date, name, address or amount to produce false "proof". Verifying the integrity of these documents is thus becoming an increasingly important concern. In this chapter, we shall present the main image analysis approaches used to verify document integrity in the context of printable and scanable documents.

3.1. Introduction

According to reports published by the ONDRP in 2017 and 2019, the number of procedures relating to document and/or identity fraud in France increased by 6.3% between 2014 and 2017 (ONDRP 2017, 2019). Note that 14,944 procedures were recorded in 2017 alone, with 43.3% relating to fake identity papers, 27% to fake vehicle documentation and 29.7% to other fake administrative documents. Counterfeiting is the most widespread type of fraud (50.3%), followed by fraudulent use (20.8%) and forgery (16%).

For a color version of all figures in this chapter, see www.iste.co.uk/puech/multimedia2.zip.

Multimedia Security 2,
coordinated by William PUECH. © ISTE Ltd 2022.

In addition to the economic impact, document fraud represents a major security issue for society. The use of false documents to obtain identity documents or visas is a major problem for administrative agencies and consulates. According to the Ministry of Foreign Affairs, 30–80% of the documents checked in countries such as Senegal, Côte d'Ivoire, the two Congos, Togo, Madagascar and the Comoros are fake[1]. A variety of techniques are used to obtain these documents; one approach involves the use of false papers that may then be used to obtain a genuine identity card or visa. According to Smith (2002), it is easier to obtain an identity card using fake documents than to counterfeit an actual identity card. This type of activity can have a significant impact; for example, the 2015 Paris terror attacks were partially financed by consumer credit obtained through the use of fake pay slips and tax documents (Brisard and Poirot 2016).

According to the 2019 ONDRP report, the majority of document fraud involves the forgery and counterfeiting of administrative documents (ONDRP 2019). Counterfeiting is the complete production of a genuine document by imitation. Interpol (2017) have also highlighted the existence of pseudo-documents, which are produced without authority and are not officially recognize; these may take very different forms and differ in physical appearance from a genuine document. Forgery is the alteration of one or more elements of an authentic document. It may relate to the date of validity, the cited identity or even a photograph. The 2017 ONDRP report also cites the example of stolen blanks, which are authentic documents that have been stolen prior to personalization and are then completed by the thief, receiver or forger (ONDRP 2017). This results in the production of a forged document.

Document integrity is the guarantee that a document has not been altered or modified. Several authors use the term "authentication" in this sense. According to the ISO15489 standard, the authenticity of a document is defined as the property of a document that can prove that it is what it claims to be, that it was created or sent by the person who claims to have created or sent it, and that it was created or sent on the date claimed. The identity of the issuer of a document, alongside document integrity, is thus at the heart of authentication.

Document integrity can now be verified automatically in the case of digital documents. These may be original digital documents, or printed and scanned versions. In this chapter, we shall focus on a variety of examples, such as administrative, commercial, financial and other supporting documents. Identity documents, which present a special case with specific security features, will not be covered here.

---

1 Available at: https://www.senat.fr/rap/r06-353/r06-35315.html.

Documents are designed by humans to be read by humans in the best conditions; thus, the main design criterion is readability. Document images are characterized by their binary character (e.g. black text on a white background) and by the presence of strong contrasts and contours. Figure 3.1 shows a comparison of the textures of an image of a page of text with a photographic image. We see that the textures in the text image are poorer: only certain frequencies are present. This fundamental difference means that the methods used to check the integrity of general images cannot be directly applied to document images; at the time of writing, few specific methods have been proposed for use in this context.

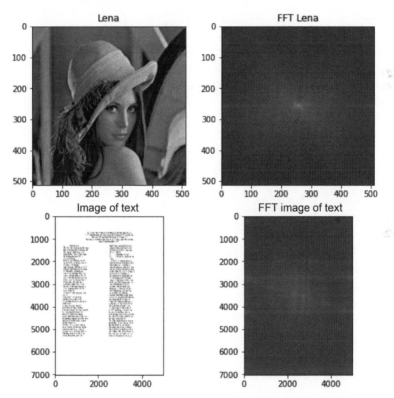

Figure 3.1. *Comparison of textures in an image of a natural scene and in an image of a printed and scanned page of text from the L3iTextCopies dataset (Eskenazi et al. 2015b) (left: image, right: magnitude of the Fourier transform)*

A distinction is made between different elements in documents, such as text, tables or graphics. Text is the element of content that contains the most information, and is most sensitive to fraudulent modification. A number of examples of fraudulent alterations to documents will be discussed in section 3.2.

Printing and scanning documents introduces degradations, which pose a major challenge for integrity verification methods. These degradations will be discussed in section 3.3. Sections 3.4 and 3.5 are devoted to different approaches to integrity verification. The first of these sections concerns active approaches, which use an extrinsic fingerprint that can be inserted into the document or transmitted with the document. The second relates to passive approaches based on the detection of intrinsic features in the document that provide information about its creation or modification.

3.2. Fraudulent manipulation of document images

In cases of forgery, a document image may be modified in different ways using image or text editing software. Modifications may be applied to the original digital document, or to a printed and scanned version. The document may then be re-digitized in order to conceal the modifications. In the case of counterfeiting, individuals attempt to reproduce an authentic document using image or text editing software. Cruz *et al.* (2018) distinguish between four different types of fraudulent manipulations applied to document images: imitation, copy-and-paste from within the same document, copy-and-paste from another document and information suppression. These will be described in detail below.

3.2.1. *Imitation*

Imitation fraud is the reproduction of the intrinsic properties of the document, including font characteristics such as type, size and color. Imitators attempt to find the most similar font to replace some of the content or add new content to a document, in the case of forgery, or to find the font that is the most similar to the document being reproduced, in the case of counterfeiting.

An example of forgery is shown in Figure 3.2(a). The date at the top of the figure is the original, while the date below has been modified, replacing the "3" with a "5". A different font has been used for this modification.

3.2.2. *Copy-and-paste of a region from the same document*

This technique is only used in cases of forgery by tampering. In this case, one part of the document is copied and pasted in a different location in order to modify or add content to the document. In this case, both source and destination are in the same document; prior to rescanning, the fraudulent document will contain two identical regions. In the field of digital forensics, this is known as copy and move forgery. An example of intra-document copy-and-paste is shown in Figure 3.2(b). The final figure of the amount (2) is copied and pasted over the first figure.

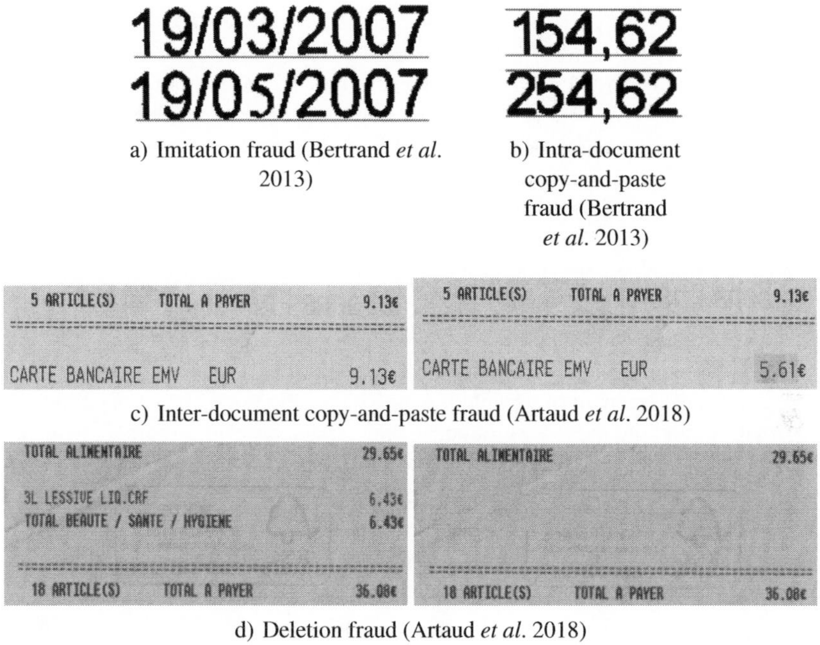

19/03/2007   154,62
19/05/2007   254,62

a) Imitation fraud (Bertrand *et al.* 2013)   b) Intra-document copy-and-paste fraud (Bertrand *et al.* 2013)

5 ARTICLE(S)	TOTAL A PAYER	9.13€		5 ARTICLE(S)	TOTAL A PAYER	9.13€
CARTE BANCAIRE EMV	EUR	9.13€		CARTE BANCAIRE EMV	EUR	5.61€

c) Inter-document copy-and-paste fraud (Artaud *et al.* 2018)

TOTAL ALIMENTAIRE		29.65€		TOTAL ALIMENTAIRE		29.65€
3L LESSIVE LIQ.CRF		6.43€				
TOTAL BEAUTE / SANTE / HYGIENE		6.43€				
18 ARTICLE(S)	TOTAL A PAYER	36.08€		18 ARTICLE(S)	TOTAL A PAYER	36.08€

d) Deletion fraud (Artaud *et al.* 2018)

Figure 3.2. *Examples of fraudulent modifications (tampering) in document images*

3.2.3. *Copy-and-paste of a region from another document*

In this case, the source and destination of the copied text are in two different documents, but the aim is the same: to modify or add content to a document. This is known in digital forensics as splicing. An example of fraudulent splicing is shown in Figure 3.2(c), where the total shown on a receipt, paid by credit card, has been modified by copying and pasting text from another receipt.

3.2.4. *Deleting information*

The purpose of this operation is to remove content from a document. As such, it only applies to cases of forgery. Information may be removed by copying and pasting a section of background over the content. Another option is to cut away the content and fill in the hold using interpolation or reconstruction techniques, such as inpainting. An example is shown in Figure 3.2(d), in which two lines of text in a receipt have been removed between the "alimentaire" (food) total and the grand total.

3.3. Degradation in printed and re-scanned documents

Scanned documents are visually similar to originals, but are deformed by the print and scan process. Figure 3.3 shows two examples of deformation resulting from the print and scan process. Two different scans of the same original character, using different printer/scanner combinations, are shown in Figure 3.3(a). The values of the pixels are not the same, particularly around the edges of the character. Figure 3.3(b) shows an original character and its deformations after one and two consecutive scans, respectively. The character, which was originally black, has become gray and the outlines have become blurred after scanning. After the second scan, there are gaps in the character. The effects of print and scan processes on colors are shown in Figure 3.4: the colors are not the same depending on the printer/scanner combination used. Color deviations appear in the graphic, which is not the same shade of yellow in the three images, and in the background, which looks blue in Figure 3.4(b). These degradations, which are associated with the print and scan process, will be described below.

a) Two scans of the same
character

b) Deformation of a character by the print and scan
process (original character, character after one
scan, character after a second consecutive scan)

Figure 3.3. *Examples of deformations resulting from the print and scan process*

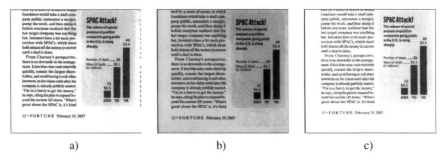

a)   b)   c)

Figure 3.4. *Extract from a journal page, printed and scanned using different printer/scanner pairings, from the L3iDocCopies dataset (Eskenazi et al. 2016)*

3.3.1. *Degradations linked to the print process*

There are several technologies used to produce paper documents from digital documents. The most commonly used are inkjet and laser printers. These printing processes are different, but in this section we shall focus on the main deformations.

When a document image is printed, users may change the size of the image or adjust margins automatically using the printing software. The result is a change of scale of the document with a possible loss of elements at the edges, such as the page number.

Screens use light to display colors and, consequently, images. Additive combinations of three colors – red, green and blue (RGB) – are used to produce different shades. Conversely, printers use subtractive color combinations – cyan, magenta, yellow and black/key (CMYK) – to produce colors. RGB colors must therefore be converted to CMYK, a conversion which may produce discrepancies in the colors. This is known as colorimetric noise.

Printers use a technique called halftoning to produce other colors from CMYK. This involves printing a pattern of colored microdots of fixed intensity. The intensity of a color is altered by acting on the size and spacing of the microdots. Different colors can be obtained by combining points of CMYK. An example is shown in Figure 3.5.

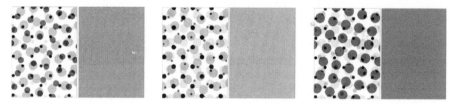

Figure 3.5. *Examples of halftoning (left: the halftone motif,*
right: the perceived color (Eskenazi 2016))

Printer resolution is specified in dpi (dots per inch), which is the number of pixels per inch in the printed image. The higher the dpi, the sharper the outline of the characters. If the dpi is too low, the outline no longer appears smooth and may have a stepped effect.

All of the mechanical elements in the printer may result in noise in the paper document. This leads to blurring or localized geometric deformations. The paper feed system can also leave traces on the paper and, if the speed is not constant, geometric deformations may be produced.

Finally, the characteristics of the paper also have an effect on the printed image. The paper may or may not be coated, and the granularity and sheet thickness may vary.

Ink is absorbed differently depending on the granularity and may run. Thickness can influence local geometric distortions. Furthermore, paper is subject to degradations associated with its lifecycle, such as creases or stains.

3.3.2. *Degradations linked to scanning*

There are several means of converting a physical document into a digital representation, such as scanning or digital photography (in still or video mode). Flatbed scanners remain the most widespread option (Barney Smith 2014).

To digitize a document using a scanner, a page is placed face-down on the glass. In the case of charged couple device (CCD) sensors, the scanner head moves from the top to the bottom of the page to acquire the image of the document line by line. A light source is used to illuminate the document, and mirrors are used to redirect the light reflected by the document through a lens onto the image sensor. The resolution of the sensor depends on the distance covered by the scanner head during the exposure time. Resolution in the opposite direction depends on the number of elements in the linear sensor and the magnification capacity of the optical system. Data from each line is accumulated to form a two-dimensional matrix of the image. Other scanners use complementary metal-oxide silicon (CMOS) sensors, which operate in two dimensions; in this case, all of the data for an image is acquired in one pass.

The digitization process converts a hard copy of a document into a matrix of two-dimensional pixels. The values of the pixels in the image depend on the color of the paper and ink, and the light intensity in the scanner. Poor placement of the page on the glass may result in distortions, such as translations or rotations.

Each element in the sensor returns a value corresponding to the mean of the light reflected from a region of the document.

The light acquired by a sensor element comes from a limited region of the paper document and is non-uniform for that region. This causes blurring in the document image, which is described by the point spread function (PSF). The document image also contains noise, which may result from variations in the paper and ink intensities, as well as from sensor noise.

The signal acquired by the sensor contains continuous values. These values must be quantized in order to be converted into a digital signal. Most scanners save the image in grayscale, but may save the image in binary (black and white) or color format depending on the settings. The image may also be compressed to reduce its size, and the compression factor plays a role in image quality. A high compression factor can result in blocky artifacts.

3.3.3. *Degradation models*

A variety of models have been proposed to describe each of these printing and scanning deformations (Mayer *et al.* 2018) for various applications, including for document analysis (Baird 2000). Baird proposed a document degradation model that takes into account the entire document creation process, including typography and acquisition. Degradations are described at page, character or pixel level. Parameters relating to document creation include the text size in points, document rotation, horizontal and vertical scaling factors and horizontal and vertical translations. Parameters for acquisition include resolution, blurring, the binarization threshold, sensitivity – which measures the noise added by the sensor – and a jitter value that describes geometric deformations at pixel level. According to this model, the image is first rotated, scaled and translated. The resolution and jitter then define the centers of each sensor element; blurring is applied to each sensor element, then noise is added and the value is thresholded in order to obtain the pixel value in the image.

Since text is the key element in documents, we have chosen to focus on methods that model character degradation. Kanungo *et al.* (2000) proposed a morphological model to model character degradations in binary images. This takes account of changes in pixel values (from black to white or vice versa) that may occur due to light fluctuations, sensor sensitivity and the value of the binarization threshold, alongside the blurring of the point spread function. The probability that the value of a background pixel will change depends on its distance d from the character outline. The model uses six parameters $\Theta = (\eta, \alpha_0, \alpha, \beta_0, \beta, k)$. Parameter η is the constant probability of all pixels toggling. The probability of a pixel switching from black to white is defined by the parameters α and α_0 and the probability of a pixel switching from white to black is defined by the parameters β and β_0. The probability of toggling decreases with the distance of the pixel from the contour. The final parameter k is the size of the disk used in a morphological closure operation to close possible holes in the characters. It takes account of the correlation introduced by the point spread function.

The degradation of an ideal binary image is calculated as follows:

1) for each pixel, calculate the distance d to the nearest contour;

2) toggle foreground pixels from black to white:

$$p(0|1, d, \alpha_0, \alpha) = \alpha_0 e^{-\alpha d^2} + \eta \qquad [3.1]$$

3) toggle background pixels from white to black:

$$p(1|0, d, \beta_0, \beta) = \beta_0 e^{-\beta d^2} + \eta \qquad [3.2]$$

4) apply a morphological closure operation with a structuring element of size k.

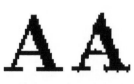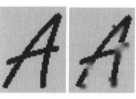

a) Character degradation in black and white (Kanungo *et al*. 2000)	b) Character degradation in grayscale (Kieu *et al*. 2012) obtained using DocCreator (Journet *et al*. 2017)	c) Character degradation in color (Do Thi *et al*. 2015)

Figure 3.6. *Examples of characters degraded using empirical models (left: original character, right: degraded character)*

Other authors have extended this model for grayscale images, taking account of additional degradations resulting from the lifecycle of the document (Kieu *et al*. 2012), and for color images (Do Thi *et al*. 2015). Examples of characters degraded using the models described here are shown in Figure 3.6. According to Baird (2000), Kanungo *et al*.'s method (Kanungo *et al*. 2000) can be used for reliable, automatic estimation of the parameters of Baird's own model (Baird 1992).

3.4. Active approaches: protection by extrinsic fingerprints

Active approaches aim to protect a document by introducing security elements in the form of extrinsic fingerprints that are used for future verification. These fingerprints may be hidden in the document itself, or transmitted with the document. There are two main types of approach: watermarking and digital signatures.

3.4.1. *Watermarking a document*

Watermarking consists of introducing invisible marks into the document. Generally, a compromise must be found between the imperceptibility of the marks, the robustness of the marks against attacks (compression, rotation, scaling, printing and scanning) and the capacity to encode information in the marks. The watermarking of document images is a special case. These methods generally have limited capacity for watermark embedding because there is no redundancy in the text, unlike natural scene images, audio or video (Nirmala *et al*. 2014). The main approaches are based on modifying the spacing between lines or words, modifying character characteristics, or modifying pixel values or frequencies in the spectral domain.

3.4.1.1. *Watermarking by space modification*

In this first class of methods, information is encoded in the white spaces of the document. The principle involves shifting words or lines slightly with respect to their normal position. Some of the most important work in this area has been carried out by Brassil *et al.* (1999, 1995).

Brassil *et al.* (1999) propose a method known as line-shift coding. A line will only be marked (shifted) if the two neighboring lines are sufficiently long. In a paragraph, only even lines will be shifted vertically by 2–3 pixels above or below their usual position.

The document is decoded using projection profiles that give information on the location of the text in the document. Let f be a page in a document with $f(x, y)$ the value of a pixel (0 or 1 for a black and white document) and $x = 0, \ldots, W$ and $y = 0, \ldots, L$. Values W and L correspond to the width and length of the page. A projection profile is the projection of a 2D matrix onto one dimension. For the horizontal profile, the sum of the pixel values for each line of the matrix is calculated:

$$h(y) = \sum_{x=0}^{W} f(x, y) \qquad [3.3]$$

Figure 3.7 shows a projection profile for three lines of text. The three peaks correspond to the lines of text, and the dips correspond to spaces between the lines. Let $[b_1, e_1]$, $[b_2, e_2]$ and $[b_3, e_3]$ be the interval, with b_i as the beginning of the line of text and e_i as the end of the line. The middle line of text $[b_2, e_2]$ is shifted, and lines 1 and 3 are the control lines.

Line shift is detected based on the baselines l_i. These are estimated as peaks in the profile in the neighborhood of e_i ($N(e_i)$):

$$l_i = \mathrm{argmax}_{y \in N(e_i)}\, g(y), \quad i = 1, 2, 3 \qquad [3.4]$$

where $g(y)$ is the profile of a block of three lines in the printed and scanned image after geometric correction.

Let l_1, l_2 and l_3 be the baselines of the lines of text $[b_1, e_1]$, $[b_2, e_2]$ and $[b_3, e_3]$. The decision rule is simply:

if $l_2 - l_1 < l_3 - l_2$, the line has been shifted upwards;
otherwise,   the line has been shifted downwards   [3.5]

The authors propose another decision rule based on the distance between the barycenters of the text lines in the original and encoded images; this approach is more robust, but access to the original image is required for decoding. The disadvantage of this method is that the shift in lines is easily perceived by the reader.

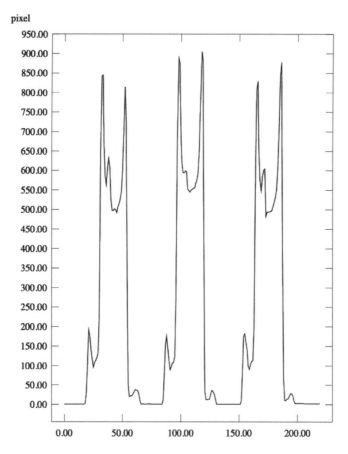

Figure 3.7. *Example of a horizontal profile of three lines of text (Brassil* et al. *1999)*

Elsewhere, Brassil *et al.* (1995) propose encoding information in the spaces between words. Each mark corresponds to a horizontal movement of a word. Words are shifted individually by adding or subtracting a constant value to the horizontal coordinate of the word.

A word is only shifted if the line in which it occurs contains enough words. If this is the case, even words, counting from the left margin, are shifted. In order to maintain text alignment, neither the first nor the last word of a line is shifted. The decoding method is similar to that used for offset lines (Brassil *et al.* 1999).

Several authors have proposed improvements for modifying word spacings, aiming to make marks more discreet and increase capacity. For example, in Huang and Yan's proposed method, words are shifted so that the spaces between the words represent a sine wave (Huang and Yan 2001). Information is encoded in the phase, amplitude and frequency of the sine waves. More recent methods have built on this notion (Kim *et al.* 2003; Zou and Shi 2005; Culnane *et al.* 2006). Nevertheless, all methods in this class assume that the spacing between words is predictable. All are robust to printing and scanning noise, but the encoding capacity remains low, as it is directly related to the number of words or lines in the document; furthermore, word or line shifting is relatively easy for readers to notice.

3.4.1.2. *Watermarking by character modification*

More recent work has focused on modifying the features of characters, in terms of either shape or color. These changes are less noticeable than shifting lines or words and the encoding capacity is greater. In this case, it is limited by the number of characters in the document.

The first methods of modifying the shape of the characters consist of changing the length (Brassil *et al.* 1995), width (Amano and Misaki 1999) or direction (Tan *et al.* 2012) of character strokes to encode information. Varna *et al.* (2009) proposed removing pixels from the left-hand contour of strokes; unfortunately, the marks remain visible for the reader. More recent methods use font generation to encode information. Several glyphs are designed for a character, each associated with a different mark. Qi *et al.* (2019) designed a vector font database, while Xiao *et al.* (2018) and Cu *et al.* (2019) used deep learning approaches to generate glyphs. Figure 3.8 shows five different generated versions of the character "a" in Times New Roman font.

Figure 3.8. *Generation of five versions of the character "a" to encode integers (Xiao* et al. *2018)*

Other approaches encode information in text by altering the luminosity, rather than the shape, of characters: this is known as text luminance modulation (TLM) (Bhattacharjya and Ancin 1999). Villán *et al.* (2006) extended this concept to color and halftones. Figure 3.9(a) shows an example of color modification. In this case, a dark character encodes a value of 0, while a light character encodes a value of 1. Figure 3.9(b) shows an example of TLM using halftones. The halftone pattern is rotated by 0° or 45° to encode values of 0 and 1, respectively. Other authors have suggested improvements to luminance modulation (Borges and Mayer 2007) and color modulation strategies (Borges *et al.* 2008). Cu *et al.* (2018) developed a luminance modulation method for encoding information in stable zones of a document, defined as the interior of segmented regions, excluding contours.

VAMOS A TRABAJAR

0 1 0 11 0 01000101

VAMOS A TRABAJAR

a) Text watermarking by color modulation. Top: original, bottom: encoded text (exaggerated)

b) Text watermarking by luminance modulation. Left: original, center: character marked with a 0, right: character marked with a 1 by halftone pattern rotation

Figure 3.9. *Examples of character watermarking by color and luminance modulation (Villán et al. 2006)*

3.4.1.3. *Watermarking by changing pixel values*

These approaches encode information by changing pixel values from black to white or vice versa, a process often known as pixel flipping. In general, pixel flipping occurs at the edges of the characters. The encoding potential of methods in this class is potentially high; however, since the watermarking approach is based on small dots, they are less robust to printing and scanning distortions. In these cases, printing and scanning must be carried out at high resolutions to limit decoding errors.

Generally, blocks are used to select regions and encode information. This sets them apart from block selection strategies and information encoding strategies. Zhao and Koch (1995) used a pseudo-random approach to choosing blocks in an image. Other methods involve dividing the whole image into blocks (Mei *et al.* 2001; Kim and Oh 2004; Zhu *et al.* 2012) before carrying out selection using a wavelet transform (Yang *et al.* 2008); another approach involves the use of character segmentation blocks (Huang *et al.* 2019; Tan *et al.* 2019). In terms of encoding, (Zhao and Koch 1995) encode values of 0 or 1 as a function of the percentage of black pixels in a block. Encoding consists of changing the pixel values on the edges. The value of the pixels with the most neighbors of the opposite value is changed. Wu and Liu (2004) further developed the method by Zhao and Koch (1995) by introducing perceptual information, such as the regularity and connectedness of the texture, into the choice of pixels to be modified. Mei *et al.* (2001) flipped pixel values in the non-smooth parts of character outlines. This method uses a base of outline patterns to add or remove pixels from the outline of a character while preserving its shape and minimizing outline artifacts and distortions. Kim and Oh (2004) presented a method of encoding information by modifying the histogram of the edge directions of the image blocks (Kim and Oh 2004).

Zhu *et al.* (2012) selected pixel positions to modify based on a perceptual model, while Tan *et al.* (2019) and Huang *et al.* (2019) based their methods on the Fourier descriptors of contours.

3.4.1.4. *Watermarking in the spectral domain*

The aim of these methods is to introduce marks into the spectral domain. The image is transformed in the spectral domain by modifying certain frequencies to insert fingerprints. A reverse transform is then applied to obtain the marked image. Approaches of this type have been developed using the wavelet transform (Liu *et al.* 1999; Nirmala *et al.* 2014; Chetan and Nirmala 2015) and the discrete cosine transform (Lu *et al.* 2002); nevertheless, the amount of research carried out in this area is limited, and the proposed methods present a number of drawbacks.

Liu *et al.* proposed coding information in the wavelet domain: however, this marking cannot withstand transformations such as binarization. Nirmala *et al.* (2014) encoded information in the LL sub-band of two-level discrete wavelets of image blocks, but the discrete nature of wavelets and rounding errors resulted in decoding errors. Chetan and Nirmala (2015) built on this work, encoding information in the LL sub-band of the integer wavelet transform. Lu *et al.* (2002) encoded information in the DC coefficients of the discrete cosine transform. However, changing the DC coefficient is equivalent to adding a constant value to all pixels in the block in the spatial domain.

3.4.2. *Digital signatures*

Digital signatures are based on content hashing techniques. In the case of natural scene images, the term "perceptual hashing" is used. These methods consist of computing a fingerprint using perceptual information in the document (the content), which is then associated with the document. The fingerprint may be inserted into the document by, for example, using a single or multi-dimensional barcode or by watermarking, or it may be transmitted separately for later integrity verification. A document is considered to have integrity if the fingerprint computed for the current document matches that transmitted with, or inserted in, the document.

Unlike cryptographic hashing methods, content hashing methods must be robust against attacks which preserve perceptive content, such as compression, rotation, brightness changes, and printing and scanning distortions. However, they must also provide the means of differentiating two different documents. For example, changing a character in the document changes its perceptual content, resulting in a different document. A trade-off needs to be made between robustness, fragility (the ability to detect content changes) and randomization.

Perceptual hashing involves three steps (Tan and Sun 2011):

1) extraction of characteristics: the robustness of the hashing method depends on the robustness of the extracted characteristics;

2) quantization: the feature vector is randomly quantized in order to increase robustness against malicious attacks. The random quantizer also ensures that different fingerprints will be independent;

3) compression: the final fingerprint is obtained by compressing intermediate fingerprints into a shorter character chain.

The main challenge in fingerprint computation lies in the extraction of robust characteristics. The quantization and compression steps are optional, but ensure that the fingerprint cannot be predicted.

Content hashing methods can be classified according to the content to which they apply: the entire page, text, layout and the images contained in documents.

3.4.2.1. *Full-page hashing*

Shimizu and Kim (2007) were the first to introduce the notion of content hashing methods for document integrity verification. In this approach, the components of the document (text and image) are identified, then a specific hashing method is applied to text, with a separate method used for images. However, the authors did not go beyond the component localization stage. Eskenazi (2016) built on this work to develop a global scheme for document hashing that applies specific algorithms for hashing text, images and layout based on a classification of regions of a document.

Malvido Garcià (2013) computed document fingerprints using a fuzzy hash, allowing modifications in document content to be located. A document is divided into blocks in order to apply quantization, a selection of discrete transform coefficients (cosine, wavelet or Fourier) and a cryptographic hash. The document fingerprint then consists of a concatenation of the hash codes of the blocks. The main drawback of this method is the very large size of the fingerprint.

3.4.2.2. *Text hashing*

Given that text is the most important element in a document, most content hashing methods focus on this aspect.

Shimizu and Kim (2007) suggested using an optical character recognition (OCR) program to extract text. Villán *et al.* (2007) also used an OCR for text extraction prior to cryptographic hashing. However, Ezkenazi *et al.*'s analysis of the impact of print and scan deformations on OCR programs showed that these are not sufficiently robust for text hashing for integrity verification purposes (Eskenazi *et al.* 2017b). The authors proposed the use of a post-treatment, known as alphabet reduction, to remove ambiguities left by the OCR. Alphabet reduction, as shown in Table 3.1, consists of merging classes of characters that are often confused in OCR. Empty lines and tabs are also removed at this stage.

Character	Replacement
Empty line	Deletion
Tabulation and space	Deletion
— (Em dash)	– (En dash)
', ' (Left and right apostrophes)	' (Centered apostrophe)
",", " (Left and right quotation marks, double apostrophes)	" (Centered quotation mark)
I, l, 1 (Upper-case I, lower-case L, number 1)	l (Vertical bar)
O (Upper-case O)	0 (zero)
fi (ligature)	f i (two letters: f and i)
fl (ligature)	f l (two letters: f and l)

Table 3.1. *Alphabet reduction (Eskenazi* et al. *2017b)*

Alternatives to OCR have also been proposed. Villán *et al.* (2007) used a random sampling of components (words or characters) in a document. Each component R, obtained by segmentation, is represented by a vector of the mean pixel values of P randomly sized and located rectangles. The vector values are then quantized and randomized to produce the final fingerprint. Tan and Sun (2011) proposed using the characteristics of character skeletons and their intersections as features; in their following work, they combined this approach with contour characteristics (Tan *et al.* 2011). Tkachenko and Gomez-Krämer (2017) studied the robustness of character classification using principal component analysis in a context of dual digitization for text hashing purposes.

3.4.2.3. *Layout hashing*

Page layout is part of the content of a document. It can have an esthetic impact on the reader and indicates the reading order of the document. Changes to the layout can also be a sign of fraudulent modifications, particularly in cases where information is added or deleted, or where the layout is not reproduced correctly in the case of counterfeiting. For this reason, the layout must also be secured. Eskenazi *et al.* (2015a) is the only study to have addressed this problem.

Eskenazi *et al.* (2015a) used the spatial relationships between regions in a document to develop a robust representation of the layout. The descriptor also gives a unique ordering of the regions of the document. The computation of the descriptor is based on a Delaunay triangulation of the barycenters of the regions, obtained by placing three fixed points outside the document, as illustrated in Figure 3.10. The barycenters of the regions are represented by vertices in the triangulation graph and the spatial relationships between the regions are shown by edges. The spatial relationships between regions can then be described by an adjacency matrix. A depth-first traversal of the graph from the upper left fixed point is used to order the vertices for this adjacency matrix. This forms the descriptor, which can then be represented by a character string or compressed by a cryptographic hash algorithm.

In the presence of printing and scanning distortions, the edges of the segmented regions may vary and the barycenters of the regions may move slightly. This can lead to a different triangulation and a different order of the regions. To take this into account, the authors recommend computing multiple descriptors by introducing variations in the triangulation. If one of these descriptors matches that of the original image, the layout is considered to have integrity.

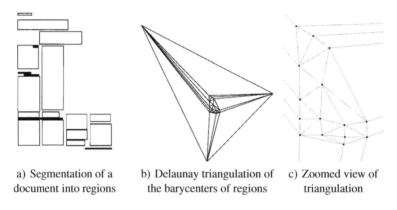

a) Segmentation of a   b) Delaunay triangulation of   c) Zoomed view of
document into regions   the barycenters of regions   triangulation

Figure 3.10. *Example of a Delaunay triangulation of the barycenters of regions (Eskenazi 2016)*

3.4.2.4. *Image hashing in documents*

This class of methods is similar to the traditional perceptual hashing methods used for natural scene images. The representation of images in documents is highly variable, from graphics to natural scenes.

Very few methods have been proposed for hashing images in a specifically documentary context. Smoacă (2011) proposes a method based on independent component analysis for hashing identity photos, but as the method is based on face recognition, it cannot be generalized. Eskenazi *et al.* (2017a) have proposed a method based on color indexing.

3.5. Passive approaches: detecting intrinsic characteristics

Passive approaches do not rely on advance security measures. These methods look for features in the document itself – intrinsic characteristics – that indicate that a document is fraudulent. Unlike extrinsic features, which are added to secure the document, intrinsic features are side effects of the creation or modification of the document. The detection of fraudulent documents may be seen as a classification task, based on finding the best indexing features or characteristics in an image, and then selecting and training the best classification algorithm. The main passive approaches include identifying the printer and scanner used (section 3.5.1), ink analysis and detection of graphic clues (section 3.5.2).

3.5.1. *Printer identification*

A document can be verified by identifying the printer that was used to produce it. In order to know whether a document is genuine, we must know what printer the original was printed on. If the document was printed by a different printer, it is considered fraudulent. Here, the intrinsic characteristics used are related to the defects and imperfections in the printer.

Printer identification can be carried out at different levels: in terms of printer type (laser printer, inkjet printer, etc.), brand, or model. One intrinsic characteristic concerns banding artifacts: light and dark lines running perpendicular to the direction of the paper (Khanna *et al.* 2008). Different models and brands are characterized by the unique frequencies of these artifacts (Ferreira *et al.* 2015), which are used in several methods. Printer identification approaches can be grouped according to whether they are designed specifically for textual content, or independently of content.

3.5.1.1. *Methods for textual content*

Methods designed specifically for textual content use imperfections in characters or words. This requires the segmentation of characters or words, or the use of OCR to compare the same characters or words. The main approaches use character texture analysis, or noise and geometric deformation analysis at the page level.

Many methods involve analyzing character texture. These methods generally involve extracting the statistical characteristics of the texture descriptors. The most common approaches are the gray level co-occurrence matrix (GLCM), discrete wavelet transform and local binary patterns (LBP). A classifier, usually a support vector machine (SVM) classifier, is then applied to identify the printer model.

Ali *et al.* (2004) have applied principal component analysis to segmented traits, notably the character "i", to reduce the dimension of the feature space before applying a Gaussian mixture model classifier.

Mikkilineni *et al.* (2005b) propose descriptors based on GLCM statistics to detect distortions of the character "e", which is the most frequently used character in the English language. The $glcm(n, m)$ entries in the GLCM matrix correspond to the number of occurrences of pixels with gray levels n and m, respectively, with a separation of (dr, dc) pixels:

$$glcm(n, m) = \sum_{(i,j),(i+dr,j+dc)\in ROI} 1_{\{Img(i,j)=n, Img(i+dr,j+dc)=m\}} \qquad [3.6]$$

with ROI as the region of interest (the segmented character) in the image Img.

The GLCM is normalized with respect to the number of pixels in the region of interest R_{glcm} to represent the probabilities of occurrence of pixels:

$$R_{glcm} = \sum_{(i,j),(i+dr,j+dc)\in ROI} 1 \qquad [3.7]$$

$$p_{glcm}(n, m) = \frac{1}{R_{glcm}} glcm(n, m) \qquad [3.8]$$

The authors use $dc = 0$, with dr in the interval $[1, 10]$. 22 statistical characteristics can be extracted from this matrix, including the marginal mean and standard deviation, entropy, maximum value and correlation. These characteristics are used to classify the five nearest neighbors. This work was later extended for an SVM classifier (Mikkilineni *et al.* 2005a), feature selections, and a metric based on Euclidean distances in a space of reduced dimensions by linear discriminant analysis (Mikkilineni *et al.* 2011). Ferreira *et al.* (2015) proposed an extension of GLCM for multi-directional and multi-scale analysis of character edges.

Joshi and Khanna (2020) used LBP-based descriptors, while Jiang *et al.* (2010) used the discrete cosine transform. Other authors propose a combination of features. Tsai *et al.* (2014) combined features from GLCM and discrete wavelet transform for documents in Chinese (Tsai and Liu 2013), using a feature selection algorithm to reduce their dimension. As in the case of English, a specific Chinese character was used. The work has been extended for Japanese using additional features from spatial, Gabor and Wiener filters (Tsai *et al.* 2015).

Recent methods have used convolutional neural networks (Ferreira *et al.* 2017; Tsai *et al.* 2019). Tsai *et al.* (2019) compared their work to an SVM architecture, similar to the one described in Tsai *et al.* (2015). Both methods were trained on a specific character for each language ("e" for English). They obtained similar results for documents printed at 300 dpi, but the results were better for microscopic images.

Other methods are based on an analysis of the noise and geometric deformations in a document. The method by Kee and Farid (2008) is based on an indirect modeling of the geometrical deformations caused by the printer. A printer profile consists of a linear base generated by principal component analysis from a set of degraded characters (the character "e"). This requires character registration. Wu *et al.* (2009) modeled geometric deformations as a projective transformation of the centers of characters and of the whole page. The original document is required in order to estimate the parameters of the projective transformation, which are then used in an SVM classifier. Jain *et al.* (2020) proposed a printer identification method based on a set of features that describe the geometric deformations at the level of the text lines. Schreyer *et al.* (2009) built on their previous work by considering the noise in an image, character contrast and the regularity of the printed character region in addition to the sharpness of character contours. This method is based on the extraction of statistical features from an analysis of noise, gradients, discrete cosine and wavelet transform frequencies.

Elkasrawi and Shafait (2014) have studied the residual noise generated around characters. Residual noise is extracted by removing the foreground from the document. Statistical descriptors are calculated for two vectors, representing, respectively, a mean of the lines and a mean of the columns of the residual noise image.

3.5.1.2. *Non-text-dependent methods*

Unlike the methods described above, which are specifically designed for textual content, the methods in this class are not tied to content and are often based on statistical characteristics at paragraph or page level. While textual content methods are designed to operate on black and white prints with binary or grayscale image analysis, methods in this class rapidly evolved from black and white to color prints. Content-independent methods are generally based on the noise analysis, geometric distortions or statistics of the transformed images.

The first approach consists of analyzing the noise generated by the printer. Methods in this class use noise extraction, statistical characteristics of the noise and classification by SVM. Choi *et al.* (2009) have proposed a method for extracting color noise in the discrete wavelet transform domain. The characteristics are statistics of the HH sub-band of the wavelet transform of RGB and CMYK images. Elsewhere, Choi *et al.* (2010) have proposed invisible noise extraction by subtraction with the Wiener filtered image in the CMYK color space. The extracted characteristics are statistics of the GLCMs of the four CMYK channels of the noise image. The method presented in Choi *et al.* (2013) is a continuation of earlier work; in this case, noise is extracted using a Wiener filter and a wavelet filter. The statistical features used include cross-correlation matrices between different RGB and CMYK color channels and statistics concerning the GLCMs of RGB and CMYK images. Tsai *et al.* (2011) also used a wavelet transform to extract characteristics, but introduced a feature selection method to reduce their dimension.

Printers produce a content-independent halftone pattern to simulate different colors and shades of gray. This halftone pattern is model and brand specific. Some methods rely on an analysis of the geometric deformations of these patterns to determine the printer model (Bulan *et al.* 2009; Wu *et al.* 2015), while others use statistical analysis of the transformed image (Ryu *et al.* 2010). Bulan *et al.* (2009) used non-uniform geometric distortions by the printer, comparing dot positions in the halftone patterns with the estimated positions. Wu *et al.* (2015) defined a pattern of hexagonal structures between the points in a halftone pattern. The distances and angles of these hexagonal structures are then used as the descriptor, and the Euclidean distance between descriptors is used to determine the printer model. Ryu *et al.* (2010) analyzed very high resolution half-tone textures for each CMYK channel. For each channel, they computed a histogram of the angles, obtained by the Hough transform, to use as a descriptor. The printer used for a page is then identified based on a correlation between the descriptor and a reference printer pattern. The reference pattern of a printer corresponds to the average of the histograms of several images printed by this printer.

Color laser printers are designed to add a pattern to printed pages that is unique to each printer. This pattern consists of small yellow dots, invisible to the naked eye, and is called the counterfeit protection system (CPS), or machine identification code (MIC). The dots form a pattern that is repeated several times on a page at a fixed horizontal and vertical distance. The spacing value is brand specific, while the pattern is printer specific and encodes the printer's serial number. van Beusekom *et al.* (2013) have proposed a method for pattern extraction and serial number decoding.

Recently, focus has shifted toward learning printer features rather than using hand-made descriptors. Bibi *et al.* (2019) propose a deep learning method for determining the printer model. The authors use a learning technique based on knowledge transfer from existing, pre-trained convolutional neural networks for feature extraction. Classification is then carried out using an SVM classifier.

3.5.2. *Detecting graphical clues*

The starting hypothesis in this case is that criminals will tend to modify elements of a document rapidly, and may not be expert users of image editing tools. On this basis, we may assume that modifications will not always be perfect, and these imperfections can be used for detection purposes. These methods are not suitable for the detection of counterfeit or pseudo-documents, but can be applied to cases of forged documents.

Several works have addressed the detection of graphical signs of modification, such as differences in the slant, size, alignment or noise of characters with respect to others (Bertrand *et al.* 2013), differences in font or character spacing within a word (Bertrand *et al.* 2015), line shifts in relation to the margins (van Beusekom *et al.* 2010), differences in the relative inclination of lines (van Beusekom *et al.* 2009) or even document texture (Cruz *et al.* 2017). For stamp verification, see Micenková *et al.* (2014).

Cruz *et al.* (2017) present a more general method, which is not connected to a specific type of forgery. This approach uses LBP texture analysis to detect discontinuities, resulting from image modification, in the background. An LBP is calculated by patch in text regions:

$$LBP_{P,R,t} = \sum_{p=O}^{P-1} s(g_p - g_c) \times 2^P \qquad [3.9]$$

where P is the set of all pixels g_p in the patch that are symmetrically and uniformly distributed in a circular neighborhood around pixel g_c with a radius R.

The uniform LBP distributor is calculated as follows:

$$LBP^u2_{P,R} = \begin{cases} \sum_{p=O}^{P-1} s(g_p - g_c), & \text{if } U(LBP_{P,R}) \leq 2 \\ P+1, & \text{otherwise} \end{cases} \qquad [3.10]$$

$$U(N_{P,R}) = |s(g_{p-1} - g_c) - s(g_0 - g_c)| + \sum_{p=1}^{P-1} |s(g_p - g_c) - s(g_{p-1} - g_c)|$$

with $s(x) = 1$ if $x \geq 0$ and 0 otherwise.

Function U measures the number of transitions between pixels in the circular representation. The authors assume that the changes are made at character or word level, and that one genuine patch will have a similar profile to other genuine patches. The difference between patches is qualified by computing the distance L^2 between the descriptors of the current patch and its neighbors. This gives a set of N values that are concatenated into the final descriptor. The authentic and modified patches are classified using an SVM classifier.

3.5.3. *Other approaches*

Scanner identification methods have been put forward alongside printer identification, although this area has received less attention. Scanner identification approaches are based on noise isolation, noise feature extraction and feature classification. Noise isolation is performed by subtracting the scanned image from the filtered scanned image. These methods are generic and not context dependent, with the exception of that developed by Khanna *et al.* (2008), using GLCM-based texture analysis of the character "e". Gaubatz and Simske (2009) proposed a method for identifying printer and scanner pairs from color test patterns.

Several different methods have been designed to verify handwritten signatures, including author identification (see the SigComp competition[2]). However, no research has yet been conducted into verifying the integrity of signatures in printed and scanned documents, in order to establish whether the re-scanned signature is authentic. Eskenazi *et al.* (2017a) discusses this problem by treating signatures as images, applying an image hashing method.

Other approaches use ink analysis to identify added words or characters. Ink analysis generally relies on chemical processes, high-resolution microscope image acquisition or multi-spectral imaging. Nevertheless, some authors have attempted to identify handwritten additions in digitized documents by analyzing the color and texture of the pen used (Kumar *et al.* 2012) or the geometric and structural characteristics of the strokes (Wadhwa *et al.* 2018).

3.6. Conclusion

Many different integrity verification methods have been proposed for images of natural scenes. These methods cannot be applied directly to document images due to the fact that documents are man-made and thus present specific characteristics. Documents are characterized by their binary character, strong contrasts and contours, and poor textures. The case of printed and scanned documents continues to present significant challenges. The amount of work carried out on the subject of document integrity verification remains low, and further research is still needed to develop reliable methods that can withstand the effects of printing and scanning distortions. In terms of active approaches, many authors have focused on watermarking; content hashing for digital signatures has attracted much less attention, and existing methods are subject to robustness problems. Many passive approaches have focused on printer identification. However, many documents are now transmitted electronically and printed by the user to serve as proof. This means that the basic assumption that the printer used to create the document can be known is no longer valid. Other approaches, such as graphical clue detection, have not yet been studied in depth and are only applicable to specific types of document fraud. Several complementary methods may need to be combined in order to develop a truly reliable system.

3.7. References

Ali, G.N., Chiang, P.-J., Mikkilineni, A.K., Chiu, G.T.-C., Delp, E.J., Allebach, J.P. (2004). Application of principal components analysis and Gaussian mixture models to printer identification. In *International Conference on Digital Printing Technologies*. NIP, Salt Lake City.

---

2 Available at: https://sigcomp2019.cursorinsight.com.

Amano, T. and Misaki, D. (1999). A feature calibration method for watermarking of document images. In *International Conference on Document Analysis and Recognition*. IEEE, Bangalore.

Artaud, C., Sidere, N., Doucet, A., Ogier, J., Poulain D'Andecy, V. (2018). Find it! Fraud detection contest report. In *International Conference on Pattern Recognition*. IEEE, Beijing.

Baird, H.S. (1992). *Document Image Defect Models*. Springer, Berlin/Heidelberg.

Baird, H.S. (2000). The state of the art of document image degradation modeling. In *International Workshop on Document Analysis Systems*. DAS, Rio de Janeiro.

Barney Smith, E.H. (2014). Document creation, image acquisition and document quality. In *Handbook of Document Image Processing and Recognition*, Doermann, D., Tombre, K. (eds). Springer, London.

Bertrand, R., Gomez-Krämer, P., Terrades, O.R., Franco, P., Ogier, J.-M. (2013). A system based on intrinsic features for fraudulent document detection. In *International Conference on Document Analysis and Recognition*. ICDAR, Washington.

Bertrand, R., Terrades, O.R., Gomez-Krämer, P., Franco, P., Ogier, J.-M. (2015). A conditional random field model for font forgery detection. In *International Conference on Document Analysis and Recognition*. ICDAR, Tunis.

van Beusekom, J., Shafait, F., Breuel, T.M. (2009). Automatic line orientation measurement for questioned document examination. In *International Workshop on Computational Forensics*. IWCF, The Hague.

van Beusekom, J., Shafait, F., Breuel, T.M. (2010). Document inspection using text-line alignment. In *International Workshop on Document Analysis Systems*. DAS, Boston.

van Beusekom, J., Shafait, F., Breuel, T.M. (2013). Automatic authentication of color laser print-outs using machine identification codes. *Pattern Analysis and Applications*, 16(4), 663–678.

Bhattacharjya, A.K. and Ancin, H. (1999). Data embedding in text for a copier system. In *International Conference on Image Processing*. IEEE, Kobe.

Bibi, M., Hamid, A., Moetesum, M., Siddiqi, I. (2019). Document forgery detection using printer source identification – A text-independent approach. In *International Conference on Document Analysis and Recognition Workshops (ICDARW)*. UTS, Sydney.

Borges, P.V.K. and Mayer, J. (2007). Text luminance modulation for hardcopy watermarking. *Signal Processing*, 87(7), 1754–1771.

Borges, P.V.K., Mayer, J., Izquierdo, E. (2008). Robust and transparent color modulation for text data hiding. *IEEE Transactions on Multimedia*, 10(8), 1479–1489.

Brassil, J., Low, S., Maxemchuk, N.F., O'Gorman, L. (1995). Electronic marking and identification techniques to discourage document copying. *IEEE Journal on Selected Areas in Communications*, 13(8), 1495–1504.

Brassil, J.T., Low, S., Maxemchuk, N.F. (1999). Copyright protection for the electronic distribution of text documents. *Proceedings of the IEEE*, 87(7), 1181–1196.

Brisard, J. and Poirot, G. (2016). Le financement des attentats de Paris (7–9 janvier et 13 novembre 2015). Report, Centre d'analyse du terrorisme.

Bulan, O., Mao, J., Sharma, G. (2009). Geometric distortion signatures for printer identification. In *International Conference on Acoustics, Speech and Signal Processing*. IEEE, Taipei.

Chetan, K. and Nirmala, S. (2015). An efficient and secure robust watermarking scheme for document images using integer wavelets and block coding of binary watermarks. *Journal of Information Security and Applications*, 24/25, 13–24.

Choi, C., Lee, M., Lee, H. (2010). Scanner identification using spectral noise in the frequency domain. In *International Conference on Image Processing*. IEEE, Hong Kong.

Choi, J.-H., Im, D.-H., Lee, H.-Y., Oh, J.-T., Ryu, J.-H., Lee, H.-K. (2009). Color laser printer identification by analyzing statistical features on discrete wavelet transform. In *International Conference on Image Processing*. IEEE, Cairo.

Choi, J.-H., Lee, H.-Y., Lee, H.-K. (2013). Color laser printer forensic based on noisy feature and support vector machine classifier. *Multimedia Tools and Applications*, 67, 363–382.

Cruz, F., Sidere, N., Coustaty, M., Poulain D'Andecy, V., Ogier, J. (2017). Local binary patterns for document forgery detection. In *International Conference on Document Analysis and Recognition*. IEEE, Kyoto.

Cruz, F., Sidère, N., Coustaty, M., Poulain D'Andecy, V., Ogier, J. (2018). Categorization of document image tampering techniques and how to identify them. In *Pattern Recognition and Information Forensics International Workshops*. CVAUI, IWCF and MIPPSNA, Beijing.

Cu, V.L., Burie, J., Ogier, J. (2018). Stable regions and object fill-based approach for document images watermarking. In *International Workshop on Document Analysis Systems*. DAS, Vienna.

Cu, V.L., Burie, J., Ogier, J., Liu, C. (2019). Hiding security feature into text content for securing documents using generated font. In *International Conference on Document Analysis and Recognition*. UTS, Sydney.

Culnane, C., Treharne, H., Ho, A.T.S. (2006). A new multi-set modulation technique for increasing hiding capacity of binary watermark for print and scan processes. In *International Conference on Digital Watermarking*. IWDW, Jeju.

Do Thi, L., Carel, E., Ogier, J., Burie, J. (2015). A character degradation model for color document images. In *International Conference on Document Analysis and Recognition*. ICDAR, Tunis.

Elkasrawi, S. and Shafait, F. (2014). Printer identification using supervised learning for document forgery detection. In *International Workshop on Document Analysis Systems*. DAS, Tours.

Eskenazi, S. (2016). On the stability of document analysis algorithms. Application to hybrid document hashing technologies. PhD Thesis, Université de la Rochelle, La Rochelle.

Eskenazi, S., Gomez-Krämer, P., Ogier, J.-M. (2015a). The Delaunay document layout descriptor. In *International Symposium on Document Engineering*. ACM, Lausanne.

Eskenazi, S., Gomez-Krämer, P., Ogier, J.-M. (2015b). When document security brings new challenges to document analysis. *Lectures Notes in Computer Science*, 8915, 104–116.

Eskenazi, S., Gomez-Krämer, P., Ogier, J. (2016). Evaluation of the stability of four document segmentation algorithms. In *12th IAPR Workshop on Document Analysis Systems*. IAPR, Santorini.

Eskenazi, S., Bodin, B., Gomez-Krämer, P., Ogier, J.-M. (2017a). A perceptual image hashing algorithm for hybrid document security. In *International Conference on Document Analysis and Recognition*. ICDAR, Kyoto.

Eskenazi, S., Gomez-Krämer, P., Ogier, J.-M. (2017b). A study of the factors influencing OCR stability for hybrid security. In *International Conference on Document Analysis and Recognition*. ICDAR, Kyoto.

Ferreira, A., Navarro, L.C., Pinheiro, G., dos Santos, J.A., Rocha, A. (2015). Laser printer attribution: Exploring new features and beyond. *Forensic Science International*, 247, 105–125.

Ferreira, A., Bondi, L., Baroffio, L., Bestagini, P., Huang, J., dos Santos, J.A., Tubaro, S., Rocha, A. (2017). Data-driven feature characterization techniques for laser printer attribution. *IEEE Transactions on Information Forensics and Security*, 12(8), 1860–1873.

Gaubatz, M.D. and Simske, S.J. (2009). Printer-scanner identification via analysis of structured security deterrents. In *International Workshop on Information Forensics and Security*. IEEE, London.

Huang, D. and Yan, H. (2001). Interword distance changes represented by sine waves for watermarking text images. *IEEE Transactions on Circuits and Systems for Video Technology*, 11, 1237–1245.

Huang, K., Tian, X., Yu, H., Yu, M., Yin, A. (2019). A high capacity watermarking technique for the printed document. *Electronics*, 8(12), 1403.

Interpol (2017). Identity and travel document fraud. Technical report, Interpol.

Jain, H., Joshi, S., Gupta, G., Khanna, N. (2020). Passive classification of source printer using text-line-level geometric distortion signatures from scanned images of printed documents. *Multimedia Tools and Applications*, 79(11), 7377–7400.

Jiang, W., Ho, A.T.S., Treharne, H., Shi, Y.Q. (2010). A novel multi-size block Benford's law scheme for printer identification. In *Advances in Multimedia Information Processing*, Qiu, G., Lam, K.M., Kiya, H., Xue, X.-Y., Kuo, C.-C.J., Lew, M.S. (eds). Springer, Berlin/Heidelberg.

Joshi, S. and Khanna, N. (2020). Source printer classification using printer specific local texture descriptor. *IEEE Transactions on Information Forensics and Security*, 15, 160–171.

Journet, N., Visani, M., Mansencal, B., Kieu, V.C., Billy, A. (2017). Doccreator: A new software for creating synthetic ground-truthed document images. *Journal of Imaging*, 3(4), 62.

Kanungo, T., Haralick, R.M., Baird, H.S., Stuetzle, W., Madigan, D. (2000). A statistical, nonparametric methodology for document degradation model validation. *IEEE Transactions on Pattern Analysis and Machine Intelligence*, 22(11), 1209–1223.

Kee, E. and Farid, H. (2008). Printer profiling for forensics and ballistics. In *Workshop on Multimedia and Security*. ACM, Oxford.

Khanna, N., Mikkilineni, A.K., Chiu, G.T., Allebach, J.P., Delp, E.J. (2008). Survey of scanner and printer forensics at Purdue University. In *International Workshop on Computational Forensic*. IWCF, Washington.

Kieu, V.C., Visani, M., Journet, N., Domenger, J., Mullot, R. (2012). A character degradation model for grayscale ancient document images. In *International Conference on Pattern Recognition*. ICPR, Tsukuba.

Kim, Y.-W. and Oh, I.-S. (2004). Watermarking text document images using edge direction histograms. *Pattern Recognition Letters*, 25(11), 1243–1251.

Kim, Y.-W., Moon, K.-A., Oh, I.-S. (2003). A text watermarking algorithm based on word classification and inter-word space statistics. In *International Conference on Document Analysis and Recognition*. IEEE, Edinburgh.

Kumar, R., Pal, N.R., Chanda, B., Sharma, J.D. (2012). Forensic detection of fraudulent alteration in ball-point pen strokes. *IEEE Transactions on Information Forensics and Security*, 7(2), 809–820.

Liu, Y., Mant, J., Wong, E.K., Low, S.H. (1999). Marking and detection of text documents using transform-domain techniques. *Security and Watermarking of Multimedia Contents*, 3657, 317–328.

Lu, H., Shi, X., Shi, Y.Q., Kot, A.C., Chen, L. (2002). Watermark embedding in DC components of DCT for binary images. In *Workshop on Multimedia Signal Processing*. IEEE, St Thomas.

Malvido Garcià, A. (2013). Secure Imprint GeNerated for PapEr Documents (SIGNED). Report, Bit Oceans.

Mayer, J., Borges, P.V.K., Simske, S.J. (2018). *Fundamentals and Applications of Hardcopy Communication: Conveying Side Information by Printed Media*, 1st edition. Springer, Cham.

Mei, Q.G., Wong, E.K., Memon, N.D. (2001). Data hiding in binary text documents. In *Security and Watermarking of Multimedia Contents*, Wong, P.W., Delp III, E.J. (eds). SPIE, San Jose.

Micenková, B., van Beusekom, J., Shafait, F. (2014). Stamp verification for automated document authentication. In *International Workshop on Computational Forensics*. IWCF, Stockholm.

Mikkilineni, A.K., Arslan, O., Chiang, P.-J., Kumontoy, R., Allebach, J., Chiu, G., Delp, E.J. (2005a). Printer forensics using SVM techniques. In *International Conference on Digital Printing Technologies*. NIP, Baltimore.

Mikkilineni, A.K., Chiang, P.-J., Ali, G.N., Chiu, G.T.C., Allebach, J.P., Delp, E.J. (2005b). Printer identification based on graylevel co-occurrence features for security and forensic applications. In *Security, Steganography, and Watermarking of Multimedia Contents VII*, Delp III, E.J., Wong, P.W. (eds). International Society for Optics and Photonics, Bellingham.

Mikkilineni, A.K., Khanna, N., Delp, E.J. (2011). Forensic printer detection using intrinsic signatures. In *Media Watermarking, Security, and Forensics III*, Memon, N.D. (ed). International Society for Optics and Photonics, Bellingham.

Nirmala, S., Naghabhushan, F., Chetan, K. (2014). A new robust watermarking scheme for document images by randomized distribution of watermark segments. In *International Conference on Recent Trends in Information, Telecommunication and Computing*. ITC, Chandigarh.

ONDRP (2017). Éléments de connaissance sur la fraude aux documents et à l'identité en 2015. Report, Observatoire national de la délinquance et des réponses pénales.

ONDRP (2019). Éléments de connaissance sur la fraude aux documents et à l'identité en 2017. Report, Observatoire national de la délinquance et des réponses pénales.

Qi, W., Guo, W., Zhang, T., Liu, Y., Guo, Z., Fang, X. (2019). Robust authentication for paper-based text documents based on text watermarking technology. *Mathematical Biosciences and Engineering*, 16, 2233–2249.

Ryu, S., Lee, H., Im, D., Choi, J., Lee, H. (2010). Electrophotographic printer identification by halftone texture analysis. In *International Conference on Acoustics, Speech and Signal Processing*. IEEE, Dallas.

Schreyer, M., Schulze, C., Stahl, A., Effelsberg, W. (2009). Intelligent printing technique recognition and photocopy detection for forensic document examination. In *Informatiktage Conference*, Gesellschaft für Informatik (ed.). Bonn.

Schulze, C., Schreyer, M., Stahl, A., Breuel, T.M. (2009). Using DCT features for printing technique and copy detection. In *Fifth IFIP WG International Conference on Digital Forensics*. IFIP, Orlando.

Shimizu, D. and Kim, H.Y. (2007). Perceptual hashing for hardcopy document authentication using morphological segmentation. In *International Symposium on Mathemathical Morphology*. ISMM, Rio de Janeiro.

Smith, A. (2002). Identity fraud: A study. Report, Economic and Domestic Secretariat, Cabinet Office.

Smoacă, A. (2011). ID photograph hashing: A global approach. PhD Thesis, Université Jean Monnet, Saint-Étienne/Politehnica University of Bucharest.

Tan, L. and Sun, X. (2011). Robust text hashing for content-based document authentication. *Information Technology Journal*, 10(8), 1608–1613.

Tan, L., Sun, X., Zhou, Z., Zhang, W. (2011). Perceptual text image hashing based on shape recognition. *Advances in Information Sciences and Service Sciences*, 3(8), 1–7.

Tan, L., Sun, X., Sun, G. (2012). Print-scan resilient text image watermarking based on stroke direction modulation for Chinese document authentication. *Radioengineering*, 21(1), 170–181.

Tan, L., Hu, K., Zhou, X., Chen, R., Jiang, W. (2019). Print-scan invariant text image watermarking for hardcopy document authentication. *Multimedia Tools and Applications*, 78(10), 13189–13211.

Tkachenko, I. and Gomez-Krämer, P. (2017). Robustness of character recognition techniques to double print-and-scan process. In *International Conference on Document Analysis and Recognition*. IAPR, Kyoto.

Tsai, M.-J. and Liu, J. (2013). Digital forensics for printed source identification. In *International Symposium on Circuits and Systems*. IEEE, Beijing.

Tsai, M.-J., Liu, J., Wang, C.-S., Chuang, C.-H. (2011). Source color laser printer identification using discrete wavelet transform and feature selection algorithms. In *International Symposium of Circuits and Systems*. IEEE, Rio de Janeiro.

Tsai, M.-J., Yin, J.-S., Yuadi, I., Liu, J. (2014). Digital forensics of printed source identification for Chinese characters. *Multimedia Tools and Applications*, 73(3), 2129–2155.

Tsai, M.-J., Hsu, C., Yin, J., Yuadi, I. (2015). Japanese character based printed source identification. In *International Symposium on Circuits and Systems*. IEEE, Lisbon.

Tsai, M.-J., Tao, Y.-H., Yuadi, I. (2019). Deep learning for printed document source identification. *Signal Processing: Image Communication*, 70, 184–198.

Varna, A.L., Rane, S., Vetro, A. (2009). Data hiding in hard-copy text documents robust to print, scan and photocopy operations. In *International Conference on Acoustics, Speech, and Signal Processing*. IEEE, Taipei.

Villán, R., Voloshynovskiy, S., Koval, O., Vila, J., Topak, E., Deguillaume, F., Rytsar, Y., Pun, T. (2006). Text data-hiding for digital and printed documents: Theoretical and practical considerations. In *Security, Steganography, and Watermarking of Multimedia Contents*, Delp III, E.J., Wong, P.W. (eds). International Society for Optics and Photonics, Bellingham.

Villán, R., Voloshynovskiy, S., Koval, O., Deguillaume, F., Pun, T. (2007). Tamper-proofing of electronic and printed text documents via robust hashing and data-hiding. In *Security, Steganography, and Watermarking of Multimedia Contents*, Delp III, E.J., Wong, P.W. (eds). International Society for Optics and Photonics, Bellingham.

Wadhwa, A., Maheshwari, M., Dansena, P., Bag, S. (2018). Geometrical and structural features for forensics in handwritten bank cheques. In *India Council International Conference*. IEEE, Coimbatore.

Wu, M. and Liu, B. (2004). Data hiding in binary image for authentication and annotation. *IEEE Transactions on Multimedia*, 6(4), 528–538.

Wu, Y., Kong, X., You, X., Guo, Y. (2009). Printer forensics based on page document's geometric distortion. In *International Conference on Image Processing*. IEEE, Le Caire.

Wu, H., Kong, X., Shang, S. (2015). A printer forensics method using halftone dot arrangement model. In *China Summit and International Conference on Signal and Information Processing*. IEEE, Chengdu.

Xiao, C., Zhang, C., Zheng, C. (2018). FontCode: Embedding information in text documents using glyph perturbation. *ACM Transactions on Graphics*, 37(2), 1–16.

Yang, H., Kot, A.C., Rahardja, S. (2008). Orthogonal data embedding for binary images in morphological transform domain – A high-capacity approach. *IEEE Transactions on Multimedia*, 10(3), 339–351.

Zhao, J. and Koch, E. (1995). Embedding robust labels into images for copyright protection. In *Procceedings of theConference on Intellectual Property Rights and New Technologies*, Brunnstein, K. and Sint, P.P. (eds). R. Oldenbourg Verlag GmbH, Hamburg.

Zhu, X., Wei, L., Chen, Y. (2012). Novel binary document image watermarking exploiting the features of double domains. *International Journal of Computer and Electrical Engineering*, 4(1), 87–92.

Zou, D. and Shi, Y.Q. (2005). Formatted text document data hiding robust to printing, copying and scanning. In *International Symposium on Circuits and Systems*. IEEE, Kobe.

4

Image Crypto-Compression

Vincent ITIER[1], Pauline PUTEAUX[2] and William PUECH[2]
[1]CRIStAL, University of Lille, CNRS, IMT Lille Douai, France
[2]LIRMM, Université de Montpellier, CNRS, France

The growing popularity of social networks and cloud computing has greatly increased the number of Joint Photographic Experts Group (JPEG)-compressed image exchanges. In this context, the security of the transmission channel and/or online storage can be sensitive to privacy leaks. Selective encryption is an effective tool for masking image content and protecting privacy while remaining consistent with the image encoding format. JPEG image encryption, also known as JPEG image crypto-compression, defines methods for encrypting a portion of the image content while still respecting the JPEG format. These methods provide a level of visual privacy while attempting to limit the file size expansion compared to classic JPEG compression. This type of method, which appeared in the early 2000s, relies on different approaches to implement the basic principles of cryptography. More recently, the question of security against decryption attacks has been the subject of increasing attention. Image processing in the crypto-compressed domain, that is, without decryption, is another new area of work.

4.1. Introduction

Over the past decade, increasing use of online storage (the cloud) and the sharing of data over networks has led to a growing demand for security and privacy with

---

For a color version of all figures in this chapter, see www.iste.co.uk/puech/multimedia2.zip.

respect to personal data; the EU's General Data Protection Regulation (GDPR)[1] is a clear illustration of this increased concern. In practice, confidentiality, authentication and integrity are under constant threat when multimedia data are transmitted and/or stored, due to hacking, copying and attempts to make malicious use of information. It is not enough to simply secure access to the file: the content itself must be protected. This can be done by encryption or data hiding.

Image encryption is an effective method of ensuring the visual privacy of image content while preserving its format and size. Unauthorized individuals are prevented from accessing the original clear image content by the introduction of randomness. Encryption may be full, where the original data are encrypted in their entirety, or selective, where only a portion of the data are protected; the choice of approach depends on the application and on the desired level of security.

The rapid growth of network usage means that bandwidth requirements are constantly increasing. Limiting bandwidth usage is an important challenge for digital productivity and environmental reasons. JPEG compression has been the most widely used compression format for storing and sharing digital images for over 25 years, since its last ISO/IEC 10918-1 ITU-T Recommendation T.81. standard was published in 1993 (Wallace 1992). JPEG is still widely used, essentially as a result of its history, alongside the fact that this format is still preferred in many applications. The vast majority of display systems, including web browsers, are compatible with the different versions and extensions of JPEG (XR, XT, etc.). Furthermore, the Independent JPEG Group (IJG)[2] produces a powerful, regularly-updated free library, libjpeg, which is widely used. The efficiency of JPEG is a result of lossy compression and the use of minimum redundancy codes. However, the quality degradation associated with JPEG compression limits its use in high-precision areas such as medical, satellite and military imagery. Hierarchical and lossless coding techniques are less commonly used, and will not be discussed here.

Format-compliant encryption methods are designed to combine efficient compression and encryption to produce encrypted content that is compatible with the format specifications. These methods are known as crypto-compression methods. The first JPEG crypto-compression methods were developed in the early 2000s, based on classic image encryption methods. However, direct application to the case of JPEG-compressed images is not trivial, as the JPEG format does not permit simple manipulation of the pixels in an image. The specificities of the format must be taken into account when applying cryptographic processes.

In section 4.2, we present an overview of the preliminary notions inherent in JPEG crypto-compression. The JPEG format, its properties and the notations used in

1 Available at: https://eur-lex.europa.eu/legal-content/FR/TXT/?uri=CELEX%3A32016R0679.
2 Available at: https//www.ijg.org/.

this chapter are presented in section 4.2.1. Section 4.2.2 is devoted to the basics of cryptography, while a description of image encryption is given in section 4.3; we also present the problems involved in compressing encrypted images. Section 4.4 provides a survey of the state of the art in JPEG crypto-compression, designed as a solution to this problem. Section 4.5 illustrates the challenge of image processing in the crypto-compressed domain, notably with respect to one of the first proposed methods, involving the recompression of crypto-compressed images. Our conclusions are presented in section 4.6.

4.2. Preliminary notions

4.2.1. *The JPEG image format*

The compression and decompression steps used in the JPEG format, set out in the JPEG standard, are shown in Figure 4.1. Compression involves six main steps. First, the color space of the image is transformed from the RGB (red, green and blue) space into another color space where luminance and chrominance are decorrelated, such as YCbCr. Monochrome planes may be downsampled (vertically, horizontally or in both directions, for chrominance and/or luminance). Each plane is then divided into non-overlapping blocks of size $N \times N$ (typically $N = 8$), and each block is projected in a frequency space using the DCT (*discrete cosine transform*). Taking a block B of size $N \times N$ from an image I, the DCT is:

$$F(u, v) = \frac{1}{\sqrt{2N}} C(u)C(v) \sum_{i=0}^{N} \sum_{j=0}^{N} p(i, j) \cos\left[\frac{(2i + 1)u\pi}{2N}\right] \cos\left[\frac{(2j + 1)v\pi}{2N}\right] \quad [4.1]$$

with $p(i, j)$, $0 \leq i, j < N$ the pixels in block B, $F(u, v)$, $0 \leq u, v < N$ the frequency coefficients and $C(\alpha) = \frac{1}{\sqrt{2}}$ if $\alpha = 0$ and 1 otherwise.

In practice, DCT computation is optimized using intermediate results and can be carried out at faster or slower speeds with more or less approximation (see the *fast, slow, float* modes in libjpeg[3]). Each block of frequency coefficients is then quantized using a quantization table Q of size $N \times N$ containing the quantization coefficients $q(u, v)$. The quantization operation involves dividing the coefficients $F(u, v)$ of the block B by the elements in the quantization matrix Q:

$$F'(u, v) = round\left(\frac{F(u, v)}{q(u, v)}\right) \quad [4.2]$$

where $round(\cdot)$ represents the rounding operator to the nearest integer.

---

3 Independent JPEG Group; available at: https//www.ijg.org/.

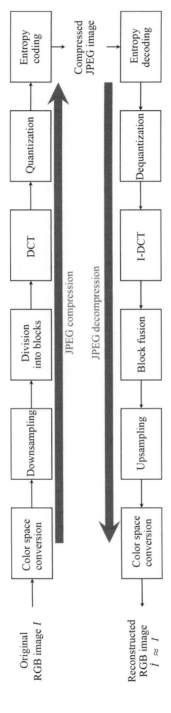

Figure 4.1. *JPEG compression and decompression steps*

This step encodes the quantized DCT coefficients $F'(u, v)$ onto 8-bit integers. Finally, the blocks are compressed, either sequentially or incrementally, using one of two specified entropy encodings, a Huffman encoding or an arithmetic encoding. The bitstream produced by the codec is usually encapsulated in EXIF (Exchangeable Image File Format) or JFIF (ISO/IEC 10918-5:2013 2013) (JPEG File Interchange Format), which establishes the form of the header and the binary markers delimiting the parameter fields.

Decompression is carried out by reversing the operations performed during compression. Since subsampling and quantization operations are not reversible, these are the two main causes of information loss during JPEG compression. Inverse quantization consists of inverting equation [4.2], multiplying the quantized DCT coefficients $F'(u, v)$ by their corresponding frequency quantizers $q(u, v)$:

$$\hat{F}(u, v) = F'(u, v) \times q(u, v)$$ [4.3]

The inverse cosine transform, noted I-DCT, makes it possible to return to the spatial domain from the frequency domain.

The downsampling and quantization operations draw on studies of the capabilities of the human visual system (HVS). Channels are often downsampled due to the low sensitivity of the HVS to chrominance. Additionally, the DCT decomposes the signal into $N \times N$ frequencies, from lowest to highest: the HVS is more sensitive to low frequencies, which provide an overview of image content, and less sensitive to high frequencies, describing details, which can thus be quantized to a greater extent. Based on this principle, the IJG proposes standard quantization tables Q_{QF}, calculated from a reference table Q_{QREF} and an integer quality factor noted QF | QF $\in [1, 100]$, where QREF = 50. For QF = 100%, all of the coefficients in the Q_{100} table are set at 1. In practice, some applications, such as Adobe Photoshop or GIMP, use their own tables. Since the tables are included in the JPEG header, they do not need to be transmitted to the decoder in advance.

Figure 4.2 shows images obtained after JPEG compression with different QF, applied to an image from the UCID database (Schaefer and Stich 2003) (Figure 4.2(a)). Note that with a high QF, the compression rate τ is already significant, but the quality of the original image is still high (Figure 4.2(b), $\tau = 12.96$ and PSNR = 41.46 dB and Figure 4.2(c), $\tau = 23.35$ and PSNR = 38.78 dB). The main problem in cases of JPEG compression with a low QF concerns degradations in texture, the appearance of granularity and block artifacts (Chan 1992), as shown in Figure 4.2(d), with QF = 25 % ($\tau = 71.18$ and PSNR = 32.82 dB).

In this chapter, we shall consider the most usual choice for JPEG options, which consists of encoding a 24-bit RGB image in a sequentially ordered bitstream, derived from a Huffman encoding. The block size is 8×8 pixels ($N = 8$). The luminance/chrominance color space (YCbCr: Y is the luminance component; Cb and Cr are the chrominance components) is used, with a standard downsampling of the chrominance channels (4:2:0) or (4:2:2: the size of the blocks is divided by two or four, respectively, by averaging the value of the neighboring pixels. The quantized frequency coefficients of each block are coded in a zigzag order on an MCU (minimum coded unit). The coefficients are then ordered by increasing frequency; since the high frequencies are quantized more strongly, the blocks tend to end in zeros, allowing for more efficient coding. The block encoding step is illustrated using an example in Figure 4.3. More generally, the coding of the DC coefficient $F'(0,0)$, proportional to the mean value, corresponds to a pair $(H_{F'(0,0)}, A_{F'(0,0)})$. The amplitude parameter $A_{F'(0,0)}$ encodes the prediction error, while the header parameter $H_{F'(0,0)}$ indicates the number of bits needed to encode it. The AC coefficients $F'(u,v)$, such that $(u,v) \neq (0,0)$, are encoded by a pair $(H_{F'(u,v)}, A_{F'(u,v)})$. $A_{F'(u,v)}$ encodes the amplitude of the coefficient, and the header $H_{F'(u,v)}$ is composed of the range of zeros – the run-length – computed earlier, alongside a parameter stating the number of bits required to encode the amplitude. When the last non-zero coefficient of the block has been encoded, an EOB (End Of Block) indicator symbol is added to the MCU. The MCU sequence is placed after the header. In the remainder of this chapter, for ease of reading, the code associated with a coefficient will be noted as the coefficient.

a)   b)   c)   d)

Figure 4.2. *Illustration of JPEG compression: a) uncompressed image (590.8 Ko) from the UCID database (Schaefer and Stich 2003), b) image compressed using JPEG at QF = 90% (45.6 Ko), c) image compressed using JPEG at QF = 75% (25.3 Ko), d) image compressed using JPEG at QF = 25% (8.3 Ko)*

4.2.2. Introduction to cryptography

Cryptography is one of the disciplines of cryptology – etymologically the *science of secrecy* – which relates to protecting messages, using one or more keys. Unlike steganography or data hiding, which consists of embedding a message within other content, cryptography makes a message unintelligible to anyone other than the intended recipient.

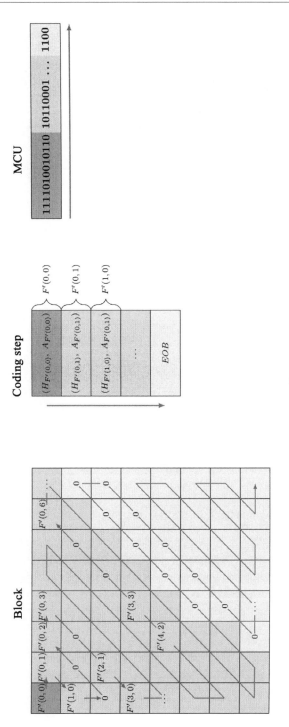

Figure 4.3. *Illustration of block code construction on an MCU (minimum coded unit)*

COMMENT ON FIGURE 4.3.– *The block is zigzagged for run-length encoding, then the coefficients are coded using Huffman tables. The DC coefficient is shown in purple, and the AC coefficients quantized in green. Starting from the position where all quantized AC coefficients are zero in the zigzag order, they are coded by an EOB signal.*

Although cryptography has been used since ancient times, it only truly took off at the end of the 20th century, notably with the development of computer science. The principles of modern cryptography are laid out by Kerckhoffs in the article *La cryptographie militaire* in the *Journal des sciences militaires* (*Journal of Military Sciences*) published in 1883 (Kerckhoffs 1883):

– security relies on the secrecy of the key, not the method;

– it should be materially, if not mathematically, impossible to decode an encrypted message without the key;

– it should not be possible to determine the key using the clear and encrypted texts.

Thus, it is assumed that all parameters of the cryptosystem other than the key must be public and universally known. Shannon, in 1949, stated the need to "assume the enemy knows the system" (Shannon 1949). The principles established by Kerckhoffs and Shannon are now considered fundamental in the implementation of any cryptosystem. This approach contrasts with that of security by obscurity, which relies on the non-disclosure of information about the structure, operation and implementation of an algorithm to be protected (e.g. by code obfuscation or remote code execution).

Two broad classes of cryptographic algorithms can be defined: symmetric cryptography – also known as secret key cryptography – and asymmetric cryptography – also known as public key cryptography.

In symmetric cryptography, the same key, called the secret key, is used to encrypt and decrypt a message. Thus, the security of the cryptosystem relies on the secure exchange of the key; only the sender and the recipient of the message must know the secret key. In addition, the key must be large enough to protect against brute-force attacks, in which all possible combinations are tested in order to find the correct key to decrypt the message. There are two categories of symmetric cryptosystems: stream ciphers and block ciphers. Stream ciphers treat the clear message as a stream of data (bits or bytes). During encryption, each character is encrypted independently, meaning that the algorithm is very fast to execute. Stream encryption can be performed in real time, without needing to wait for all of the data for encryption to be received. The stream cipher principle, also known as a disposable mask or Vernam cipher, was first defined in Vernam (1926). A secret key is used as the initialization seed for a cryptographically secure pseudo-random number generator (PRNG) to generate a pseudo-random binary sequence, called the encryption stream, of the same size as the message to be encrypted. Messages are then encrypted by performing an exclusive-or between the data to be encrypted and the generated pseudo-random binary sequence. In block cipher algorithms, on the other hand, clear data are split into blocks of fixed size (often 64, 128 or 256 bits); blocks are then encrypted one by one. There are several different block cipher methods (Dworkin 2001), such as ECB (electronic code book), CBC (cipher block chaining), CFB (cipher feedback), OFB (output feedback) or CTR (counter-based cipher). The best-known block encryption algorithms include the Data Encryption Standard (DES), published in 1976 (Davis 1978), the Triple DES (3DES) (Karn *et al.* 1995), derived from the DES, and the Advanced Encryption Standard (AES) (Daemen and Rijmen 1999), which is currently the benchmark standard for block encryption. Note that the DES algorithm uses a single 56-bit key, while 3DES uses two or three keys of the same size. AES encryption traditionally uses a key of between 128 and 192 bits, and recent cases have extended to 256 bits (Singh 2013).

In asymmetric cryptography, two keys are used: a public key and a private key. These keys are generated by the user who wishes to receive the messages. They are mathematically related insofar as the decryption operation is the inverse of the encryption operation. For this purpose, one-way functions, which are easy to evaluate but difficult to reverse, are used. The public key is generated by computing the image of the private key via the chosen one-way function. In other words, even if the public key is known, it is very difficult to retrieve the associated private key (which is impossible to compute in polynomial time). Thus, the public key can be transmitted openly, but the private key must remain secret and is never transmitted. Asymmetric encryption algorithms can be used for two purposes:

– to encrypt the message before sending to guarantee its confidentiality: the sender uses the recipient's public key to encrypt the message and the recipient uses their private key to decrypt it;

– to digitally sign a message to guarantee its authenticity: the sender uses their own private key to encrypt the message, and the recipient uses the sender's public key to decrypt it, thus authenticating the sender.

The first asymmetric protocol was described by Merkle in a paper written in 1975 (Merkle 1978); however, due to a 3-year publication delay, the concept of secure cryptographic key exchange over a public channel is generally attributed to Diffie and Hellman (1976). Using their method, two people who do not know each other can jointly establish a shared secret key over a non-secure channel. This key can then be used to encrypt subsequent communications between these two people. The first asymmetric encryption method, named RSA, was developed by Rivest *et al.* (1978). This approach is based on the problem of factorizing large numbers as a product of two prime numbers. Other methods used other difficult problems, such as the discrete logarithm (El Gamal 1985) or quadratic residuality (Paillier 1999). Note that the size of the keys used in asymmetric cryptosystems varies from 1,024 to 4,096 bits.

There are advantages and disadvantages to both symmetric and asymmetric algorithms. One notable difference is that symmetric cryptography requires key exchange, which is not necessary in asymmetric cryptography. Asymmetric algorithms are more complicated to implement, slower and require greater hardware resources than symmetric algorithms. PGP software aims to combine the advantages of these two classes of cryptographic algorithms by offering a hybrid system. A secret one-time key is generated in order to send messages securely, encrypting the message using a symmetric algorithm. The key itself is then encrypted using an asymmetric encryption algorithm such as RSA. The sender then transmits both the encrypted message and key to the recipient. The time needed to execute the asymmetric algorithm is considerably reduced as only the key is encrypted in this manner.

The latest developments in cryptology research relate to quantum and post-quantum cryptography. Quantum cryptography draws on the properties of quantum physics – notably the Heisenberg principle – and of information theory in order to develop cryptographic algorithms, resulting in proven or conjecturally unattainable levels of security. For example, in quantum key distribution, a key can be transmitted between two remote parties on demand with demonstrable security. If the information is intercepted and read by a third party, errors will be introduced so that the attack is detected. The aim of post-quantum cryptography is to create cryptographic methods that are resistant to an attacker using a quantum computer. Cryptographic algorithms that rely on the discrete logarithm problem or on the product of two integers problem for security are no longer guaranteed to be secure when faced with quantum computing power. Nevertheless, since quantum technology is not yet operational, this theoretical research has very few practical applications at present.

4.3. Image encryption

The purpose of image encryption is to ensure visual privacy of the clear content of an image. Encryption is said to be "full" when the original content of the image is protected in its entirety: in this case, no information about the clear image can be extracted from the encrypted image. In contrast, "selective" encryption conceals only part of the data. Finally, in "partial" encryption, only a specific area of the image is encrypted, and pixels outside of this area are clearly visible. The difference between these three types of encryption is illustrated in Figure 4.4.

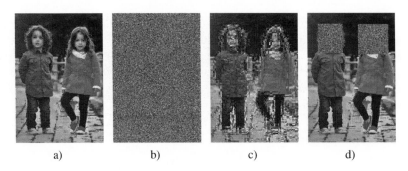

a)   b)   c)   d)

Figure 4.4. *Illustration of the difference between three types of encryption:*
a) original image, b) full encryption, c) selective encryption and d) partial encryption

Image encryption methods must verify two properties:

– format conformity: the encrypted image must have the same format as the original image;

– size preservation: the encrypted and original images must be the same size.

The first property implies that data must be structured in the same way before and after encryption. This means that classic cryptographic methods cannot be directly applied to images without being adapted to take account of the specificities of image formats. Furthermore, the format conformity property implies that encrypted data can be viewed using the same image editing software as the original data.

In terms of the second property, note that a limited increase in data size after encryption can be acceptable in certain applications.

Moreover, following Shannon (1949), an encryption method must result in confusion and diffusion. In the case of images, the confusion principle implies that the relationship between the encryption key and the encrypted image must be as complex as possible. The diffusion property indicates that the statistical redundancy between pixels in a clear image must be dissipated in the statistics of the encrypted image. In other words, the correlation between pixels in the clear image should not be reflected in the encrypted image. Pixel permutation and substitution operations are used to introduce confusion and increase diffusion.

While the classical cryptographic algorithms described in section 4.2.2 have been adapted for image formats, specific algorithms have also been developed. Note that these algorithms are generally based on a symmetric encryption method; asymmetric encryption is less widespread due to the large volume of data to process. Asymmetric encryption is much more costly in terms of computing time and results in an increase in the size of the original data.

In the following section, we shall describe naive approaches to image encryption, based on the use of a PRNG and on the substitution or permutation principle (section 4.3.1). We will then explain how chaos theory has been applied to image encryption (section 4.3.2). Finally, we will briefly touch on encryption-then-compression approaches, in which images are encrypted before being compressed (section 4.3.3).

4.3.1. *Naive methods*

Image encryption approaches based on substitution and/or permutation operations involve the use of cryptographically secure PRNGs, as described in section 4.2.2. As input, these generators rely on a secret key, K, the type of elements and the length of the sequence to be generated.

The objective of shuffle encryption methods, which are efficient and easy to implement, is to transform a clear image into an unintelligible one by permuting the positions of pixels. Take an image $I = \{p(i)\}_{0 \leq i < m \times n}$ of $m \times n$ pixels. I is shuffle-encrypted as follows. A PRNG is used with a secret key K to define the new pixel positions of I. A sequence $S = \{s(i)\}_{0 \leq i < m \times n}$ of $m \times n$ pseudo-random positions $s(i)$ such that $0 \leq s(i) < m \times n$ and $\forall\, i,\, \forall\, j,\, 0 \leq j < m \times n,$ $i \neq j \Rightarrow s(i) \neq s(j)$ (in order to avoid collisions) is generated. The encrypted image $I_e = \{p_e(i)\}_{0 \leq i < m \times n}$ is obtained by copying the pixel values of I at pseudo-random positions given by the sequence S:

$$p_e(i) = p(s(i)) \tag{4.4}$$

Certain authors have suggested random permutations of rows and columns in an image (Usman *et al.* 2007; Premaratne and Premaratne 2012) or pixel blocks (Wright *et al.* 2015), rather than switching the locations of all of the pixels.

Substitution-based encryption methods have also been developed. These use an exclusive-or operation between the generated pseudo-random sequence and the content of a clear image. The operation can be performed in two different ways. The image can be encrypted pixel by pixel, bit by bit (e.g. from the least significant bit to the most significant bit), or bit-plane by bit-plane (e.g. from the least significant plane to the most significant plane). Consider an image $I = \{p(i)\}_{0 \leq i < m \times n}$ of $m \times n$ pixels. The pixel-by-pixel encryption of I is performed as follows. A pseudo-random binary sequence $S = \{s(i)\}_{0 \leq i < m \times n}$, of $m \times n$ bytes $s(i)$, is generated using a secret key K and a PRNG. The encrypted image $I_e = \{p_e(i)\}_{0 \leq i < m \times n}$ is then obtained by performing an exclusive-or between each pixel $p(i)$ in the image I and the associated byte $s(i)$ in the pseudo-random sequence S:

$$p_e(i) = p(i) \oplus s(i) \tag{4.5}$$

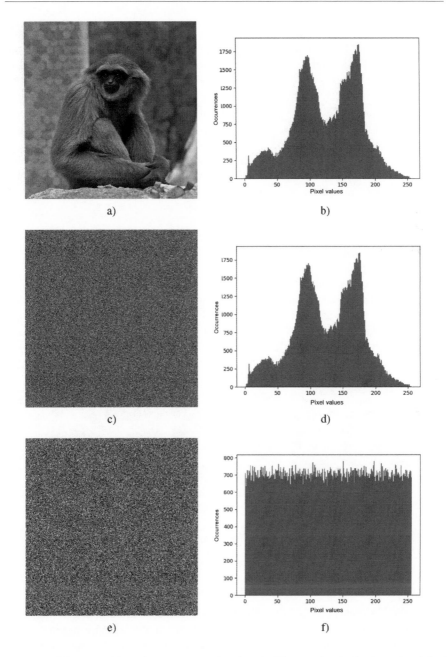

Figure 4.5. *Illustration of image encryption by shuffling and substitution. a) original image, b) histogram associated with (a), c) image (a) encrypted by pixel shuffling, d) histogram associated with (c), e) image (a) encrypted by substitution, pixel by pixel, and f) histogram associated with (e)*

Figure 4.5 shows a clear image, encrypted versions using shuffling and substitution, and the associated histograms. We see from Figure 4.5(b) that the distribution of pixels in the clear image includes a certain number of modes relating to the content. Furthermore, as we see from Figure 4.5(d), the histograms of pixels in the encrypted and clear images are identical. While this encryption method is easy to apply, certain statistical properties of the original image are preserved. In the case of pixel substitution (Figure 4.5(f)), on the other hand, the pixel distribution is almost uniform. While neighboring pixels have similar values and are strongly correlated in the clear domain, these relationships are removed by this form of encryption. Thus, analysis of an image encrypted using substitution methods – unlike shuffling methods – does not give any information about the original content of the clear image.

4.3.2. *Chaos-based methods*

The rapid development of chaos theory and associated applications has resulted in the creation of a variety of encryption techniques. The first method using chaos was published by Arnold and Avez in 1967 and is known as Arnold's cat map (Arnold and Avez 1967). Later, Scharinger and Pichler applied the baker's map to image encryption (Scharinger and Pichler 1996). These two well-known methods are illustrated in Figure 4.6.

a)   b)   c)

Figure 4.6. *Illustration of two image encryption methods using chaos theory: a) original image, b) Arnold's cat map (Arnold and Avez 1967) and c) baker's map (Scharinger and Pichler 1996)*

Fridrich extended the discretized version of this map into three dimensions (3D) and combined it with a scattering mechanism (Fridrich 1997, 1998). In most cases, later encryption algorithms incorporate both permutation and substitution mechanisms and use a combination of several chaotic maps. Chaos-based cryptosystems can be divided into two distinct classes. In the first class, a pixel is considered to be the smallest element (Chen *et al.* 2004; Mao *et al.* 2004; Guan *et al.* 2005), while in the second class, binary operations are applied to the bits making up a pixel (Xiang *et al.* 2007; Zhu *et al.* 2011). In Chen *et al.* (2004), the authors applied Arnold's cat map in three dimensions, while in Mao *et al.* (2004), baker's map is used in three dimensions to swap pixel positions during the substitution phase. Guan *et al.* (2005) applied Arnold's cat map to shuffle the pixel positions of an image in the spatial domain, before using the chaotic system defined in Chen and Ueta (1999) to change the pixel values. To reduce the execution time, Xiang *et al.* (2007) defined a chaotic selective encryption method, encrypting only the four most significant bits of each pixel and leaving the four least significant bits clear. In 2011, Zhu *et al.* (2011) proposed a cryptosystem in which Arnold's cat map is used to perform permutations at the binary level, allowing both the location and values of pixels in the image to be changed. A logistic map is then used to introduce diffusion.

4.3.3. *Encryption-then-compression*

Encryption-then-compression methods, as their name suggests, work by encrypting then compressing an image. The challenge with this type of method is that compression must be carried out in the encrypted domain, without access to the secret key or the original, clear image. At first glance, the compression of encrypted data appears impossible since the redundancies between pixels are removed by the encryption operation. However, in 2004, Johnson *et al.* (2004) showed that stream-encrypted data can be compressed without altering its security level. Following on from these theoretical results, practical algorithms for lossless compression of encrypted binary images have been developed. Kumar and Makur (2008) applied this method to prediction errors computed in the encrypted domain, improving the compression rate. Lazzeretti and Barni (2008) have presented several methods for lossless compression of grayscale and color encrypted images. The authors divided images into binary planes before exploiting intra- and inter-plane correlation. Other encryption-then-compression methods rely on shuffling blocks in an image (Kurihara *et al.* 2015, 2017). The original image is divided into blocks of 16×16 pixels, which are then pseudo-randomly swapped using a first secret key. A second secret key is used to perform rotations and/or inversions on the blocks. A transformation is also applied to the pixels of each block: the highest order bit of some pixels is modified using a third secret key. Finally, in the case of color images, the three components are permutated using a fourth secret key. The resulting encrypted image is robust to conventional JPEG compression.

Despite considerable efforts made in recent years, encryption-then-compression systems still perform poorly in terms of compression performance, compared to lossy or lossless image and video encoders using clear data input. Moreover, many of these approaches are vulnerable to puzzle attacks (Cho *et al.* 2010). Given that JPEG is the most widely used compressed image format, many methods rely on joint encryption and JPEG compression together. The challenges and operation of these image crypto-compression approaches will be described in section 4.4.

4.4. Different classes of crypto-compression for images

In this section, we shall present a state of the art of the broad categories of crypto-compression methods that are compatible with JPEG format, with examples selected on the basis of performance and diversity. These methods may be extended to other formats.

Encryption and compression steps were carried out separately in early crypto-compression methods. The main problem with this strategy is that encryption significantly alters the statistical characteristics of the image: efficient substitution-based encryption methods tend to result in a distribution of the encrypted image which is close to a uniform distribution of random variables. Furthermore, shuffling-based encryption methods remove spatial coherences. This means that compression efficiency is greatly reduced if encryption is performed first. In this context, interest in JPEG-compressed image encryption has increased in recent years. The main aim is to encrypt images in such a way that the encrypted data can always be represented in a meaningful format (i.e. preserving format conformity). In the JPEG format, not all binary data need to be encrypted: encryption methods can thus focus on image-specific data rather than format. When decompressing without the encryption key, the image in pixel form is selectively encrypted since not all of the information is encrypted, unlike full pixel encryption methods (used in a non-compressed format). A visual security level (transparent, sufficient or confidential) must be defined in accordance with the application. Keyless decryption must, by definition, be very complex. In methods of this new type, compression and JPEG encryption are either performed together or after compression. There are three main categories of methods: sign bit encryption, DCT coefficient encryption and methods based on shuffling DCT coefficients or JPEG blocks. Shi and Bhargava designed one of the first crypto-compression approaches to directly encrypt the binary JPEG stream (Shi and Bhargava 1998). The authors suggest encrypting the sign bit of the AC and DC coefficients (the sign of the difference in the case of DC coefficients). A binary pseudo-random sequence is generated based on a secret key and encryption is performed by an exclusive-or operation on this sequence with the sequence of all sign bits. This method preserves the JPEG structure of the image, which can be viewed using standard image editing software. Furthermore, the compression ratio is hardly (if at all) changed, since the number of bits remains the same. Nevertheless, Said (2005) was able to demonstrate weaknesses in this method. Given that the image respects the JPEG format, the majority of the bitstream remains unchanged even if the clear image seems to be encrypted. It is therefore easy to guess the original value of the encrypted bits. Recent methods have attempted to increase security and visual privacy, focusing on increasing the confusion and diffusion properties using substitution and/or shuffling-based crypto-compression techniques.

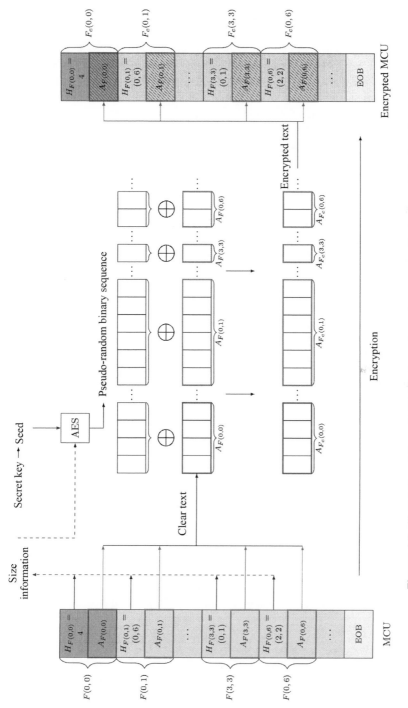

Figure 4.7. *Illustration of the substitution-based crypto-compression approach designed by Puech and Rodrigues (2005). ⊕ represents the exclusive-or operator*

4.4.1. *Substitution-based crypto-compression*

Methods in the substitution-based crypto-compression class operate by replacing clear values with encrypted values. In general, values are encrypted using the exclusive-or operator between the clear values and a pseudo-random sequence generated using a secret key. This operation maintains format compatibility and limits file size inflation. Van Droogenbroeck and Benedett (2002) suggest encrypting AC coefficients after the DCT transformation, but not the DC coefficients, since they contain important visible information and are predictable. Building on this idea, Puech and Rodrigues have proposed a selective encryption method for JPEG images that encrypts both DC and AC coefficients (Puech and Rodrigues 2005).

In this method, shown in Figure 4.7, all the DC coefficient codes (optional) and the non-AC coefficients are concatenated to form a 128-bit bitstream. This bitstream is then encrypted using the AES algorithm (Daemen and Rijmen 1999) in OFB mode. Finally, the JPEG image is constructed using the encrypted coefficient values. Since the size of the coefficients, alongside the zero-range encoding, remains unchanged, the Huffman encoding is also unchanged and the resulting JPEG file has the same size as if it had been compressed without encryption, using the same parameters. When decoded without decryption, the image is not easily understandable by the HVS. If the DC coefficients are encrypted, then the image is incomprehensible. If the AC coefficients alone are encrypted, however, then the low-resolution image will be accessible. Rodrigues *et al.* (2006) extended this concept to protect individual anonymity, rather than the entire image: in this case, encryption is performed on regions of interest, such as human skin, detected automatically. These regions are detected using the clear DC coefficients of the Cb and Cr color components. Selective encryption is applied to blocks of the luminance component Y during the entropy coding phase. As the HVS has relatively low sensitivity to chrominance information, it is usually highly quantized and downsampled. The impact of encrypting the corresponding channel coefficients is only minor. The quantized AC coefficients of the region of interest are encrypted using the CFB mode of the AES algorithm. This method respects the JPEG format, and the resulting crypto-compressed JPEG image is the same size as that obtained using the standard JPEG algorithm. Furthermore, partial encryption is sufficient to hide sensitive information, such as text (Pinto *et al.* 2013). The advantage of these encryption methods is that the compression ratio is the same as that of a conventional JPEG compression using the same parameters. However, information is not shuffled during transmission, meaning that the resulting crypto-compressed images are more vulnerable to brute force attacks.

4.4.2. *Shuffle-based crypto-compression*

Just like shuffle encryption, shuffle crypto-compression consists of rearranging the elements of an image using a PRNG. In the case of JPEG compression, the most obvious elements to shuffle are the JPEG blocks. This introduces distortion into the image at the decoding stage due to the predictive coding of the DC coefficients, but does not change the size of the image, since the blocks (except the DC coefficients) are independently coded.

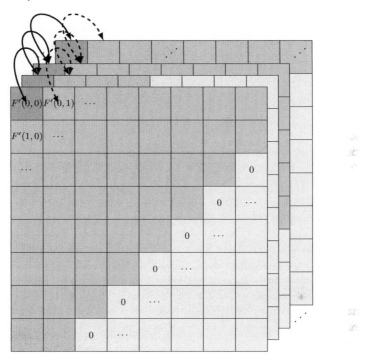

Figure 4.8. *Illustration of the full inter-block shuffle method (FIBS)*
for frequency coefficients, proposed by Li and Yuan (2007)

However, the blocks remain clear, and security is not guaranteed. Kurihara *et al.* (2017) designed an encryption-then-compression approach in which blocks are permuted in the spatial domain. This approach is vulnerable to puzzle solver attacks, as demonstrated by Chuman *et al.* (2017). The method has been further developed to use other elements of the compressed JPEG image, which permit efficient and secure information transmission while limiting the inflation of the JPEG file size. In natural images, the distribution of coefficients of the same frequency follows a Laplacian distribution (Lam and Goodman 2000). Shuffling non-zero coefficients of the same frequencies seems to give good security while preserving the overall file size. The run-length coding is identical, but the value of the coefficient can be changed, resulting in a change in the Huffman code. However, Li and Yuan (2007) have shown that this approach can be attacked to generate a sketch of the image, and visual privacy is therefore not guaranteed. The authors suggested a solution to this problem in the form of the FIBS (Full Inter-Block Shuffle) method, which consists of shuffling coefficients of the same frequency between blocks, as shown in Figure 4.8. The decoded image is then unintelligible (if the DC coefficients are encrypted); however, since the coefficients are mixed, the entropy coding step is less efficient than with standard JPEG compression. This is due to the fact that the zero-range coding is less efficient, since successive zeros in the blocks are scattered. This may lead to a change in the position of the end-of-block code, so that the MCUs require more bits. Furthermore, the header of the code for a coefficient may be modified according to the size of the zero range preceding it. Note that non-textured areas are affected by the encryption due to the shuffling of zeros. Shuffling methods do not permit the introduction of confusion: the distribution of DCT coefficients always follows the same frequency distribution after naive shuffling (Reininger and Gibson 1983).

Figure 4.9 shows the results obtained after applying three different crypto-compression methods with QF = 90% to the UCID database image (Schaefer and Stich 2003) shown in Figure 4.2(a). The crypto-compressed images in the first line were obtained by encrypting the AC coefficients of the three YCbCr components alone. The images in the second line were obtained by encrypting both AC and DC coefficients. Figures 4.9(a) and (d) are obtained by applying Puech and Rodrigues' substitution method (Puech and Rodrigues 2005). The crypto-compressed images in Figures 4.9(b) and (e) are obtained by shuffling. Note that, for both methods, when only the AC coefficients are encrypted, the crypto-compressed images are the same size as the JPEG image with QF = 90% (Figure 4.2(b)). Finally, the size inflation observed in Li and Yuan's FIBS method (Li and Yuan 2007) results from the loss of efficiency of zero-range coding (59.5 KB in the case of Figure 4.9(c) and 63.3 KB in the case of Figure 4.9(f)).

4.4.3. *Hybrid crypto-compression*

Certain authors have turned to hybrid approaches in order to benefit from the advantages of both confusion and diffusion properties. The encryption capacity of the methods presented earlier is only low if the quality factor is low, since there are few non-zero coefficients. The advantage of hybrid approaches is that an accumulation of different steps with a low impact on file size results in a low overall size increase, but with higher visual privacy and security. Minemura *et al.* (2012) took this approach in shuffling JPEG blocks. Within each block, the AC coefficients with a null zero range are shuffled then the sign bits are encrypted using a pseudo-random sequence and the XOR operation to increase perturbations. These three steps do not increase file size. DC coefficients are then grouped by close values using frequency-domain edge detection for processing; this may result in a small increase in the number of bits. In concrete terms, if only the AC coefficients are shuffled then the edges of the image will still be perceptible. Taking a similar approach, Unterweger and Uhl (2012) described a three-step crypto-compression method. The first step is to shuffle the order of the code coefficients (of the form $(H_{F'(u,v)},\ A_{F'(u,v)})$) in an MCU using the AES algorithm (Daemen and Rijmen 1999) in OFB mode, as shown in Figure 4.10. Non-zero coefficients and the zero coefficients coded together are shuffled: this operation does not increase the size of the code, but changes the position of the frequency coefficients. The bits of the coefficient values $(A_{F'(u,v)})$ are then inverted as a function of the output (binary, 0 or 1) of the AES-based PRNG used in the previous step. Finally, a pseudo-random approach is used to modify the order of MCUs sharing the same Huffman tables, which gives additional security to an extent dependent on the number of Huffman tables. This method is secure in the sense that a brute force attack on the AES key will be more effective than trying all possible combinations.

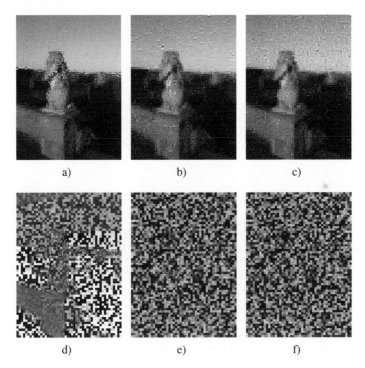

a)   b)   c)

d)   e)   f)

Figure 4.9. *Crypto-compressed images with QF = 90%, with encrypted AC coefficients (first line) and encrypted DC and AC coefficients (second line) for the three YCbCr components of the image shown in Figure 4.2(a)*

COMMENT ON FIGURE 4.9.– *(a) and (d) obtained using Puech and Rodrigues' method (Puech and Rodrigues 2005) (45.6 KB and 48.9 KB); (b) and (e) obtained by shuffling non-zero coefficients (45.9 KB and 49.5 KB); (c) and (f) obtained using Li and Yuan's FIBS method (Li and Yuan 2007) (59.5 KB and 63.3 KB).*

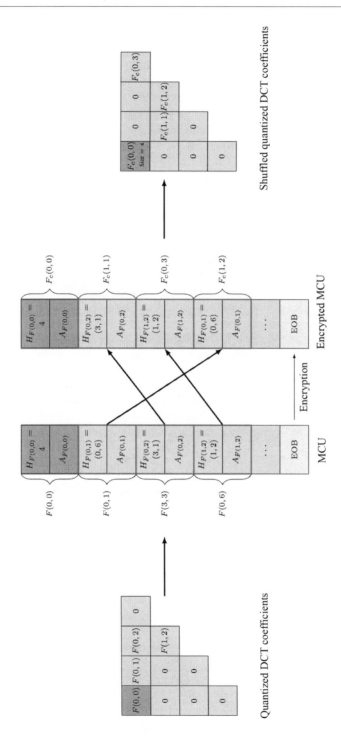

Figure 4.10. *Illustration of Unterweger and Uhl's intrablock coefficient code shuffling method (Unterweger and Uhl 2012)*

The methods presented here can be used to encrypt JPEG images in an efficient and effective manner, both in terms of visual privacy and file size limitation. Security analysis of crypto-compression methods, as found in Unterweger and Uhl (2012), is currently lacking, but current trends point toward this analysis becoming increasingly systematic. Although most methods are based on the JPEG format, and thus on the discrete cosine transform (DCT), other schemes exist and have been popularized in recent years. A variety of JPEG2000 compatible image crypto-compression methods are presented in Engel *et al.* (2009). Other methods work by encrypting the sign of wavelet coefficients (Dufaux *et al.* 2004), on permutations (Norcen and Uhl 2004; Lian *et al.* 2004) or on randomized arithmetic coding (Grangetto *et al.* 2006). Shahid *et al.* (2011) adapted these methods for video by designing a selective encryption technique for the H.264/AVC video codec for the CAVLC and CABAC standards. Encryption is performed during the entropy coding phase using the AES algorithm in CFB mode. To conserve file size and preserve the H.264/AVC format, encryption is only applied to CAVLC keywords and CABAC bitstreams. An in-depth study of HEVC crypto-compression methods has recently been published (Hamidouche *et al.* 2017). Crypto-compression methods for video files will be discussed in greater depth in Chapter 5.

The advantage of crypto-compression methods is that crypto-compressed images can be handled in the same way as conventional JPEG images in terms of sharing, storage or viewing. However, some tasks can no longer be carried out using these files, such as computer visualization algorithms, quality enhancement or the application of a second compression; these operations all require decryption. In this context, homomorphic encryption methods have been designed to allow operations to be performed directly in the encrypted domain (see Chapter 6).

4.5. Recompressing crypto-compressed JPEG images

Let us suppose that an individual – let us call her Alice – wishes to use a JPEG crypto-compression system to prevent malicious use of her images and to use as little space as possible. Alice wants to store her images in the Cloud in order to back up her data and access her files from anywhere. JPEG crypto-compression is a suitable solution in this case, as it offers a degree of confidentiality with respect to attacks on the platform, or to data analysis by the web host. Most cloud services impose limitations on image submission (in terms of either size or format) in order to optimize storage and bandwidth usage. If Alice crypto-compresses her images with a quality factor QF, the network administrator may want to recompress them. Recompression is usually carried out by applying a new JPEG compression with a specific quantization table. However, while simple recompression of a crypto-compressed image is possible, Alice will no longer be able to decrypt her images using her secret key: the content of the original image is lost. Crypto-compression methods are not robust to simple recompression. Alice could, theoretically, transit her secret key to the host to permit crypto-compression with a lower quality factor, but this solution is not secure. Ideally, a method is needed to permit recompression of crypto-compressed JPEG images without using the secret key. In this case, the images transferred by Alice would be recompressed directly on the cloud server, with a new quality factor QF* such that QF* < QF.

In this section, we present a method for recompressing crypto-compressed JPEG images without knowing the secret key used during encryption (Itier *et al.* 2020). We shall begin by describing the different steps of the proposed new crypto-compression method, which is based on the study of Puech *et al.* (2013). As we shall see, JPEG compression and encryption are performed jointly during Huffman coding. We then describe an efficient method to recompress crypto-compressed JPEG images directly in the encrypted domain. Note that this approach preserves the security level of the crypto-compression method. The general scheme of this method for recompressing crypto-compressed JPEG images is shown in Figure 4.11.

4.5.1. *A crypto-compression approach robust to recompression*

The crypto-compression method used here draws on the work of Puech *et al.* (2013). Our aim is to adapt this approach in order to make it robust to the application of one or more recompression operations following the initial crypto-compression. If an image is crypto-compressed using the approach described in Puech *et al.* (2013) then recompressed without adaptation, then desynchronization with the pseudo-random binary sequence used for decryption will occur during the decoding phase, and it will be impossible to reconstruct the content of the original image. To solve this problem, we propose a reordering of the JPEG coefficients during the encryption phase. Figure 4.11 shows a general overview of the crypto-compression method is presented.

The standard JPEG compression steps are applied to the original image I up to quantization of the frequency coefficients. Encryption is then carried out during the Huffman coding phase. At the very least, the luminance component Y must be encrypted to preserve the confidentiality of the original image. We recall that the two chrominance components, Cb and Cr, can also be encrypted; however, as we see from Figure 4.12, this is not crucial, since the HVS is not particularly sensitive to them. All coefficients in each MCU which are non-zero $F'(u, v)$ after quantization are encrypted. The non-zero AC $F'(u, v)$ coefficients are then reordered according to their size in descending order. The recompression step described in section 4.5.2 corresponds to dividing all non-zero AC coefficients $F'(u, v)$ by two. Note that reordering of the coefficients makes it possible to resynchronize the PRNG, even for a coefficient $F'(u, v)$ with a coded amplitude of one bit, reduced to zero after recompression. Without the reordering step, it would be impossible to differentiate between these coefficients and those that were already zero before the recompression, resulting in desynchronization with the pseudo-random binary sequence.

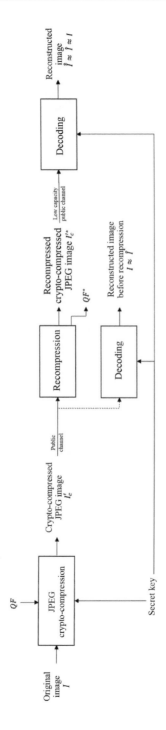

Figure 4.11. *General scheme of the recompression method for crypto-compressed JPEG images*

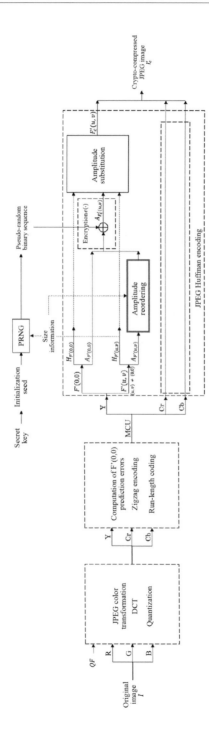

Figure 4.12. *Crypto-compression method, designed to be robust to recompression*

Once the non-zero AC coefficients $F'(u, v)$ have been selected and re-ordered, a secret key is used to generate a different seed for each MCU. This seed is used to initialize a PRNG to obtain a pseudo-random binary sequence. The size of this sequence is computed by adding the sizes of each non-zero AC coefficient $F'(u, v)$, giving a number of bits which is sufficient to encrypt all of their amplitudes. Thus, the value of an encrypted coefficient $F'_e(u, v)$ is:

$$
\begin{aligned}
F'_e(u, v) &= \mathcal{E}\left(F'(u, v),\ \mathrm{size}(F'(u, v))\right) \\
&= \mathcal{E}\left(\left\{H_{F'(u,v)}, A_{F'(u,v)}\right\},\ \mathrm{size}(F'(u, v))\right) \\
&= \left\{H_{F'_e(u,v)}, A_{F'_e(u,v)}\right\}
\end{aligned}
\qquad [4.6]
$$

where $H_{F'_e(u,v)} = H_{F'(u,v)}$.

As we see from Figure 4.12, the encryption function $\mathcal{E}(\cdot)$ consists of applying an exclusive-or operation between the amplitude value of a clear coefficient $F'(u, v)$ and the corresponding part of the pseudo-random binary sequence, according to its size and position in the MCU. The amplitude values $A_{F'(u,v)}$ of the original binary stream are replaced with the encrypted values $A_{F'_e(u,v)}$ to obtain the encrypted MCU. In this sequence, the encrypted equivalent of a coefficient $F'(u, v)$, coded by a pair $(H_{F'(u,v)},\ A_{F'(u,v)})$, is $F'_e(u, v)$, coded by a pair $(H_{F'_e(u,v)},\ A_{F'_e(u,v)})$, of which the header remains unchanged. Note that the encrypted coefficient is coded on the same number of bits as the original version, since only an exclusive-or is applied. Finally, the crypto-compressed JPEG image I'_e is obtained.

4.5.2. Recompression of a crypto-compressed image

As we see from Figure 4.13, recompression is applied directly to the encrypted JPEG bitstream for each component. Following crypto-compression, each MCU is made up of one or more coefficients, encoded by $(H_{F'_e(u,v)},\ A_{F'_e(u,v)})$ pairs. The first step in recompression is to remove the least significant bit from the amplitude parameter of each coefficient $F'_e(u, v)$. The recompressed coefficients $F'^*_e(u, v)$ are calculated as follows:

$$
F'^*_e(u, v) =
\begin{cases}
\left\lfloor \dfrac{F'_e(u,v)}{2} \right\rfloor, & \text{if } |F'_e(u, v)| > 1 \\[2mm]
0, & \text{if } |F'_e(u, v)| = 1
\end{cases}
\qquad [4.7]
$$

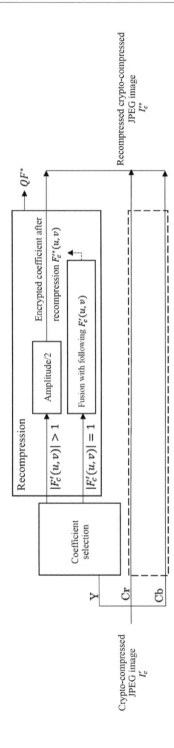

Figure 4.13. *Recompression of a crypto-compressed image*

Removing the last bit of each non-zero coefficient causes a one-bit reduction in the size of their binary code. The size parameter in the header should therefore be adjusted accordingly. Moreover, if the amplitude of a coefficient $F'_e(u, v)$ is encoded on one bit before recompression, its recompressed version $F'^*_e(u, v)$ will be a null coefficient. Thus, this coefficient must be encoded in the zero range of the next coefficient $F'^*_e(u, v)$, which must be non-zero by construction. The value of the zero range of its header $H_{F'^*_e(u,v)}$ is adjusted by taking account of the number of preceding coefficients, which are equal to zero. The new value of the zero range is equal to the initial value of the zero range, plus that of the previous coefficient, plus one:

$$H_{F'^*_e(u,v)} = (\text{new zero range, size} - 1) \tag{4.8}$$

Finally, the recompressed encrypted coefficients in each MCU are coded by the pair $(H_{F'^*_e(u,v)}, A_{F'^*_e(u,v)})$. The coefficients $q_{\mathrm{QF}^*}(u, v)$ in the updated quantization table Q_{QF^*} are:

$$q_{\mathrm{QF}^*}(u, v) = \begin{cases} 2 \times q_{\mathrm{QF}}(u, v), & \text{if } 2 \times q_{\mathrm{QF}}(u, v) \le 255 \\ 255, & \text{otherwise} \end{cases} \tag{4.9}$$

The main advantage of the proposed method is that it is easy to locate the deleted bits after recompression. This means that synchronization with the pseudo-random binary sequence remains possible, enabling error-free decryption. The fact that non-zero coefficients are reordered by amplitude means that those that become zero after recompression are located at the end of the MCU.

The format preservation property of our method means that the recompressed crypto-compressed image I'^*_e remains in JPEG format. The image may be decrypted using the secret key used for encryption, but only if the image is known to have been recompressed. A flag may be added to the comment section of the JFIF file to indicate the number of recompressions that have been performed.

4.5.3. *Decoding a recompressed version of a crypto-compressed JPEG image*

As we see from Figure 4.14, the decoding phase consists of four main steps: decrypting the JPEG binary flow encrypted during Huffman decoding, inverse quantization, the I-DCT transform and inversion of the color space change (from YCbCr back to RGB).

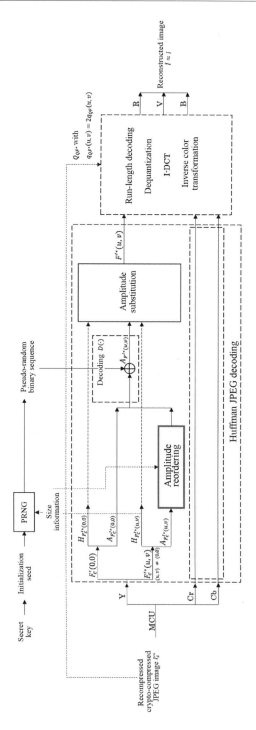

Figure 4.14. *Decoding a recompressed version of a crypto-compressed JPEG image*

The decryption operation can be carried out by anyone with access to the secret key used during encryption. By referring to the comment part of the JFIF file, it is possible to know whether the encrypted image has been recompressed. The first step of decryption is to use the secret key as an initialization seed for the PRNG in order to generate the pseudo-random binary sequence required for decryption. The decryption process thus takes account of the fact that the encrypted binary sequence must be shifted in order to decrypt each coefficient; remember that these coefficients were divided by two during the recompression phase. As the last bit of each code is removed during recompression, the last bit of each part of the pseudo-random binary sequence associated with a coefficient must also be ignored. The decryption function $\mathcal{D}(\cdot)$ is similar to the encryption function. It requires two input parameters: a recompressed encrypted coefficient $F_e'^*(u, v)$ and its size, which is specified in the header. The associated clear coefficient is obtained by applying an exclusive-or between the magnitude of the encrypted coefficient and the associated part in the pseudorandom binary sequence:

$$F'^*(u, v) = \mathcal{D}\left(F_e'^*(u, v), \ \text{size}(F_e'^*(u, v))\right)$$

$$= \mathcal{D}\left(\left\{H_{F_e'^*(u,v)}, A_{F_e'^*(u,v)}\right\}, \ \text{size}(F'(u, v)) - 1\right) \qquad [4.10]$$

$$= \left\{H_{F'^*(u,v)}, A_{F'^*(u,v)}\right\}$$

where $H_{F'^*(u,v)} = H_{F_e'^*(u,v)}$.

Note that applying the proposed recompression method to the clear JPEG image I', we obtain exactly the same coefficients $F'^*(u, v)$ as after decrypting the coefficients $F_e'^*(u, v)$. The encryption/decryption method is commutative with the recompression method, since the exclusive-or operation is commutative with the floor function:

$$F'^*(u, v) = \mathcal{D}\left(\left\lfloor \frac{\mathcal{E}(F'(u,v), \ \text{size}(F'(u,v)))}{2} \right\rfloor, \ \text{size}(F'(u, v)) - 1\right)$$

$$= \left\lfloor \frac{\mathcal{D}(\mathcal{E}(F'(u,v), \ \text{size}(F'(u,v))), \ \text{size}(F'(u,v))-1)}{2} \right\rfloor \qquad [4.11]$$

$$= \left\lfloor \frac{F'(u,v)}{2} \right\rfloor$$

After decryption, Huffman decoding is applied and the quantized DCT coefficients are reconstructed. The inverse quantization operation is then performed in order to obtain the dequantized values $\hat{F}(u, v)$. As we have seen, the decrypted image corresponds to the recompressed compressed image I'^*. Its quantization table Q_{QF^*} is derived from the quantization table Q_{QF} of the compressed image I', of which the coefficients have been multiplied by two:

$$\hat{F}(u, v) = F'^*(u, v) \times q_{QF^*}(u, v)$$
$$= \begin{cases} F'^*(u, v) \times 2 \times q_{QF}(u, v), & \text{if } 2 \times q_{QF}(u, v) \leq 255 \\ 255, & \text{otherwise} \end{cases} \quad [4.12]$$

Finally, the decompressed RGB image $\hat{I}$ image is obtained by applying the I-DCT transformation to convert the frequency coefficients into pixels, then the inverse color space change to convert the YCbCr image into RGB. As in the case of a standard JPEG compression, depending on the quality factor QF, the content of the reconstructed image $\hat{I}$ will be more or less faithful to the original image I.

4.5.4. *Illustration of the method*

Figure 4.15 was obtained by applying the crypto-compressed JPEG image recompression method to the *Peppers* image (321×481 pixels) using a quality factor of QF = 75% for the first JPEG compression. The first step in the method is to crypto-compress the original image. In this example, the AC and DC coefficients of the three components (Y, Cb and Cr) are encrypted to preserve the visual privacy of the original image content. We see that it is difficult to distinguish details, and that the value of the color PSNR is very low (11.74 dB). After the decoding phase, we see that the decrypted crypto-compressed JPEG image is very similar to the original image (PSNR = 38.59 dB). Note that this image is identical to the one obtained after a classic non-encrypted JPEG compression with QF = 75%. The obtained crypto-compressed image is then recompressed directly in the encrypted domain (i.e. without decrypting the crypto-compressed image). By analyzing the quantization table, we can estimate the quality factor after recompression as EQF* = 50% (Itier *et al.* 2020). Finally, the recompressed crypto-compressed JPEG image can be perfectly decrypted with the secret key used for crypto-compression. The PSNR value is high (35.21 dB), indicating strong similarity between the resulting image and the original *Peppers* image.

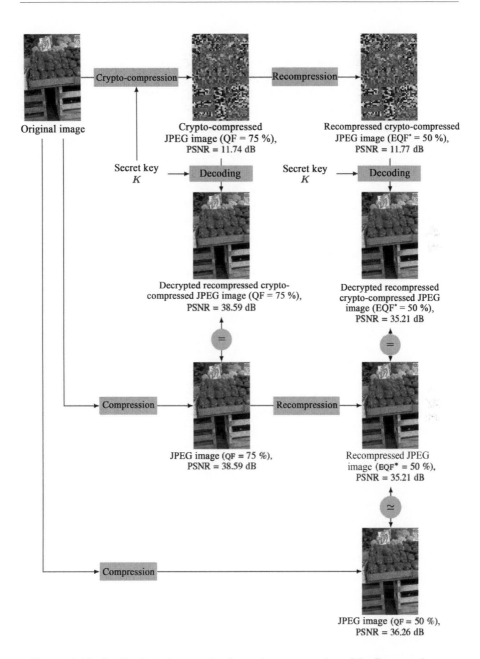

Figure 4.15. *Application of our method: crypto-compression of the* Peppers *image (QF = 75%, encryption of the AC and DC luminance coefficients and the two chrominance components) and recompression of the crypto-compressed image*

4.6. Conclusion

In this chapter, we have described the development of JPEG crypto-compression methods over the last two decades. State-of-the-art methods draw on essential encryption concepts alongside in-depth knowledge of the JPEG compression format. Crypto-compression operations are not limited to the JPEG format; however, the widespread use of this format for sharing and viewing images makes it particularly suitable for a presentation of this type. Generally speaking, image crypto-compression methods aim to fulfill three aims: providing a satisfactory compression ratio (which must be comparable to conventional compression), visual privacy, and encryption security (vs. brute force attacks, key estimation, etc.). As we have seen, systematic security analysis of these methods is a growing area of research. These methods are designed to provide a certain level of visual security (via selective encryption), which can be estimated based on the encryption parameters. However, there is no guarantee of a fixed privacy level, and two images encrypted in the same way may present significant differences in visual privacy levels as perceived by an observer. Visual privacy is often evaluated using conventional image quality metrics such as PSNR or SSIM. Since these methods are designed to compare "high"-quality images, however, their effectiveness in estimating the "badness" of an image is limited. In this context, new methods have recently been proposed for assessing visual privacy assessment. These methods or principles may be used to design crypto-compression methods to meet user-imposed levels of visual privacy.

Images can be processed within the JPEG crypto-compressed domain, permitting applications such as the recompression of crypto-compressed images described above. The field of image encryption is currently evolving due to the development of homomorphic encryption methods, which offer a level of security comparable with that of conventional methods while still permitting data processing. The use of these methods in the context of crypto-compression presents a significant challenge due to the need to respect the size constraints of compressed files.

4.7. References

Arnold, V.I. and Avez, A. (1967). *Problèmes ergodiques de la mécanique classique*. Gauthier-Villars, France.

Chan, S. (1992). Recompression of still images. Report, University of Kent, Canterbury.

Chen, G. and Ueta, T. (1999). Yet another chaotic attractor. *International Journal of Bifurcation and Chaos*, 9(7), 1465–1466.

Chen, G., Mao, Y., Chui, C.K. (2004). A symmetric image encryption scheme based on 3D chaotic cat maps. *Chaos, Solitons & Fractals*, 21(3), 749–761.

Cho, T.S., Avidan, S., Freeman, W.T. (2010). A probabilistic image jigsaw puzzle solver. In *Conference on Computer Vision and Pattern Recognition (CVPR)*. IEEE, San Francisco.

Chuman, T., Kurihara, K., Kiya, H. (2017). On the security of block scrambling-based ETC systems against jigsaw puzzle solver attacks. In *International Conference on Acoustics, Speech and Signal Processing (ICASSP)*. IEEE, New Orleans.

Daemen, J. and Rijmen, V. (2002). *The Design of Rijndael: AES, the Advanced Encryption Standard*. Springer, Berlin.

Davis, R. (1978). The data encryption standard in perspective. *IEEE Communications Society Magazine*, 16(6), 5–9.

Diffie, W. and Hellman, M. (1976). New directions in cryptography. *IEEE Transactions on Information Theory*, 22(6), 644–654.

Dufaux, F., Wee, S., Apostolopoulos, J., Ebrahimi, T. (2004). JPSEC for secure imaging in JPEG 2000. In *Electronic Imaging, Applications of Digital Image Processing*, Tescher, A. (ed). The International Society for Optical Engineering, Bellingham.

Dworkin, M. (2001). Recommendation for block cipher modes of operation: Methods and techniques. Report, National Institute of Standards and Technology, Computer Security Division, Gaithersburg.

El Gamal, T. (1985). A public key cryptosystem and a signature scheme based on discrete logarithms. *IEEE Transactions on Information Theory*, 31(4), 469–472.

Engel, D., Stütz, T., Uhl, A. (2009). A survey on JPEG2000 encryption. *Multimedia Systems*, 15(4), 243–270.

Fridrich, J. (1997). Image encryption based on chaotic maps. In *International Conference on Systems, Man, and Cybernetics (SMC)*. IEEE, Orlando.

Fridrich, J. (1998). Symmetric ciphers based on two-dimensional chaotic maps. *International Journal of Bifurcation and Chaos*, 8(6), 1259–1284.

Grangetto, M., Magli, E., Olmo, G. (2006). Multimedia selective encryption by means of randomized arithmetic coding. *IEEE Transactions on Multimedia*, 8(5), 905–917.

Guan, Z.-H., Huang, F., Guan, W. (2005). Chaos-based image encryption algorithm. *Physics Letters A*, 346(1), 153–157.

Hamidouche, W., Farajallah, M., Sidaty, N., El Assad, S., Deforges, O. (2017). Real-time selective video encryption based on the chaos system in scalable HEVC extension. *Signal Processing: Image Communication*, 58, 73–86.

ISO/IEC 10918-5:2013 (2013). Information technology – Digital compression and coding of continuous-tone still images: JPEG File Interchange Format (JFIF) – Part 5. Report, International Organization for Standardization.

Itier, V., Puteaux, P., Puech, W. (2020). Recompression of JPEG crypto-compressed images without a key. *IEEE Transactions on Circuits and Systems for Video Technology*, 30(3), 646–660.

JEITA CP-3451E (2002). Exchangeable image file format for digital still cameras: Exif Version 2.32. Report, Japan Electronics and Information Technology Industries Association.

Johnson, M., Ishwar, P., Prabhakaran, V., Schonberg, D., Ramchandran, K. (2004). On compressing encrypted data. *IEEE Transactions on Signal Processing*, 52(10), 2992–3006.

Karn, P., Metzger, P., Simpson, W. (1995). The ESP triple DES transform. *RFC*, 1851, 1–11.

Kerckhoffs, A. (1883). La cryptographie militaire. *Journal des sciences militaires*, IX, 5–38, 161–191.

Kumar, A.A. and Makur, A. (2008). Distributed source coding based encryption and lossless compression of gray scale and color images. In *Workshop on Multimedia Signal Processing (MMSP)*. IEEE, Cairns.

Kurihara, K., Shiota, S., Kiya, H. (2015). An encryption-then-compression system for JPEG standard. In *Picture Coding Symposium (PCS)*. IEEE, Cairns.

Kurihara, K., Imaizumi, S., Shiota, S., Kiya, H. (2017). An encryption-then-compression system for lossless image compression standards. *IEICE Transactions on Information and Systems*, 100(1), 52–56.

Lam, E.Y. and Goodman, J.W. (2000). A mathematical analysis of the DCT coefficient distributions for images. *IEEE Transactions on Image Processing*, 9(10), 1661–1666.

Lazzeretti, R. and Barni, M. (2008). Lossless compression of encrypted grey-level and color images. In *European Signal Processing Conference*. EUSIPCO, Lausanne.

Li, W. and Yuan, Y. (2007). A leak and its remedy in JPEG image encryption. *International Journal of Computer Mathematics*, 84(9), 1367–1378.

Lian, S., Sun, J., Wang, Z. (2004). Perceptual cryptography on JPEG2000 compressed images or videos. In *International Conference on Computer and Information Technology (CIT)*. IEEE, Wuhan.

Mao, Y., Chen, G., Lian, S. (2004). A novel fast image encryption scheme based on 3D chaotic baker maps. *International Journal of Bifurcation and Chaos*, 14(10), 3613–3624.

Merkle, R.C. (1978). Secure communications over insecure channels. *Communications of the ACM*, 21(4), 294–299.

Minemura, K., Moayed, Z., Wong, K., Qi, X., Tanaka, K. (2012). JPEG image scrambling without expansion in bitstream size. In *International Conference on Image Processing (ICIP)*. IEEE, Orlando.

Norcen, R. and Uhl, A. (2004). Encryption of wavelet-coded imagery using random permutations. In *International Conference on Image Processing (ICIP)*. IEEE, Singapore.

Paillier, P. (1999). Public-key cryptosystems based on composite degree residuosity classes. In *International Conference on the Theory and Applications of Cryptographic Techniques*. EUROCRYPT, Prague.

Pinto, M., Puech, W., Subsol, G. (2013). Protection of JPEG compressed e-comics by selective encryption. In *International Conference on Image Processing (ICIP)*. IEEE, Melbourne.

Premaratne, P. and Premaratne, M. (2012). Key-based scrambling for secure image communication. In *International Conference on Intelligent Computing*. ICIC, Huangshan.

Puech, W. and Rodrigues, J.M. (2005). Crypto-compression of medical images by selective encryption of DCT. In *European Signal Processing Conference*. EUSIPCO, Antalya.

Puech, W., Bors, A.G., Rodrigues, J.M. (2013). Protection of colour images by selective encryption. In *Advanced Color Image Processing and Analysis*, Fernandez-Maloigne, C. (ed.). Springer, New York.

Reininger, R. and Gibson, J. (1983). Distributions of the two-dimensional DCT coefficients for images. *IEEE Transactions on Communications*, 31(6), 835–839.

Rivest, R.L., Shamir, A., Adleman, L. (1978). A method for obtaining digital signatures and public-key cryptosystems. *Communications of the ACM*, 21(2), 120–126.

Rodrigues, J.M., Puech, W., Bors, A.G. (2006). Selective encryption of human skin in JPEG images. In *International Conference on Image Processing (ICIP)*. IEEE, Atlanta.

Said, A. (2005). Measuring the strength of partial encryption schemes. In *International Conference on Image Processing (ICIP)*. IEEE, Genoa.

Schaefer, G. and Stich, M. (2003). UCID: An uncompressed color image database. In *Electronic Imaging: Storage and Retrieval Methods and Applications for Multimedia*. SPIE, San Jose.

Scharinger, J. and Pichler, F. (1996). Efficient image encryption based on chaotic maps. In *Proceedings of the 20th Workshop of the Austrian Association for Pattern Recognition (OAGM/AAPR) on Pattern Recognition*, Pinz, A. (ed.). R. Oldenbourg Verlag GmbH, Munich.

Shahid, Z., Chaumont, M., Puech, W. (2011). Fast protection of H. 264/AVC by selective encryption of CAVLC and CABAC for I and P frames. *IEEE Transactions on Circuits and Systems for Video Technology*, 21(5), 565–576.

Shannon, C.E. (1949). Communication theory of secrecy systems. *Bell System Technical Journal*, 28(4), 656–715.

Shi, C. and Bhargava, B. (1998). A fast MPEG video encryption algorithm. In *International Conference on Multimedia (MM)*. ACM, Bristol.

Singh, G. (2013). A study of encryption algorithms (RSA, DES, 3DES and AES) for information security. *International Journal of Computer Applications*, 67(19), 33–38.

Unterweger, A. and Uhl, A. (2012). Length-preserving bit-stream-based JPEG encryption. In *Workshop on Multimedia and Security (MMSec)*. ACM, Warwick.

Usman, K., Juzoji, H., Nakajima, I., Soegidjoko, S., Ramdhani, M., Hori, T., Igi, S. (2007). Medical image encryption based on pixel arrangement and random permutation for transmission security. In *International Conference on e-Health Networking, Application and Services (Healthcom)*. IEEE, Taipei.

Van Droogenbroeck, M. and Benedett, R. (2002). Techniques for a selective encryption of uncompressed and compressed images. In *Advanced Concepts for Intelligent Vision Systems (ACIVS)*, Springer, Ghent.

Vernam, G.S. (1926). Cipher printing telegraph systems: For secret wire and radio telegraphic communications. *Journal of the AIEE*, 45(2), 109–115.

Wallace, G.K. (1992). The JPEG still picture compression standard. *IEEE Transactions on Consumer Electronics*, 38(1), XVIII–XXXIV.

Wright, C.V., Feng, W.-C., Liu, F. (2015). Thumbnail-preserving encryption for JPEG. In *Workshop on Information Hiding and Multimedia Security (IH&MMSec)*. ACM, Portland.

Xiang, T., Wong, K.-W., Liao, X. (2007). Selective image encryption using a spatiotemporal chaotic system. *Chaos: An Interdisciplinary Journal of Nonlinear Science*, 17(2), 023115.

Zhu, Z.-L., Zhang, W., Wong, K.-W., Yu, H. (2011). A chaos-based symmetric image encryption scheme using a bit-level permutation. *Information Sciences*, 181(6), 1171–1186.

Zimmermann, P.R. (1995). *The Official PGP User's Guide, Volume 5*. MIT Press, Cambridge.

5

Crypto-Compression of Videos

Cyril BERGERON[1], Wassim HAMIDOUCHE[2]
and Olivier DÉFORGES[2]

[1]*Thales SIX GTS France, Gennevilliers, France*
[2]*IETR, INSA Rennes, Univ Rennes, France*

Recent developments in digital communication systems and the widespread use of video content have raised new concerns about media security and privacy. This chapter addresses these emerging security issues by providing a state of the art of partial, perceptual and selective encryption approaches. We also present recent work in the field of video crypto-compression, with a particular focus on selective encryption adapted to video compression standards. In this context, methods are proposed for evaluating the visual privacy offered by these solutions.

5.1. Introduction

5.1.1. *Background*

The quest for confidentiality in communications has long been a subject of interest for scholars, dating back to ancient times (with examples including Caesar's code, Al-Kindi's cryptanalysis, Vigenère's cipher, etc.). Over the centuries, what began as a form of art evolved into a fully fledged science in its own right under the name of cryptology (including cryptography and cryptanalysis). The notion of

---

For a color version of all figures in this chapter, see www.iste.co.uk/puech/multimedia2.zip.

Multimedia Security 2,
coordinated by William PUECH. © ISTE Ltd 2022.

secrecy in communications was initially brought into focus by the need to protect crucial data in the military and diplomatic fields (Kerckhoffs 1883); it was later adopted in the civilian world in order to preserve the confidentiality of information and messages, notably in an industrial context, for the protection of commercial exchanges, exclusive knowledge and innovations. Finally, the digital revolution (with the rise of telecommunications, computers, the Internet and social networks) created a need for new methods of storing and transmitting digital data in order to prevent undesirable disclosure and fraudulent copying.

Claude Shannon, the founding father of information theory, actually developed his mathematical theory through his work in the field of cryptology at Bell Labs during World War II. His seminal work on the notion of secrecy, "Communications Theory of Secrecy Systems" (Shannon 1949), was written in 1945 (although it would only be declassified by the U.S. Department of Defense in 1949), predating the work that would lead to his two fundamental theorems on source and channel coding. Information security thus forms an integral part of the information theory "triptych" of source coding, cryptography and channel coding.

5.1.2. *Video compression*

The recent evolution of digital communication systems (xDSL, 3G, 4G and 5G) has led to an explosion of multimedia services and applications (IPTV, content sharing and social networking); the vast majority of data exchanged over networks now consists of video content[1]. Video compression is an integral part of many multimedia applications available today and is essential for meeting the needs of users (for applications such as digital TV, streaming and videoconferencing). Numerous video coding standards have been developed over recent decades, created by standardization committees such as ITU-T (the International Telecommunication Union-Telecommunication standardization sector), or ISO/IEC JTC1/SC29/WG11 by MPEG (the Moving Picture Experts Group). Codecs such as Advanced Video Coding (AVC) and High Efficiency Video Coding (HEVC) (ITU-T 2013) mean that video service providers are still able to maintain good quality content, despite demands for higher video resolutions, and to adapt to a variety of different transmission rates. For example, the latest HEVC video encoding standard, published in 2013, went well beyond the compression performance of existing video encoders, allowing up to 50% bitrate reduction over AVC for equivalent subjective video quality (Sullivan *et al.* 2012).

---

1 According to the Cisco Visual Networking Index (VNI), video content is expected to account for 82% of all consumer Internet traffic in 2021 (Cisco 2017).

5.1.3. *Video security*

The increased use of video compression in various video-on-demand systems, video communication services, social networks and media sharing platforms has raised not only public knowledge and use of these services, but also raises crucial security challenges in terms of copyright protection, data protection and privacy. For example, the widespread use of social networks means that people may now be recorded anywhere, with or without their knowledge, and published on the Internet without their consent: this directly impacts their privacy rights.

Security and content protection in the field of video have thus become an important issue in the last decades and have attracted considerable scientific research (in the areas of steganography, watermarking, partial encryption, etc.). By analogy with channel coding, source coding and cryptography have long been studied separately. The idea of combining source coding and security aspects under the term crypto-compression has opened up promising new avenues alongside work on joint source-channel coding.

Selective encryption appears to be one of the most promising new tools combining compression and cryptography, and has received most attention in the scientific literature over the past few years.

In this chapter, we present different approaches to protection used and studied in the state of the art, including crypto-compression systems. We notably focus on the selective encryption scheme used in video compression standards: AVC, HEVC and its scalable extension SHVC. Finally, we shall present different methods used to objectively measure and subjectively evaluate selective encryption in order to quantify the level of visual security offered by various approaches.

Section 5.2 presents the state of the art in encryption systems, while section 5.3 is devoted to different aspects of selective encryption. Approaches to measuring image and video quality are presented in section 5.4. Section 5.5 concerns perspectives for further development in this area, and some conclusions are presented in section 5.6.

5.2. State of the art

Traditionally, encryption schemes are considered to be distinct and independent from information compression approaches. Standard symmetric encryption algorithms, such as AES and DES, are used to encrypt all bits in a video stream (Wu and Kuo 2005), in the same way as a text file, that is, without considering the specific structure of the video stream. Unfortunately, this general approach, based on successive compression and encryption phases, is not optimized for video content.

Several different video encryption systems have been presented in the literature over the past three decades (Liu and Koenig 2010; Jolly and Vikas 2011; Stutz and Uhl 2012).

As we see from Figure 5.1, video encryption methods can be grouped into three broad categories, operating at different stages in the transmission process:

– visual encryption methods, where modifications are applied in the spatial (or pixel) domain before compression;

– crypto-compression methods, in which encryption occurs as part of the compression process;

– naive encryption methods, which are applied after compression at system/transport level.

The families and sub-families of methods presented in the following sections are also clearly illustrated in Figure 5.1.

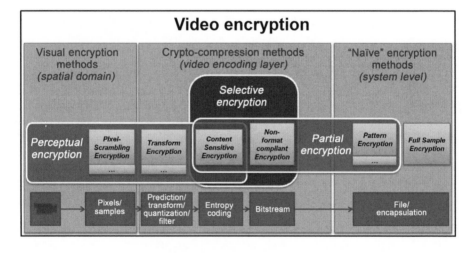

Figure 5.1. *Video encryption methods*

5.2.1. *Naive encryption*

The simplest and most common method used in secure video transmission is to encrypt the entire video stream. This approach is called full sample encryption, and was standardized by MPEG under the name of Common Encryption (CENC) for files (ISO/IEC 23001-7 2016) and MPEG-2 video transport streams (ISO/IEC 23001-9 2016). Using this technique, which is also known as full encryption, all compressed video streams are treated as opaque data; the attention to the structure and specificity of the compressed content is not taken into account, meaning that the video stream cannot be analyzed at the transport or low-level layers. The fact that the video data are encrypted in their entirety makes this method computationally complex and ill-suited to the transmission of a high bitrate video streams, with low latency and low complexity constraints (Tawalbeh *et al.* 2013; Asghar *et al.* 2014). Furthermore, the bitstreams encrypted using these standards can only be decoded following the application of the corresponding decryption process (as the encryption process breaks the syntax of the video bitstream).

These two challenges have been handled independently by two broad subsets of encryption methods proposed in the literature: partial encryption methods (section 5.2.2) and perceptual encryption methods (section 5.2.3), shown in Figure 5.1.

5.2.2. *Partial encryption*

Partial encryption involves protecting a portion of the bitstream (bytes or bits) while leaving the remainder *clear* (i.e. unchanged). Limiting the number of encrypted bits considerably reduces the complexity of cryptographic operations (XOR) and the use of the encryption algorithm itself, without compromising the security of the process. The MPEG CENC standard also defines subsample encryption and pattern encryption, where only the data relating to entropically compressed video streams is partially encrypted. Pattern encryption, as the name suggests, involves the encryption of only certain sequences of data bytes, leaving other sequences unencrypted, following a regular user-defined pattern (Figure 5.2). This method greatly reduces use of the encryption system (in this case AES), thus decreasing the latency induced at both the encoder and decoder ends of the process.

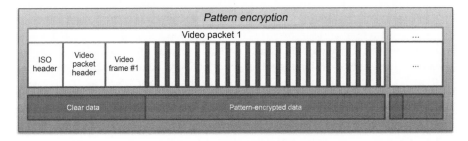

Figure 5.2. *Principle of pattern encryption*

Furthermore, leaving the headers of the video frames unencrypted means that certain information, such as the frame number, remains accessible, so that specific portions of the video can be decrypted without needing to process the entire video. Nevertheless, as in the case of full encryption, encrypted bitstreams cannot be decoded without the correct decryption mechanism: the encrypted video cannot be displayed.

5.2.3. *Perceptual encryption*

The second main subset includes all methods of encryption where video content is visually degraded, either completely or locally (i.e. in only one or more areas of the image). Unlike naive encryption, these methods generate a protected bitstream that can be decoded without requiring access to the encryption key. For this reason, some authors use the term format compliant encryption (or the more general term format-preserving encryption, which is wider than image/video encryption), since these approaches preserve the format and syntax of the resulting stream. Others have used the term "transparent encryption", highlighting the fact that the protected video sequence cannot be detected as "encrypted" at any point in the transmission chain.

Note that these perceptual encryption methods also have the property of adjusting the level of visual degradation obtained after decoding. This adjustment means that a person who does not have access to the decryption key may be authorized to visualize a low-quality, but interpretable, version of the protected video. In the case of on-site video surveillance, for example, individual identification is not relevant for detecting suspicious events or crowd movements, except to law enforcement officers who may request authorization from the authorities to obtain a decryption key, notably in investigative contexts.

Methods in this subset often rely on pixel scrambling, an approach which degrades visual content prior to compression using a cryptographic mechanism (Podesser *et al.* 2002; Ye 2010; Liu *et al.* 2013). Unfortunately, this method also has certain drawbacks: modifying pixels in the spatial domain (i.e. the sample domain) alters the compression efficiency of the video codec. In the case of lossless compression, based on a modification of the statistics of the samples to be processed, operations such as entropy coding no longer effectively reduce the bitrate. Moreover, in the case of lossy compression, reversibility is not guaranteed as compression artifacts may prevent correct retrieval of the original protected content.

5.2.4. *Crypto-compression methods*

In response to these issues, several authors have proposed encryption methods that operate on the video coding layer by modifying the compression algorithm. Thus, information is compressed and protected in a single pass through cryptographic mechanisms within the different compression stages, as shown in Figure 5.3.

One example is the transform encryption approach, where the selected transform (DCT (Liu *et al.* 2006; Weng and Preneel 2007), DWT (Zeng and Lei 1999; Lian *et al.* 2004)) differs from the normalized version, although the syntax obtained in this way remains compatible with the chosen compression format. These methods, therefore, intrinsically modify the steps in the compression process and, in most cases, modify the compression performance of encoders, which may be problematic if the bitrate allocated to video transmission is limited. For example, randomly permuting the transformed coefficients (TC) has been shown to "distort" the probability distribution of these coefficients, making entropy coding less efficient and thus increasing the compressed video bitrate (Tang 1997; Shi *et al.* 1999).

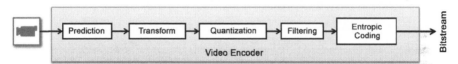

Figure 5.3. *Stages in the video compression process*

5.2.5. *Selective encryption methods*

As we saw in section 5.2.1, C. Shannon carried out an in-depth study of the close relationship between data compression and encryption (Shannon 1949). Shannon demonstrated that removing redundancy in a source could strengthen the encryption process. In section 5.2.4, we saw that video encryption involves compressing data using a video encoder that eliminates most of the redundancy in the source before encrypting the entire bitstream, assuming that the resulting bits have the same importance and statistics. This theoretical approach thus implies the use of a perfect encoder that removes all statistical redundancy in the source prior to encryption. However, despite the ever-increasing efficiency of video codecs in terms of compression, their associated bitstreams have their own syntax and structure that can be considered as a bias for cryptanalysis attacks. It is worth noting that some joint source-channel coding solutions rely on this statistical bias and have proven to be effective in recovering errors in compressed bitstreams transmitted over noisy channels (Bergeron and Lamy-Bergot 2004; Sabeva *et al.* 2006). Selective encryption, on the other hand, takes the coding structure of the video bitstream into account and encrypts only the most sensitive information. Note that the term "selective" relates directly to the choice of information to protect.

Selective encryption methods evolved as an efficient alternative to existing encryption methods for different video and image codecs (Wen *et al.* 2002; Bergeron and Lamy-Bergot 2005; Dufaux and Ebrahimi 2008; Shahid *et al.* 2011; Stutz and Uhl 2012; Peng *et al.* 2013; Van Wallendael *et al.* 2013a, 2013b; Shahid and Puech 2014; Farajallah *et al.* 2015; Boyadjis *et al.* 2017).

As the selective encryption operation is carried out during the final stage of video compression, that is, entropy encoding, this encryption can also be carried out independently of the compression (or decompression) process by means of transcoding, as some authors have suggested (Boyadjis *et al.* 2014).

In this sense, selective encryption may be considered as a subset of partial encryption methods, since only part of the information is protected. However, it cannot be automatically considered as a subset of perceptual encryption methods, since some of the selective encryption methods described in the literature do not necessarily provide a format compliant bitstream: this is known as non-format compliant selective encryption (Lian *et al.* 2006).

Section 5.3 presents solutions where the encrypted bitstream remains standard-compliant, taking advantage of both the benefits of perceptual encryption methods (decodability, visual degradation adjustment and spatially or temporally localized encryption) and the partial encryption methods described earlier (low computational cost of encryption/decryption, lower latency, and information accessibility).

5.3. Format-compliant selective encryption

5.3.1. *Properties*

In this chapter, we have chosen to focus on format-compliant selective encryption methods, which combine the advantages of the partial encryption (section 5.2.2) and perceptual encryption (section 5.2.3) methods described above. This type of encryption approach respects certain key properties:

– the syntax of the compression standard is preserved so that the compressed stream remains readable by any format-compliant decoder, and cannot be identified as such; this element of discretion is particularly valuable if communications are being monitored;

– the approach is guaranteed to be efficient in terms of rate/distortion, avoiding non-controlled fluctuations in bitrate which may exceed or "clog" the available capacity;

– the complexity and processing times involved in these approaches are moderate, and the number of encryption (and decryption) operations is limited;

– encryption may be temporally and locally restricted within the video, and the level of encryption (with associated levels of visual degradation) can be adjusted by selecting the appropriate number of elements within the video content.

These selective encryption methods thus imply modifying the entropy encoder within the compression step by partially encrypting the symbols resulting from the compression algorithm. The challenge lies in determining which data should be selected for this encryption.

It is hard to understand the challenges inherent in modifying the entropy encoder without a clear understanding of the process. To illustrate these issues, let us consider the CAVLC (Context Adaptive Variable Length Coding) entropy encoder of the H.264/AVC standard. This encoder transforms each symbol resulting from the various compression steps (intra prediction, motion vector, TC, etc.) into a variable length codeword (VLC), where each associated length is directly related to the probability of the symbol occurring. To encode motion vectors (specifically, the difference with respect to the default motion vector), the standard uses a look-up table (see Table 5.1) to entropically encode the (x, y) coordinates of the vector.

Index	VLC codeword	Mvd_IX
0	1	0
1	010	1
2	011	−1
3	00100	2
4	00101	−2
5	00110	3
6	00111	−3
7	0001000	4
8	0001001	−4
...	...	...

Table 5.1. *VLC codewords: differences in movement vectors (CAVLC H.264/AVC). For a color version of this table, see www.iste.co.uk/puech/multimedia2.zip*

Note that when the coordinate values are of low amplitudes (compared to the default motion vector), they are coded using short code words; this is statistically consistent since motion vectors generally have values close to those of their collocated neighbors.

In the case of CABAC (Context-Adaptive Binary Arithmetic Coding), used in H.264/AVC and HEVC, the entropy encoder is based on an adaptive binary arithmetic coding technique using context models. The arithmetic coding step and context modeling mean that the bits in CABAC compressed streams are highly interdependent, as shown in Figure 5.4.

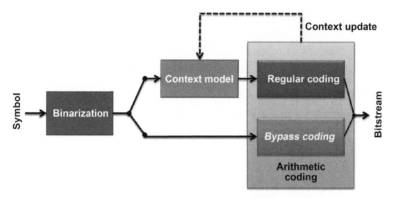

Figure 5.4. *Diagram of the CABAC encoder*

However, the arithmetic encoder only uses context models for regular coding; these models are not used in bypass encoding, and, in this case, the probability models are not updated during arithmetic encoding so that modifications to these values have no impact on the CABAC encoding.

There are two ways of applying selective encryption in this case:

– encrypt the symbols directly and generate a new codeword from the look-up table or from the CABAC encoder. This method maintains standard compatibility but can modify the length of the generated codeword, meaning that the size of the post-compression stream may be different;

– encrypt certain bits of the VLC (such as those shown in blue in Table 5.1) or, in the case of CABAC, bits that have been encoded using Bypass Coding. This approach limits possibilities, but the bitsize of the video stream is preserved.

The majority of the algorithms used in the state of the art are of the first type, and therefore bitrate preservation is not guaranteed. Some authors (Van Wallendael *et al.* 2013a) have studied the impact of all the encryptable parameters in the HEVC syntax in terms of video quality and bitrate: the degradations obtained with constant bitrate selective encryption algorithms were essentially similar. Furthermore, changing the compression efficiency of a compression chain is not recommended and can also present a bias for statistical attacks based on the probability of occurrence of the compressed symbol.

5.3.2. *Constant bitrate format compliant selective encryption*

In this section, we shall consider methods that present no additional cost in terms of rate, ensuring that the transport layer will not be affected by the encryption process, while preserving the advantages of the solutions described above. The main challenge in this case concerns the selection of the sensitive data to encrypt from within the possibilities offered by the video format, without affecting compression efficiency.

In our case, the only way to ensure bitrate conservation is to select only "cipherable" bits, which will only produce valid codewords of identical size when modified by a classic cryptographic algorithm. This selection of cipherable bits also entails identifying parts of the data stream that do not influence the decoding process, that is, where modifications resulting from encryption do not result in desynchronization or create non-compatible bit streams. For example, if the number of non-zero coefficients (the values of which will be modified) is encrypted, then the expected number of coefficients would be different and the rest of the decoding would be desynchronized; a compatible decoder would thus be unable to interpret the rest of the stream, and an error message would result. The set of eligible cipherable bits is known as the encryption space (ES), and is different for each codec.

Certain authors have provided more or less complete encryption space solutions (specifying the set of symbols and associated cipherable bits) for different video compression formats. Bergeron and colleagues (Bergeron and Lamy-Bergot 2005; Bergeron 2007) proposed a selective encryption scheme for H.264/AVC (CAVLC) bitstreams based on a selection of certain bits in different codewords, such as the luma prediction modes Intra4 × 4 and Intra16 × 16, intra-chroma prediction modes, coefficient values suffixes and motion vectors. Shahid *et al.* proposed a selective encryption scheme for CABAC with AVC (Shahid *et al.* 2011) and for HEVC (Shahid *et al.* 2009). Hamidouche *et al.* (2015) introduced a more thorough selection approach for HEVC and its scalable extension SHVC, encrypting motion vectors, TC and intra-prediction modes.

As we see from Figure 5.5, all of these solutions maintain the conformity of the bitstream format without altering compression efficiency. Nevertheless, note that these solutions use different standard cryptographic schemes to generate pseudo-random numbers (PRNG) to modify the cipherable bits: AES-CTR (Bergeron and Lamy-Bergot 2005), AES-CFB (Shahid *et al.* 2009, 2011) and chaos coding (Hamidouche *et al.* 2015).

For each symbol considered, it is important to note that the bits designated as cipherable must retain this capability in any bitstream, and that cases where a given configuration would permit delayed resynchronization cannot be considered. Cipherable bits correspond to cases where several codewords of the same length are available and no *a posteriori* change in context will occur when switching from one to the other, and encryption consists of swapping from one value of a symbol to another. This presents a twofold advantage: first, compatibility with the requirements of the video standard in question is guaranteed; second, it makes it difficult to find an angle of attack to try to break the encryption key, as it aims to make all solutions possible, hence removing the possibility of ruling out some cases based on non-respect of standard syntax.

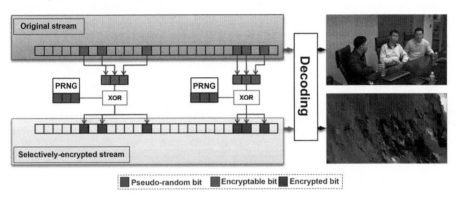

Figure 5.5. *Constant bitrate format compatible selective encryption: key principle*

5.3.3. *Standardized selective encryption*

In 2019, the MPEG standardization committee (ISO/IEC JTC1/SC29/WG11) began work on standardizing a selective encryption process compatible with the H.264/AVC and H.265/HEVC video compression formats (alongside a new image compression standard, HEIF (High Efficiency Image Format), a file format for images and image sequences recently standardized by MPEG (ISO/IEC 23008-12 2017), based on the ISOBMFF format (ISO/IEC 14496-12 2012) and using AVC and HEVC intra-mode encoders for still images), under the name MPEG A-VIMAF: Visual Identity Management Application Format (ISO/IEC 23000-21 2019). These selective solutions are compliant with their respective standards, and are thus compatible with the constant bitrate format; they have also been integrated into the CENC (Common Encryption Standard) for the ISOBMFF – *ISO Base Media File Format* – (ISO/IEC 23001-7 2016) under the name of content sensitive encryption (CSE).

For simplicity's sake, we will not go into detail concerning all partially cipherable symbols and their associated restrictions here. In this section, we shall simply present lists of codewords containing cipherable bits in Tables 5.2 (AVC CAVLC mode), 5.3 (AVC CABAC mode) and 5.4 (HEVC mode).

Codewords	Cipherable bits	Constraints?
Slice QP Delta	Suffix bits	No
Macroblock QP Delta	Suffix bits	No
Macroblock type	Certain suffix bits	Yes
IPCM	All bits	No
Intra Luma Prediction	All bits	Yes
Intra Chroma Prediction	Final bit	Yes
Motion prediction reference	Suffix bits	Yes
Motion prediction vector	Suffix bits	No
Trailing ones	All bits	No
Level Suffix	All bits	No
Total zeros	Final bit	Yes
Run Before	Certain bits	Yes

Table 5.2. *Cipherable codewords for AVC (CAVLC)*

Codewords	Cipherable bits	Constraints?
IPCM	All bits	No
Motion prediction vector	Suffix bits	Yes
Motion prediction vector sign	All bits	No
Sign of coefficient level	All bits	No
Absolute value of coef. level	Suffix bits	Yes

Table 5.3. *Cipherable codewords for AVC (CABAC)*

For reasons of efficiency, the pseudo-random number generator (PRNG) used by MPEG for the CSE standard is the AES Counter Mode (CTR). Figure 5.6 shows how AES-CTR generates a pseudo-random sequence from a 128 bit block, an initialization vector (IV) which is incremented for each block and a chosen encryption key (of 128, 192 or 256 bits). AES-CTR mode offers a number of advantages:

– its robustness to errors and loss has been widely validated (Isa *et al.* 2011; Boyadjis *et al.* 2015);

– the algorithm is fast and parallel-friendly for software/hardware optimization (Gueron and Krasnov 2014);

– its symmetry properties mean that autonomous encryption/decryption systems can be designed by transcoding (Boyadjis *et al.* 2014).

Codewords	Cipherable bits	Constraints?
Motion vector difference	Suffix bits	Yes
Motion vector difference sign	All bits	No
Delta QP sign syntax element	All bits	Yes
Transform coefficient sign	All bits	Yes

Table 5.4. *Cipherable codewords for HEVC*

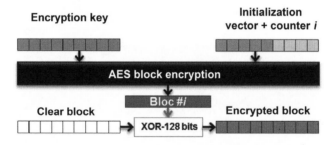

Figure 5.6. *Standard AES-CTR operating mode*

Obviously, the generated 16-byte (128-bit) block cipher cannot be applied directly to the compressed stream: as we saw previously, a video parser is used to locate cipherable bits. The encryption or decryption processes are performed using a simple XOR operation between the identified bits and the generated cipher blocks, as shown in Figure 5.7.

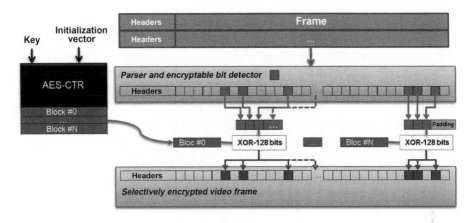

Figure 5.7. *Content sensitive encryption process*

5.3.4. *Locally applied selective encryption*

Many countries have rules and regulations issued by local authorities concerning video surveillance and the protection of personal data (for example, the GDPR in Europe). For example, in France, cameras can be installed in or adjacent to public spaces, but must be registered with the CNIL (*Commission nationale de l'informatique et des libertés*). Devices used to visualize either live or recorded images must only be accessible to authorized individuals, and can only be used by the police or legal authorities in the context of judicial requisition following an incident. Thus, it may be necessary to mask certain fixed areas in the camera's field of vision (if part of this field is private and filming is not authorized), and individual anonymization by dynamic masking (blurring) of faces or any other identifying features may be required. In this context, the selective encryption method can also be used to protect regions of interest (ROI) in the video content (such as human faces or predefined areas) and leave the rest of the video (background) unencrypted, meaning that it is not subject to visual degradation (except as a result of compression). Since the process is reversible, authorized individuals in possession of the key have the ability to reconstruct the content of the video in its entirety, including masked areas, where necessary. The first stage in this approach is to divide the video into independent regions, in which non-confidential "clear" zones and confidential "protected" zones will be defined, as shown in Figure 5.8.

Since each codec has its own specificities, we have chosen to focus on the most widespread examples, AVC and HEVC. Nevertheless, this approach may be generalized to other codecs using different terminologies and constraints.

In the AVC and HEVC codecs, slice and tile concepts can be used to divide video frames into independent regions. This is possible due to the fact that dependencies between neighboring blocks and entropy coding dependencies are reset at slice (or tile) boundaries, preventing reconstruction issues in clear areas (see section 5.3.4.1). Furthermore, certain coding restrictions are taken into account in order to prevent the propagation of encryption errors outside the ROI in the inter-coding configuration (as in the case of predicted frames, such as P- and B-frames); these are presented in section 5.3.4.2.

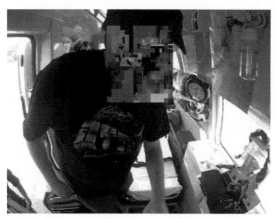

Figure 5.8. *Example of zone (selective) encryption*

5.3.4.1. *Controlling the propagation of selective encryption in intra-coding*

In conventional compression approaches, the first frame of a video is intra-coded, that is, coded intrinsically without using previous frames, and successively compressed blocks may use pre-coded pixels in a process known as intra-prediction. This coding scheme is very efficient, since it avoids re-encoding some of the information that has already been encoded in the neighborhood of the block in question. However, in the case of selective encryption, if a block is encrypted, the resulting degradation may be propagated to adjacent blocks. The AVC and HEVC standards include tools to control error propagation, designed to prevent the emergence of unwanted effects as a result of noisy transmission: slices, slice groups (AVC only) and tiles (HEVC only). For region-selective encryption, these tools can be used to prevent uncontrolled degradation of adjacent zones (which should remain clear), as shown in Figure 5.9.

5.3.4.2. *Controlling the propagation of selective encryption in inter-coding*

Coding processes using predictions based on previously coded images are subject to reconstruction dependencies; in the context of region-selective encryption, certain tools must therefore be used to prevent drift error propagation.

To ensure perfect reconstruction over the video sequence in the clear (unencrypted) area, the motion prediction mechanism is constrained to the clear area, to point exclusively to previous frames inside another clear area, as shown in Figure 5.10.

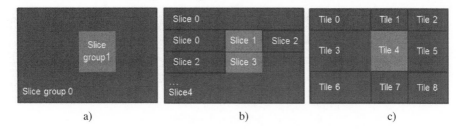

a)   b)   c)

Figure 5.9. *Image split into two zones, "protected" in green and "clear" in blue: a) by slice groups, b) by slices and c) by tiles*

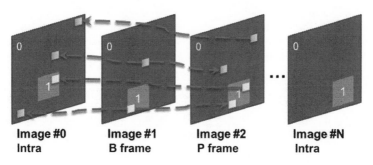

| Image #0 | Image #1 | Image #2 | Image #N |
| Intra | B frame | P frame | Intra |

Figure 5.10. *Management of the motion vector constraint with a protected zone and a clear zone*

SEI (Supplemental Enhancement Information) messages can be used to indicate this constraint for motion vectors, known as the motion-constrained slice group set in AVC and motion-constrained tile-based adaptation in HEVC. In HEVC specifically, the merge mode derives motion vector information from a list of neighboring spatial and temporal candidates; both decoding operations may thus propagate errors from encrypted tiles to unencrypted areas if content is not properly decrypted (with no key or using the wrong decryption key). In merge mode, temporal candidates for clear zone tiles must be taken from within the clear zone of the reference frames. In order to prevent the propagation of encryption outside the ROI tile, additional encoding constraints must be applied:

– motion vectors are restricted to referring only to the colocalized tile in the predicted block;

– in-loop filters must be disabled on the boundaries of the tile or slice (as in the case of intra-coding, to prevent them from being used as a reference).

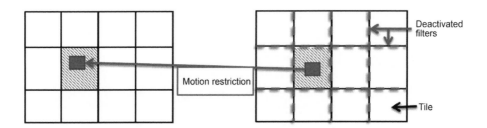

Figure 5.11. *Restriction of motion vectors*
and in-loop filters on tile boundaries

Although selective encryption does not directly increase the bit rate of the video stream, the constraints imposed in the case of region-selective encryption tend to have a negative impact on compression performance, depending on the resolution and content of the video. However, they are necessary and permit "clean" reconstruction, even at tile boundaries, as shown in Figure 5.11. These restrictions ensure perfect reconstruction of clear areas, even if part of the reference frame is encrypted using a region-selective encryption method.

5.3.4.3. *Differentiated access in selective encryption*

Given the possibility of defining and encrypting multiple regions in a dynamic manner, for certain applications, different encryptions may be applied to different zones, enabling differentiated access, as shown in Figure 5.12.

Figure 5.12. *Multi-access to protected*
multimedia streaming content

For example, consider the case of a personal video shared on social networks. The individuals featuring in the video may be blurred by selective encryption. Based on the individuals present, different access rights may be assigned to different users with access to the media file, as shown in Figure 5.13.

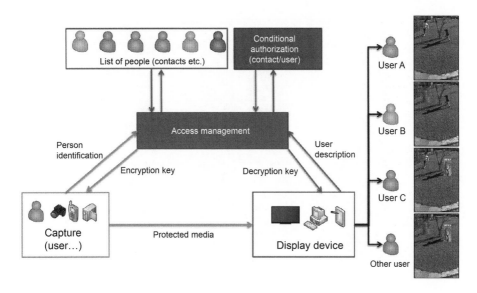

Figure 5.13. *Example of selective encryption*
using type-conditional user access

In this figure, a user *A* records a video and identifies the people in the video; they may then "anonymize" each individual using a different key via selective encryption. When another user wishes to decode the video, they must retrieve the keys associated with each protected zone from a user, but the available keys will vary depending on their assigned access rights. In our case, user *A* is able to access all zones, but users *B* and *C* can only access certain, different parts of the video, as a function of the privacy restrictions imposed by the individuals featuring in the film. Finally, for any other unauthorized user, the two encrypted zones will remain anonymized. Other approaches based on image sharing will be presented in Chapter 8.

Recent work by the ISO/IEC on standardized protection, in the form of common encryption (CENC) (ISO/IEC 23001-7 2016) and MPEG A-VIMAF (ISO/IEC 23000-21 2019), has enabled the use of multiple decryption keys for the same mutimedia content (Bergeron *et al.* 2017). Each key is linked to an identifier and an encrypted zone, as shown in Figure 5.14.

ISOBMFF media files can now contain a combination of encrypted and unencrypted sets with multiple keys; note, however, that it is not possible to use multiple keys for the same zone in the context of common encryption.

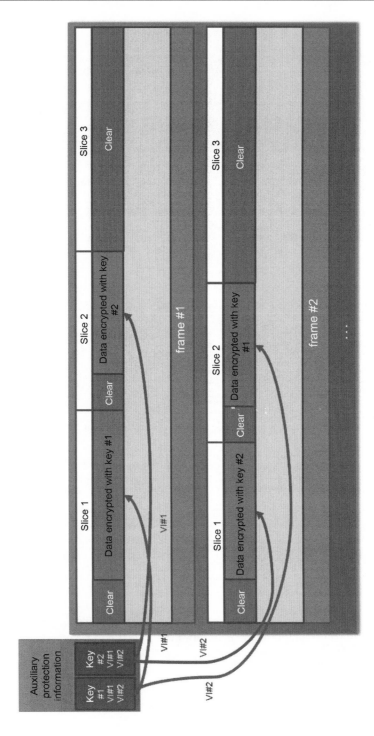

Figure 5.14. *Example of an ISOBMFF file with two key identifiers, where selective encryption is applied to certain slices of different frames*

5.3.5. *Decrypting selective encryption*

The subject of robustness to attacks has received relatively little attention in the context of research on selective encryption. As part of the CSE standardization process, MPEG launched a challenge to test the scheme (Bergeron *et al.* 2018). Three HEVC and three AVC bitstreams encrypted by CSE (Figure 5.15), along with the three open source software packages (Kvazaar (Tampere University of Technology 2015), GPAC (Telecom ParisTech 2008) and OpenHEVC (IETR-INSA Rennes 2015)) used to compress-encrypt and decompress-decrypt HEIF images and video sequences, were provided in order to evaluate the robustness of these solutions to different types of attacks.

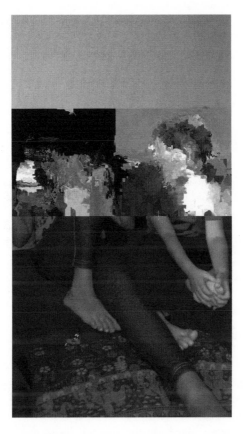

Figure 5.15. *Extract from an encrypted video sequence used in the "Break the Content Sensitive Encryption Challenge"*

The challenge website[2] supplies all the necessary information concerning the generation and decryption of HEVC bitstreams encrypted using CSE on various platforms. To date, there have been no successful attacks on this content.

In terms of security in selective encryption, although these solutions require relatively few encrypted bits (approximately 15–20% for AVC and HEVC) and the modifications made to compressed symbols do not affect the coherence of the syntax (while degrading visual reconstruction), it is hard to estimate and perfectly reconstruct the original bitstream: any attempt to identify the original message will be coherent and valid in terms of the syntax, and will thus be decodable.

Furthermore, it is important to note that video compression algorithms are not systematic and that each standard offers a variety of methods for compressing the same information. This means that it is not easy to find the original coded (and encrypted) bitstream, despite the fact that part of the information remains unencrypted.

The size of encrypted symbols is preserved during the process (the number of bits is unchanged), and also have the particularity of being intrinsically statistically similar since they are entropically designed by the standard (the size of a symbol depends on its probability of occurrence). These properties mean that formal statistical biases will not appear during a frequency attack.

5.4. Image and video quality

The relevance of encryption is an important question to consider. From a *security* perspective, the coded element must offer a high level of protection against cryptographic attacks. This level is generally estimated using statistical or correlation measurements. For images and videos, histogram analysis is also commonly used. In this case, *perceptual quality* is also an issue, and is even harder in cases of selective encryption where differences in the encryption level have a significant impact on image rendering.

The perceptual quality of images is based on image quality metrics, which may be split into two categories. The first group of *subjective* metrics rely on testing by human observers. These methods are time-consuming to implement, but are essential for calibration purposes. The second group of metrics are *objective*: in this case, distortion is estimated based on measurements in the image, with the goal of replicating subjective scores as closely as possible. There are two types of objective metrics: *Full Reference* (FR), as in the case of the MSE (Mean Squared Error), PSNR or SSIM (Structural Similarity Index) (Wang *et al.* 2004), where the distortion

---

2 Available at: http://openhevc.insa-rennes.fr/press-release/avc-and-hevc-selective-video-encryption-decryption-challenge/.

between the source and the coded image is estimated, or *No Reference* (NR), such as the NIQE (Natural Image Quality Evaluator) (Mittal *et al.* 2013), which operates blindly without knowledge of the reference. All of these metrics are widely known and used in quality optimization approaches.

The use of encryption, whether local or total, raises new questions to which responses are not always available in the present state of the art (Reza and Barbeau 2012):

– Which are the best methods to use for subjective quality testing?

– Which quality metrics are best-suited to the type of degradations resulting from encryption?

– What is the appropriate visual degradation threshold for a given application?

For images, various studies have shown that the usual objective quality metrics are no longer effective when applied to encrypted data (Hofbauer and Uhl 2010, 2016).

This is due to the fact that the relationship between visual quality and security is not symmetrical. Furthermore, these metrics have been developed to estimate a level of quality but do not directly indicate the intelligibility of the content. While certain image-specific metrics have been proposed (Xiang *et al.* 2016), no solutions have yet been developed for encrypted videos, to the best of our knowledge. A further explanation relates to the lack of existing work on subjective evaluations of visually encrypted videos to use as a starting point. In terms of databases, there are only two available in this context and they only contain images. Both relate to selective encryption, the first for images encoded in JPEG2000 format (Autrusseau *et al.* 2010) and the second for JPEG (Le Philippe *et al.* 2017).

In sections 5.4.1 and 5.4.2, we present a thorough study of the objective and subjective quality of selectively encrypted videos. At the end of section 5.4.2, we also present a complete public database on encrypted HEVC videos (Fezza *et al.* 2019a, 2019b).

5.4.1. *Experiments on encryption solutions*

5.4.1.1. *Content-sensitive encryption: a subjective approach*

The robustness of an encryption scheme can be evaluated using different tools. The vast majority of studies make a strong link between the degree of perceptual encryption and video quality. Metrics of the video quality assessment (VQA) type have been widely used to assess the security of visual encryption. Yao *et al.* (2008), for example, used three objective quality metrics: image entropy, structural distortion and spatial correlation. A range of VQAs have been proposed to improve measurement accuracy: the correlation coefficient (CC) (Jagadeesh *et al.* 2013), the edge similarity score (ESS), the luminance similarity score (LSS) (Mao and Wu 2004), the similarity of local entropy (SLE) (Sun *et al.* 2011) and encryption quality (EQ) (Ahmed *et al.* 2007). Hu *et al.* introduced a metric known as semantic distortion measurement (SDM), which measures the degree of semantic distortion in a video.

The main shortcoming of these encryption-oriented metrics is that they focus on only one specific parameter of the video, neglecting the multimodal character of human perception. Moreover, there are no studies on subjective quality that assess the user-perceived quality of encrypted videos. The objective measures mentioned above process videos as a binary sequence without taking into account the properties of the human visual system (HVS). In the rest of this chapter, we shall present a comprehensive study of both objective and subjective evaluation methods for assessing the quality of encrypted images.

In this context, the selective encryption solution introduced in section 5.3 and standardized by MPEG is used. While maintaining compatibility, we encrypt a set of HEVC syntax elements including motion vector differences "*MV*", the signs of these differences "*MVs*", the coefficients of the transforms "*TC*" and their sign "*TCs*". The configuration "*All*" corresponds to the encryption of all of these elements. This solution is implemented in Kvazaar (Viitanen *et al.* 2015), an open source free HEVC encoder, to create a new version (called *secure Kvazaar*) with the ability to compress and encrypt UHD HEVC video in real time. The subjective and objective studies conducted took account of different possible encryption scenarios and quantization parameters.

Three levels were considered for the basic CSE scheme:

– encryption of TC alone: *TC*;

– encryption of the signs of the transformed coefficients alone: *TCs*;

– encryption of all syntax elements: *All* = {*TC; TCs; MV; MVs*}.

Similarly, for the extension of the scheme to the scalable SHVC coder, the objective study covers three scenarios:

– base layer encryption only: {*SE-SHVC-BL*;

– enhancement layer encryption only: *SE-SHVC-EL*;

– encryption of both the base and enhancement layers: *SE-SHVC-All* = {*SE-SHVC-BL; SE-SHVC-EL*.

5.4.1.2. *Test environment and apparatus*

Subjective tests were carried out in the psychovisual laboratory at the IETR (INSA Rennes), which follows the recommendations of the ITU-R (ITU-R 2012). A

40-inch Full HD Samsung UE40F6640SS screen was used to view video sequences. Thirty-three observers – 24 men and 9 women, aged from 20 to 55 – participated in the experiment. All subjects were checked for color perception and visual acuity (10/10 in each eye, without correction).

As video content can have a significant impact on visual perception, we selected a set of sequences from the MPEG test base used by the JCT-VC expert group. Videos were primarily selected on the basis of their color, movement and texture characteristics. Five source sequences, each 10 s long but with different resolutions (classes), were selected for testing (see Table 5.5). The video sequences are compressed and encrypted in real time using the Kvazaar encoder with three levels of quantization for QP (22, 27 and 32) and for a low delay IPPP configuration. Syntax elements were encrypted in one of the three modes described above: *TC*, *TCs* and *All*. Finally, these different coding configurations give a set of 45 encrypted sequences: 5 sources × 3 QP × 3 encryption schemes.

Class	Resolution	Images per second	Video
B	1,920 x 1,080	50	*BasketballDrive, Cactus*
D	1,280 x 720	60	*FourPeople*
B	1,920 x 1,080	24	*Kimono*
E	416 x 240	60	*BQSquare*

Table 5.5. *Set of video sequences used in the experiment*

5.4.1.3. *Evaluation procedure*

The quality assessment used here is based on the Double Stimulus Continuous Quality Scale (DSCQS) (ITU-R 2012). Observers viewed each encrypted video twice, along with the original video. Participants were asked to quantify the degree of visibility of the content of encrypted videos, assigning a numerical score to each encrypted video according to a scale shown in Table 5.6, ranging from 1 (video content completely invisible) to 5 (video content clearly visible).

Degree of content visibility	Score
Clearly visible	5
Visible	4
Somewhat visible	3
Barely visible	2
Completely invisible	1

Table 5.6. *Subjective scoring scale*

At the end of each test, a graphical interface was displayed for 10 s for users to indicate their scores. Additional sequences were displayed prior to the experiment so that users were comfortable with the testing process. Finally, in order to prevent the occurrence of memorization phenomena, sequences were mixed so that two successive videos presented different characteristics.

5.4.2. *Video quality: experimental results*

5.4.2.1. *Objective measures of selective encryption*

The new encryption schemes presented above were implemented in the SHVC reference program, the Scalable Reference software Model (SHM), version 4.1 (Boyce *et al*. 2016). For this measure, we considered the classic test conditions used in SHVC, including two video sequences of size 2,560 × 1,600 (class A) and five sequences of size 1,920 × 1,080 (class B) (Seregin and He 2013). These videos were configured using a low delay P configuration (image I followed by P images), two layers ($L = 2$) and three scalability configurations: 2x, 1.5x and SNR. The PSNR was used to assess the quality of the decoded video.

Table 5.7 shows mean performances in terms of the PSNR and encryption space (ES, ratio of encrypted bits in the SHVC stream) of the three proposed encryption schemes, for videos in classes A and B and using different quantization values for QP. We see that the PSNR drops off sharply in the case of SE-SHVC-BL and SE-SHVC-All (PSNR of Y less than 10 dB); the first of these options encrypts the base layer (BL) alone, while the second applies encryption to all layers. Furthermore, we see that the SE-SHVC-BL scheme encrypts less than 7.5% of the SHVC video stream for all three scalability configurations.

Class	Scalability	Orig. PSNR Y	SE-SHVC-BL		SE-SHVC-All		SE-SHVC-EL	
			PSNR Y	ES (%)	PSNR Y	ES (%)	PSNR Y	ES (%)
A	SNR	41.12	8.28	7.27	8.25	15.06	23.69	7.79
	2x	41	9.04	5.62	8.96	16.61	17.72	10.98
	HEVC	41.25	8.55	17.83	–	–	–	–
B	SNR	39.54	9.18	6.23	9.13	15.72	25.77	9.49
	2x	39.6	9.82	4.11	9.66	17	18.65	12.89
	1.5x	39.57	9.11	6.31	9.03	16.41	21.97	10.1
	HEVC	39.6	9.29	18.27	–	–	–	–

Table 5.7. *Video quality and ES analysis for* $QP_{EL} = 22$

Figure 5.16 shows the visual quality of the ninth image from the *BasketballDrive* video, selectively encrypted using the SE-SHVC-BL and SE-SHVC-EL schemes.

Note, too, that the SE-SHVC-BL, in which only the BL is encrypted, also affects the quality of the enhancement layer EL. The reason for this is that inter-layer prediction, which is based on the decoded BL image and its motion vector, propagates errors to the EL layer. However, the SE-SHVC-EL scheme, in which only the EL is encrypted and the BL remains unchanged, has less of an impact on the quality of the EL image than the SE-SHVC-BL scheme. This is explained by the fact that most of the information is contained in the BL layer, while the EL layer only contains details.

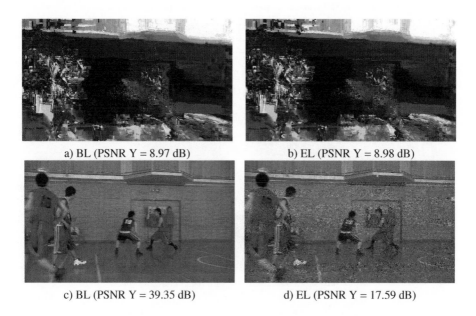

a) BL (PSNR Y = 8.97 dB)   b) EL (PSNR Y = 8.98 dB)

c) BL (PSNR Y = 39.35 dB)   d) EL (PSNR Y = 17.59 dB)

Figure 5.16. *Visual quality of image #9 from the BasketballDrive video sequences with SNR scalability configuration a) and b) SE-SHVC-BL, c) and d) SE-SHVC-EL*

Table 5.8 shows the encryption quality EQ and the Hamming distance of the three coding schemes in different scalability configurations for the *Traffic* video sequence. The EQ is the average frequency difference between the bytes in the source and encrypted videos. The security level of the proposed schemes is assessed by calculating the HD between the original and coded images in the same sequence. The HD value between a source image P and an encrypted image C, which gives the probability of a bit change, should be close to 50% (Wang *et al.* 2014). In this case, a classic plain-text sensitivity attack becomes ineffective. The results shown in Table 5.8 demonstrate the robustness of the proposed selective encryption solution.

To evaluate the ROI-based secure coding solution introduced previously, seven other video sequences with different resolutions and temporal frequencies were considered, maintaining the same SHVC (Seregin and He 2013) test conditions. These videos were simultaneously compressed and encrypted using the Kvazaar encoder in an IPPP-type inter-coding configuration. The videos were coded using a uniform 4 × 4 tile distribution (i.e. four tiles wide, four tiles high), applying restrictions to the motion vector and preventing the use of in-loop filters across tile boundaries (as explained in section 5.3.4). The PSNR and SSIM values between the source and ROI-encrypted images are given in Table 5.9.

Schemes	EQ		HD	
	2x	SNR	2x	SNR
SE-SHVC-BL	10,942	15,499	0.48	0.51
SE-SHVC-All	11,056	15,439	0.48	0.51
SE-SHVC-EL	2,880	1,561	0.37	0.32

Table 5.8. *Encryption quality for the Traffic sequence*

Schemes	Unencrypted		ROI encryption	
	PSNR	SSIM	PSNR	SSIM
PeopleOnStreet	42.8	0.93	11.2	0.23
Kimono	42.2	0.96	9.9	0.22
ParkScene	43.3	0.91	10.7	0.20
Cactus	42.5	0.94	10.4	0.23
BQTerrace	41.8	0.90	10.8	0.24
BasketballDrive	41.5	0.96	10.1	0.23
Vidyo1	45.2	0.92	11.3	0.21

Table 5.9. *PSNR (dB) and SSIM between source and encrypted videos (QP = 22)*

We also note that, compared to a compressed but unencrypted image, the quality of the encrypted image is significantly lower. The average PSNR within the ROI remains below 11.4 dB for all of the encrypted sequences. Similarly, the mean SSIM values are under 0.24. These objective measurements show that the proposed schemes permit secure and adaptive ROI encryption.

Figure 5.17 shows videos that have been decoded and decrypted using the correct key, on the left, and without a key, on the right.

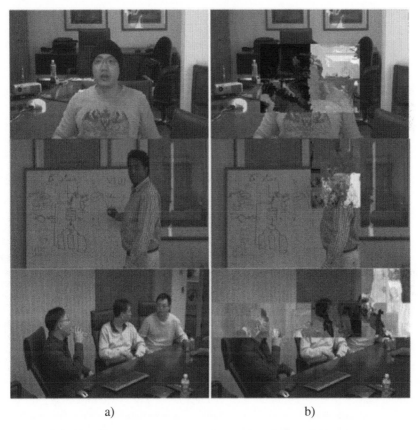

a)   b)

Figure 5.17. *Image #9 from HEVC videos encrypted using the proposed scheme: a) correctly decrypted, b) encrypted*

As we have seen, the proposed encryption method is format-compatible and does not increase encoding cost. However, in the specific case of ROI encoding, an average loss of 12% compression efficiency is observed. This is directly linked to the tiling operation, and to the restrictions preventing error propagation outside the ROI. The loss is therefore highly dependent on the tiling configuration.

5.4.2.2. *Subjective verification of selective encryption*

Subjective quality analyses are generally based on the Mean Opinion Score (MOS) for each video used in the test. This value is obtained using equation [5.1], where s_{ijk} is the score assigned by participant i for the degree of visibility j of sequence k and N is the number of observers:

$$MOS_{jk} = \frac{1}{N} \sum_{i=1}^{N} s_{ijk} \qquad [5.1]$$

To obtain a better assessment of result compliance, a confidence interval, typically 95%, is associated with each MOS. This is given by equation [5.2]. Thus, scores must be contained in the interval $[MOS_{jk} - IC_{jk}, MOS_{jk} + IC_{jk}]$ to respect the experimental conditions:

$$IC_{jk} = 1.95 \frac{\delta_{jk}}{\sqrt{N}}, \quad \delta_{jk} = \sqrt{\sum_{i=1}^{N} \frac{(s_{ijk} - MOS_{jk})}{N}} \qquad [5.2]$$

Before analyzing the data, we assessed the distribution of the scores given by each participant. The goal here is to eliminate observer scores that would be significantly inconsistent, and would therefore interfere with the results. We applied a filtering procedure based on the recommendations of the ITU-R (ITU-R 2012). Following this stage, two participants were rejected and 31 were retained.

The subjective scores assigned by participants, collected via a dedicated graphical interface, were then used to measure the perceptual quality of encrypted videos. Figure 5.18 shows the perceived degree of visibility (expressed by the MOS) of different selective encryption schemes and for different quantization levels with QP = 22, QP = 27 and QP = 32. It shows that the scores assigned by the subjects fall within a range from 3 (somewhat visible) down to 1 (completely invisible), depending on the chosen encryption scheme. This implies that visibility to a human observer is very significantly degraded when only the TC are encrypted. The score of 3 on the scale reflects a perceptual level of "somewhat visible": the observer is able to recognize the overall context of the video (sports, movie, nature) without seeing its details. The same results were obtained by encrypting the sign bit of the transformed coefficients (TCs), with a slight variation in the MOS depending the video content and QP.

However, the results change completely for the final encryption scheme (All). In this case, observer scores varied from "barely visible" (2) to "completely invisible" (1). A score of 2 indicates that subjects are able to perceive some elements of the video, but without recognizing the context.

Figure 5.18 also shows that MOS values are highly dependent on video class (resolution). Thus, "*BQSquare*" (class E) is completely invisible with a MOS of $\simeq 1$ and very little variation as a function of QP. *BasketballDrive*, on the other hand, obtained high visibility scores for both TC and TCs, due to the strong motion component of this particular sequence. In this case, there is a very significant drop in perceptual level for the (All) configuration, notably when the motion vector is encrypted.

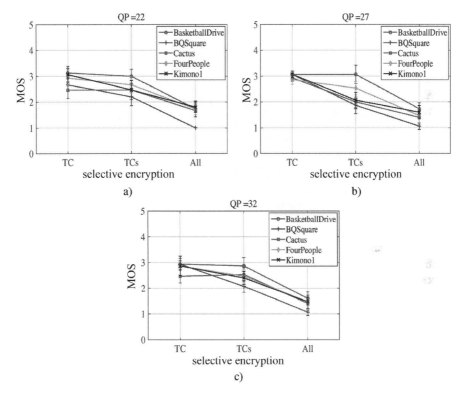

Figure 5.18. *Subject visibility scores including a confidence interval of 95% for a) QP = 22, b) QP = 27 and c) QP = 32*

5.4.2.3. *A new encrypted video database*

We recently developed a new public database of selectively encrypted HEVC videos alongside their subjective measures. The main characteristics are outlined below (Fezza *et al.* 2019a, 2019b).

5.4.2.3.1. Preparing the database

A total of seven original videos were selected: *FourPeople*, *Pontoon*, *Crowd_run*, *Djoko*, *Voiles*, *Fallout4* and *Pedestrian_area*. These sequences provide a variety of content, including interior and exterior, with a wide range of color, texture and movement. Sequences are classified according to their spatial and temporal complexities, using spatial information (SI) and temporal information (TI) indicators (ITU-T 2008).

Each sequence has a 10 s duration, and different resolutions and temporal image rates were considered, as shown in Table 5.10. Two further sequences, *BasketballDrive* and *GTAV*, were used in the learning phase.

Name	Resolution	Images/second
Pontoon, Crowd_run, Djoko, Voiles	1,920 × 1,080	50
Fallout4	1,920 × 1,080	60
FourPeople	1,280 × 720	60
Pedestrian_area	1,920 × 1,080	25

Table 5.10. *Video sequences used in testing*

The video sequences were encoded using the HEVC (HM) reference program. Four quantization levels were applied: $QP \in \{22, 27, 32, 37\}$. We chose to use a Random Access (RA) coding configuration, given that neither low latency contexts nor ROI encryption will be considered in this case. A new syntax element encryption element, *IPM*, corresponding to intra-prediction mode, was used in addition to the four previous elements (*TC*, *TCs*, *MV*, *MVs*).

Table 5.11 shows the different coding configurations as a function of encrypted syntax elements, with $\{\cdot\}$ indicating the set of elements taken into account.

The five encryption schemes were selected in order to cover a broad image quality spectrum, as shown in Figure 5.19. We thus have a total of 140 encrypted videos: 7 original sequences × 4 QP × 5 encryption schemes. We also have 28 compressed but non-encrypted video sequences (7 originals × 4 QP), included in the database as references, giving a grand total of 168 sequences.

5.4.2.3.2. Test environment and methodology

Tests were carried out in the psychovisual laboratory at the IETR, as before, in compliance with the ITU recommendations (ITU-R 2012; ITU-T 2008). A 75-inch 4K Sony Bravia X94C screen was used for display purposes.

Configurations	QP	Encrypted syntax elements
Config1	22, 27, 32, 37	{IPM}
Config2	22, 27, 32, 37	{TC}
Config3	22, 27, 32, 37	{TC, TCs}
Config4	22, 27, 32, 37	{IPM, MV, MVs}
Config5 (All)	22, 27, 32, 37	{IPM, TC, TCs, MV, MVs}

Table 5.11. *5 encryption schemes with corresponding syntax elements*

a) Unencrypted video   b) Config1   c) Config2

d) Config4   e) Config5

Figure 5.19. *Examples for the Pontoon video sequence with different levels of encryption*

The scoring scale used here is that presented in section 5.4.1.3, ranging from 1, where the content is completely invisible, to 5, for perfectly visible. A single stimulus (SS) protocol, in which each sequence was presented individually without the reference, was used. Non-encrypted sequences were included in the test set for scoring alongside the other sequences. A total of 18 subjects (6 women, 12 men) participated in the test. Due to the number of sequences to view, each session was split into two parts so that each viewing period lasted no more than 20 min. MOS values were calculated for each sequence, after the definition of a confidence interval and elimination of incoherent results (of which there were no instances in this case).

5.4.3. *CSE: a complete real-time solution*

Alongside our work with MPEG on standardizing the specificities of ROI encryption, we worked with researchers at Tampere University of Technology, Finland, to develop a complete end-to-end standardized selective encryption solution (CSE, see section 5.3.3) based on tile configurations (Abu Taha *et al.* 2020).

The system relies entirely on open-source programs: as we see from Figure 5.20, HEVC compression was carried out using Kvazaar (Tampere University of Technology 2015), encapsulation using GPAC and decompression using OpenHEVC (IETR-INSA Rennes 2015). Encryption and selective decryption, which in this solution are based on the AES standard, were integrated into Kvazaar and OpenHEVC, respectively. The Siru SDR20 transceiver platform, which is scalable and at the heart of future developments in radio systems, was used for wireless transmission.

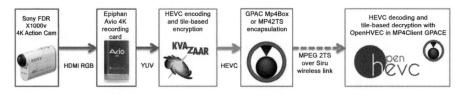

Figure 5.20. *End-to-end encryption solution*

Two examples of solutions developed for 4K TV content, in a secure production and transmission context with low latency and in a dense environment, will be presented below. In this case, there were two video streams to manage in parallel: A, for 4K video with wired transmission, and B, for encrypted HD video:

– *A*: 4K video recorded by the 4K camera, encoded in real time by Kvazaar using a 22-core Xeon processor, sent over a wired IP connection, decoded and displayed by OpenHEVC on a portable computer.

– *B*: HD video processed in the same way as for stream A, but with selective encryption performed at the encoding stage and with wireless transition over an SDR Siru connection. One portable computer was used for simultaneous decryption and decompression, displaying a high-quality video. A second computer was used for decompression without decryption, displaying correct content for non-protected zones alone (background).

Figure 5.21 shows a screenshot of decoded images at the end of the process. A 6×3 tile configuration was used in this case.

Figure 5.21. *Encrypted and unencrypted HEVC tiles*

5.5. Perspectives and directions for future research

Despite the high levels of effort dedicated to developing encryption and video encoding approaches in recent years, further work is still needed in many different areas. Some of these prospects will be explored below.

5.5.1. *Versatile Video Coding*

While the HEVC standard brought about significant improvements in terms of the development of new products and services, video is now being used in unprecedented ways, creating new needs. For example, applications are being developed to provide immersive, natural visualization experiences: these rely on very high resolutions (4K, 8K) to ensure a correct quality of service.

Furthermore, the use of video services is increasing exponentially with the proliferation of mobile components, leading to greater reliance on video in daily life, whether for social networking, video-on-demand, television, online gaming or e-learning.

In response to these new challenges, the Joint Video Expert Team (JVET) standardization group launched a new coding standard, applicable to both MPEG and ITU, in July 2020: this is Versatile Video Coding (VVC) (ITU-T 2020). VVC far exceeds HEVC in terms of performance, with an objective quality increase of around

35% (Schwarz *et al.* 2007; Alshina *et al.* 2016) and, more importantly, a subjective increase of 50% (Sidaty *et al.* 2017). This comes at the cost of a significant increase in complexity, with a ratio of around 10 at the coder level and of around 3 for the decoder.

The general principle of the codec remains a hybrid scheme: this new development is not a new or groundbreaking approach, and essentially consists of improving certain elements of the existing method. VVC is based on a reference program VTM, which integrates all of the basic building blocks of the codec.

New tools in the standard include (1) quadtree image coding, using a classic Quad-Tree Binary Tree or advanced Triple Tree approach (QTBT + TT); (2) advanced intra-prediction, with 67 modes; (3) improved inter prediction using affine motion estimation; (4) improved transforms, using Adaptive Multiple Transforms (AMT) and Non-Separable Secondary Transforms (NSST); (5) new filtering schemes in the form of Adaptive In-Loop Filters (ALF). Conversely, other functions have barely changed: for example, the entropy coding approach still relies on CABAC.

The adaptation of existing encryption schemes to a new standard such as VVC can, to a great extent, be based on existing concepts, although the specific characteristics of new elements must also be taken into account. We are in the final stages of adaptations to our own approach. Another interesting strategy could be to integrate selective encryption into the AV1 (Alliance for Open Media 2018) codec, developed by the Alliance for Open Media, which offers similar performance and presents similar characteristics to HEVC.

5.5.2. *Immersive and omnidirectinal video*

We are currently witnessing an upsurge in interest for immersive media technologies, such as virtual reality (VR), and omnidirectional video streaming. Omindirectional videos are spherical, panoramic videos, allowing spectators to view a scene from all directions (see Figure 5.22).

Full spherical coverage requires significantly higher resolutions than classic 2D content in order to meet consumer expectations.

The compression solutions used in these cases must facilitate both transmission and storage. One conventional method is to project 360° images onto a 2D support (typically with 8K resolution) before applying a classic codec. Unfortunately, the projection phase creates sampling problems and results in distortions. A more sophisticated approach is to take account of the intrinsic spherical nature of omnidirectional content within the definition of coding schemes. Several techniques have been proposed, aiming to improve compression efficiency by taking account of geometric representations (Li *et al*. 2016) or the spherical nature of visual content (Simone *et al*. 2016), or via the use of adaptive distribution methods (Hosseini and Swaminathan 2016).

Figure 5.22. *Immersive application using a VR headset*

Incorporating geometric representations within encryption schemes may offer the means of obtaining private, secure omnidirectional HEVC videos, with reduced complexity for the decryption phase.

5.6. Conclusion

In this chapter, we have presented different ways of protecting compressed videos, explaining the different terminologies used in the state of the art over the past two decades. We chose to focus on selective encryption methods, combining different advantages which are, in our view, essential: namely, selective encryption of parts of information to avoid excessive use of the cryptographic system and visual encryption, which we have shown to be relevant for a variety of video applications.

The video crypto-compression methods presented here respect compression rates (preserving the efficiency of compression models), maintain visual confidentiality (as demonstrated in this chapter) and offer robust resistance to cryptanalysis attacks. The methods that we have presented and proposed for visual privacy evaluation make it possible to design perceptual encryption systems with different levels of visual security, adapted to the specific needs of the user. The availability of multiple levels of degradation (and thus of confidentiality) opens up new and interesting perspectives for application, notably with respect to anonymization in the context of video surveillance.

Standardization within MPEG highlights the interest of this solution and shows promise in terms of use in the near future. Furthermore, the standard allows images in HEIF format to be protected in the same way: this format has come to replace JPEG in some contexts, notably for Apple devices. The advent of the new H.266/VVC codec (ISO/IEC MPEG I Part 3) also offers interesting perspectives for future investigation in the field of selective encryption: as we have shown in this chapter, the CSE methods presented here may be adapted and applied theoretically to any video or image codec.

5.7. References

Abu Taha, M., Hamidouche, W., Sidaty, N., Viitanen, M., Vanne, J., El Assad, S., Deforges, O. (2020). Privacy protection in real time HEVC standard using chaotic system. *Cryptography*, 4(2), 18.

Ahmed, H.E.H., Kalash, H.M., Allah, O.S.F. (2007). Encryption efficiency analysis and security evaluation of RC6 block cipher for digital images. In *International Conference on Electrical Engineering*. IEEE, Lahore.

Alliance for Open Media (2018). Press release – Videolan joins the alliance for open media. VideoLAN [Online]. Available at: https://www.videolan.org/press/aomedia.html.

Alshina, E., Alshin, A., Choi, K., Park, M. (2016). Performance of JEM 1 tools analysis. *2nd JVET Meeting*. San Diego.

Asghar, M., Ghanbari, M., Fleury, M., Reed, M.J. (2014). Confidentiality of a selectively encrypted H.264 coded video bit-stream. *Journal of Visual Communication and Image Representation*, 25(2), 487–498.

Autrusseau, F., Stuetz, T., Pankajakshan, V. (2010). Subjective quality assessment of selective encryption techniques [Online]. Available at: http://www.irccyn.ecnantes.fr/ãutrusse/Databases.

Bergeron, C. (2007). Optimisation conjointe source/canal d'une transmission vidéo H.264/AVC sur un lien sans fil. PhD Thesis, Télécom ParisTech [Online]. Available at: https://pastel.archives-ouvertes.fr/pastel-00004234/file/these_final_bergeron.pdf.

Bergeron, C. and Lamy-Bergot, C. (2004). Soft-input decoding of variable-length codes applied to the H.264 standard. In *6th Workshop on Multimedia Signal Processing*. IEEE, Siena.

Bergeron, C. and Lamy-Bergot, C. (2005). Compliant selective encryption for H.264/AVC video streams. In *7th Workshop on MMSP*. IEEE, Shanghai.

Bergeron, C., Sidaty, N., Hamidouche, W., Boyadjis, B., Feuvre, J.L., Lim, Y. (2017). Real-time selective encryption solution based on ROI for MPEG – A visual identity management AF. In *2017 22nd International Conference on Digital Signal Processing*. IEEE, London.

Bergeron, C., Hamidouche, W., Feuvre, J.L., Boyadjis, B. (2018). Content sensitive encryption: Decryption challenge [Online]. Available at: http://open-hevc.insa-rennes.fr/press-release/avc-and-hevc-selective-video-encryption-decryption-challenge/.

Boyadjis, B., Perrin, M.-E., Bergeron, C., Lecomte, S. (2014). A real-time ciphering transcoder for H.264 and HEVC streams. In *International Conference on Image Processing (ICIP)*. IEEE, Paris.

Boyadjis, B., Bergeron, C., Lecomte, S. (2015). Auto-synchronized selective encryption of video contents for an improved transmission robustness over errorprone channels. In *International Conference on Image Processing (ICIP)*. IEEE, Quebec.

Boyadjis, B., Bergeron, C., Pesquet-Popescu, B., Dufaux, F. (2017). Extended selective encryption of H.264/AVC (CABAC) and HEVC-encoded video streams. *IEEE Transactions on Circuits and Systems for Video Technology*, 27(4), 892–906.

Boyce, J.M., Ye, Y., Chen, J., Ramasubramonian, A.K. (2016). Overview of SHVC: Scalable extensions of the high efficiency video coding standard. *IEEE Transactions on Circuits and Systems for Video Technology*, 26(1), 20–34.

Cisco (2017). Cisco visual networking index: Forecast and methodology, 2016–2021. White paper, Cisco.

Dufaux, F. and Ebrahimi, T. (2008). Scrambling for privacy protection in video surveillance systems. *IEEE Transactions on Circuits and Systems for Video Technology*, 18(8), 1168–1174.

Farajallah, M., Hamidouche, W., Déforges, O., El Assad, S. (2015). ROI encryption for the HEVC coded video contents. In *International Conference on Image Processing (ICIP)*. IEEE, Quebec.

Fezza, S.A., Hamidouche, W., Kamraoui, R.A., Déforges, O. (2019a). Encrypted HEVC videos database and MOS values [Online]. Available at: https://sites.google.com/view/ietr-selectvidencrypt-database.

Fezza, S.A., Hamidouche, W., Kamraoui, R.A., Déforges, O. (2019b). Visual security assessment of selective video encryption. In *Eleventh International Conference on Quality of Multimedia Experience*. QoMEX, Berlin.

Gueron, S. and Krasnov, V. (2014). Speeding up counter mode in software and hardware. In *Eleventh International Conference on Information Technology: New Generations*. ITNG, Las Vegas.

Hamidouche, W., Farajallah, M., Raulet, M., Déforges, O., El Assad, S. (2015). Selective video encryption using chaotic system in the SHVC extension. In *International Conference on Acoustics, Speech and Signal Processing (ICASSP)*. IEEE, Brisbane.

Hofbauer, H. and Uhl, A. (2010). Visual quality indices and low quality images. In *European Workshop on Visual Information Processing*. EUVIP, Paris.

Hofbauer, H. and Uhl, A. (2016). Identifying deficits of visual security metrics for images. *Signal Processing: Image Communication*, 46(2), 60–75.

Hosseini, M. and Swaminathan, V. (2016). Adaptive 360 VR video streaming: Divide and conquer! In *IEEE International Symposium on Multimedia (ISM)*. IEEE, San Jose.

Hu, Y., Zhou, W., Zhao, S., Chen, Z., Li, W. (2018). SDM: Semantic distortion measurement for video encryption. In *International Conference on Automatic Face Gesture Recognition*. IEEE, Xi'an.

IETR-INSA Rennes (2015). OpenHEVC decoder, LGPLv3 [Online]. Available at: https://github.com/OpenHEVC/openHEVC.

Isa, H., Bahari, I., Sufian, H., Z'aba, M.R. (2011). AES: Current security and efficiency analysis of its alternatives. In *7th International Conference on Information Assurance and Security (IAS)*. IEEE, Malacca.

ISO/IEC 14496-12 (2012). ISOBMFF ISO base media file format. ISO/IEC JTC1/SC29/WG11 (MPEG). Tokyo.

ISO/IEC 23000-21 (2019). VIMAF Visual Identity Management Application Format. ISO/IEC JTC1/SC29/WG11 (MPEG). Tokyo.

ISO/IEC 23001-7 (2016). Common encryption in ISO base media file format files. ISO/IEC JTC1/SC29/WG11 (MPEG). Tokyo.

ISO/IEC 23001-9 (2016). Common encryption of MPEG-2 transport streams. ISO/IEC JTC1/SC29/WG11 (MPEG). Tokyo.

ISO/IEC 23008-12 (2017). HEIF High Efficiency Image File Format. ISO/IEC JTC1/SC29/WG11 (MPEG), Tokyo.

ITU-R (2012). Methodology for the subjective assessment of the quality of television picture. Recommendation, ITU-R, Geneva.

ITU-T (2004). AVC Advanced Video Coding standard. Recommendation, ITU-T, Geneva.

ITU-T (2008). Subjective video quality assessment methods for multimedia applications. Recommendation, ITU-T, Geneva.

ITU-T (2013). HEVC High Efficiency Video Coding standard. Recommendation, ITU-T, Geneva.

ITU-T (2020). VVC Versatile Video Coding standard. Recommendation, ITU-T, Geneva.

Jagadeesh, P., Nagabhushan, P., Pradeep Kumar, R. (2013). A novel perceptual image encryption scheme using geometric objects based kernel. *International Journal of Computer Science and Information Technology*, 5, 165–173.

Jolly, S. and Vikas, S. (2011). Video encryption: A survey. *International Journal of Computer Science*, 8(2), 525–534.

Kerckhoffs, A. (1883). La cryptographie militaire. *Journal des sciences militaires*, IX, 5–38, 161–191.

Le Philippe, N., Itier, V., Puech, W. (2017). Visual saliency-based confidentiality metric for selective crypto-compressed JPEG images. In *International Conference on Image Processing (ICIP)*. IEEE, Beijing.

Li, J., Wen, Z., Li, S., Zhao, Y., Guo, B., Wen, J. (2016). Novel tile segmentation scheme for omnidirectional video. In *International Conference on Image Processing (ICIP)*. IEEE, Phoenix.

Lian, S., Sun, J., Wang, Z. (2004). Perceptual cryptography on SPIHT compressed images or videos. In *International Conference on Multimedia and Expo*. IEEE, Taipei.

Lian, S., Liu, Z., Ren, Z., Wang, H. (2006). Secure advanced video coding based on selective encryption algorithms. *IEEE Transactions on Consumer Electronics*, 52(2), 621–629.

Liu, F. and Koenig, H. (2010). A survey of video encryption algorithms. *Computers & Security*, 29(1), 3–15.

Liu, G., Ikenaga, T., Goto, S., Baba, T. (2006). A selective video encryption scheme for MPEG compression standard. *IEICE Transactions on Fundamentals of Electronics, Communications and Computer*, E89-A(1), 194–202.

Liu, Z., Li, S., Liu, W., Wang, Y., Liu, S. (2013). Image encryption algorithm by using fractional Fourier transform and pixel scrambling operation based on double random phase encoding. *Optics and Lasers in Engineering*, 51(1), 8–14.

Mao, Y. and Wu, M. (2004). Security evaluation for communication-friendly encryption of multimedia. In *International Conference Image Processing*. IEEE, Singapore.

Mittal, A., Soundararajan, R., Bovik, A.C. (2013). Making a completely blind image quality analyzer. *IEEE Signal Process. Letters*, 20(3), 209–212.

Peng, F., Zhu, X.-W., Long, M. (2013). An ROI privacy protection scheme for H.264 video based on FMO and chaos. *IEEE Transactions on Information Forensics and Security*, 8(10), 1688–1699.

Podesser, M., Schmidt, H.P., Uhl, A. (2002). Selective bitplane encryption for secure transmission of image data in mobile environments. In *5th Nordic Signal Processing Symposium on Mobile Environments*. Hurtigruta, Tromsø-Trondheim.

Reza, T.A. and Barbeau, M. (2012). QoS aware adaptive security scheme for video streaming. In *International Symposium on Foundations and Practice of Security*. FPS, Montreal.

Sabeva, G., Jamaa, S.B., Kieffer, M., Duhamel, P. (2006). Robust decoding of H.264 encoded video transmitted over wireless channels. In *Workshop on Multimedia Signal Processing*. IEEE, Victoria.

Schwarz, H., Marpe, D., Wiegand, T. (2007). Overview of the scalable video coding extension of the H.264/AVC standard. *IEEE Transactions on Circuits and Systems for Video Technology*, 17, 1103–1120.

Seregin, V. and He, Y. (2013). Common SHM test conditions and software reference configurations. Document, JCTVC, Geneva.

Shahid, Z. and Puech, W. (2014). Visual protection of HEVC video by selective encryption of CABAC binstrings. *IEEE Transactions on Multimedia*, 16(1), 24–36.

Shahid, Z., Chaumont, M., Puech, W. (2009). Selective and scalable encryption of enhancement layers for dyadic scalable H.264/AVC by scrambling of scan patterns. In *International Conference on Image Processing*. IEEE, Cairo.

Shahid, Z., Chaumont, M., Puech, W. (2011). Fast protection of H.264/AVC by selective encryption of CAVLC and CABAC for I&P frames. *IEEE Transactions on Circuits and Systems for Video Technology*, 21(5), 565–576.

Shannon, C.E. (1949). Communication theory of secrecy systems. *Bell System Technical Journal*, 28(4), 656–715.

Shi, C., Wang, S.-Y., Bhargava, B. (1999). MPEG video encryption in real-time using secret key cryptography. In *International Conference on Parallel and Distributed Processing Techniques and Applications*. PDPTA, Las Vegas.

Sidaty, N., Hamidouche, W., Déforges, O., Philippe, P. (2017). Compression efficiency of the emerging video coding tools. In *International Conference on Image Processing (ICIP)*. IEEE, Beijing.

Simone, F.D., Frossard, P., Wilkins, P., Birkbeck, N., Kokaram, A. (2016). Geometry-driven quantization for omnidirectional image coding. In *Picture Coding Symposium (PCS)*. IEEE, Nuremberg.

Stutz, T. and Uhl, A. (2012). A survey of H.264 AVC/SVC encryption. *IEEE Transactions on Circuits and Systems for Video Technology*, 22(3), 325–339.

Sullivan, G.J., Ohm, J.-R., Han, W.-J., Wiegand, T. (2012). Overview of the High Efficiency Video Coding (HEVC) standard. *IEEE Transactions on Circuits and Systems for Video Technology*, 22(12), 1649–1668.

Sun, J., Xu, Z., Liu, J., Yao, Y. (2011). An objective visual security assessment for cipher-images based on local entropy. *Multimedia Tools Appl.*, 53, 75–95.

Tampere University of Technology (2015). Kvazaar HEVC encoder, LGPLv2.1 [Online]. Available at: https://github.com/ultravideo/kvazaar.

Tang, L. (1997). Methods for encrypting and decrypting MPEG video data efficiently. In *Fourth ACM International Conference on Multimedia*. ACM, Boston.

Tawalbeh, L.A., Mowafi, M., Aljoby, W. (2013). Use of elliptic curve cryptography for multimedia encryption. *IET Information Security*, 7(2), 67–74.

Telecom ParisTech (2008). GPAC, GPAC Licensing [Online]. Available at: https://github.com/gpac/gpac.

Van Wallendael, G., Boho, A., De Cock, J., Munteanu, A., Van de Walle, R. (2013a). Encryption for high efficiency video coding with video adaptation capabilities. *IEEE Transactions on Consumer Electronics*, 59(3), 634–642.

Van Wallendael, G., De Cock, J., Van Leuven, S., Boho, A., Lambert, P., Preneel, B., Van de Walle, R. (2013b). Format-compliant encryption techniques for high efficiency video coding. In *International Conference on Image Processing (ICIP)*. IEEE, Melbourne.

Viitanen, M., Koivula, A., Lemmetti, A., Vanne, J., Hamalainen, T.D. (2015). Kvazaar HEVC encoder for efficient intra coding. In *International Symposium on Circuits and Systems (ISCAS)*. IEEE, Lisbon.

Wang, Z., Bovik, A.C., Sheikh, H.R., Simoncelli, E.P. (2004). Image quality assessment: From error visibility to structural similarity. *IEEE Transactions on Image Processing*, 13(4), 600–612.

Wang, X., Luan, D., Bao, X. (2014). Cryptanalysis of an image encryption algorithm using Chebyshev generator. *Digital Signal Processing*, 25, 244–247.

Wen, J., Severa, M., Zeng, W., Luttrell, M., Jin, W. (2002). A format-compliant configurable encryption framework for access control of video. *IEEE Transactions on Circuits and Systems for Video Technology*, 12, 545–557.

Weng, L. and Preneel, B. (2007). On encryption and authentication of the DC DCT coefficient. In *International Conference on Signal Processing and Multimedia Applications*. INSTICC, Barcelona.

Wu, C.-P. and Kuo, C.-C. (2005). Design of integrated multimedia compression and encryption system. *IEEE Transactions on Multimedia*, 7(5), 828–839.

Xiang, T., Guo, S., Li, X. (2016). Perceptual visual security index based on edge and texture similarities. *IEEE Transactions on Information Forensics and Security*, 11(5), 951–963.

Yao, Y., Xu, Z., Li, W. (2008). Visual security assessment for video encryption. In *Third International Conference on Communications and Networking in China*. Chinacom, Hangzhou.

Ye, G. (2010). Image scrambling encryption algorithm of pixel bit based on chaos map. *Pattern Recognition Letters*, 31(5), 347–354.

Zeng, W. and Lei, S. (1999). Efficient frequency domain video scrambling for content access control. In *International Conference on Multimedia*. ACM, Orlando.

6

Processing Encrypted Multimedia Data Using Homomorphic Encryption

Sébastien Canard[1], Sergiu Carpov[2], Caroline Fontaine[3] and Renaud Sirdey[4]

[1] Orange Labs, Applied Crypto Group, Caen, France
[2] Inpher, Lausanne, Switzerland
[3] LMF, ENS Paris-Saclay, University of Paris-Saclay, CNRS, Gif-sur-Yvette, France
[4] CEA, LIST, University of Paris-Saclay, Gif-sur-Yvette, France

In this chapter, we present the state of the art in homomorphic encryption techniques, which make it possible to process encrypted data. These techniques are very costly, but impressive progress has been made in recent years; experiments have already been carried out for industrial applications, including in the multimedia field. We shall present the results of some of these experiments, along with the theoretical background needed to understand their development.

6.1. Context

This chapter concerns encryption techniques in the cryptographic sense of the term, that is, techniques designed to ensure the confidentiality of data in general,

---

For a color version of all figures in this chapter, see www.iste.co.uk/puech/multimedia2.zip.

Multimedia Security 2,
coordinated by William Puech. © ISTE Ltd 2022.

regardless of its nature. We consider the data to be protected as bits, bit vectors or numbers. These data are first encoded in an alphabet or a suitable mathematical structure, depending on the chosen encryption technique.

Encryption techniques have been used since ancient times; their general development will not be discussed here. In this chapter, we shall focus on *homomorphic* techniques, in which operations performed on encrypted data are also performed, indirectly, on the underlying clear data. The result of the operation performed on the encrypted data remains encrypted, and is decryptable only by the holder of the private decryption key sk, who is thus the only person with access to the result of the computation in clear. For example, to move the computation of a function $P(x_1, x_2)$, the client may encrypt sensitive data x_1 and x_2 locally using the public encryption key[1] pk, and provide the server with the encrypted values HomEnc(x_1) and HomEnc(x_2). The server then evaluates a function $f_P($HomEnc(x_1), HomEnc(x_2)$)$ such that, when the resulting encrypted value is transmitted to the client, it can be decrypted to obtain HomDec($f_P($HomEnc(x_1), HomEnc(x_2)$)) = P(x_1, x_2)$. This capability opens up numerous perspectives for applications, as shown in Figure 6.1. For example, in the context of cloud computing, this approach reconciles the interests of both service providers and users (in the broadest sense: ordinary individuals, companies or even public authorities). Users can encrypt their data before transmitting it to service providers, meaning that the latter can process these data without ever accessing the clear text, eliminating any risk of data leaks.

This secure computation paradigm first appeared in the late 1970s, in a famous paper published by Rivest *et al.* (1978). In this paper, the authors defined and studied the applicative potential of a new notion of private homomorphism, conjecturing the existence of cryptosystems that would be malleable, but still offer a sufficient level of security[2].

---

1 Symmetric homomorphic systems do exist, but are extremely rare. For this reason, in this chapter, homomorphic encryption systems are presumed to be asymmetric, with two distinct keys pk (public, to encrypt) and sk (private, to decrypt). However, our presentation can be transposed to symmetric systems if necessary by considering that the encryption key pk and the decryption key sk are both secret. Moreover, for reasons of simplicity, we shall not explicitly specify the keys used when this is obvious.

2 An encryption system is said to be malleable when the encrypted version of a message, HomEnc(m), can be used to calculate the encrypted version of another message of the form HomEnc($P(m)$) for a certain function P, without ever needing to know the plaintext value of the message m. This property is seen, a priori, as a weakness in terms of security, but can be tolerated if the gain in terms of functionality is sufficient to compensate for the decrease in security.

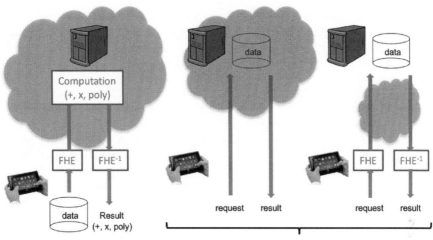

Figure 6.1. *Typical usage scenarios for homomorphic encryption techniques. Data can be processed by the service provider without access to the clear information. The result is also encrypted, and it can only be decrypted by individuals with the appropriate key. Clear data are shown in green, with encrypted data in orange*

In other words, the authors conjectured the existence of cryptosystems that would allow general computations to be performed directly on encrypted data without weakening them excessively from a security point of view. This idea remained purely theoretical for several years; the homomorphic properties (limited to one operation) of several famous cryptosystems, such as ElGamal or Goldwasser-Micali, were noted but tolerated, since the degree of malleability was considered acceptable in terms of security.

Important developments were made in this area in the late 1990s, driven by the wave of enthusiasm that followed the publication of Paillier's cryptosystem (Paillier 1999). Besides offering high levels of performance, the Paillier cryptosystem stood out due to the fact that additions, and multiplications by a public integer, could be performed in the encrypted domain. It thus became possible to apply any linear (public) operator directly to encrypted data at reasonable computational cost. This possibility rapidly gave rise to new fields of applied research exploiting the properties of homomorphic encryption. An important step was reached in 2005 with the publication of the BGN scheme by Boneh *et al.* (2005), followed, in 2008–2010, by important publications by Aguilar-Melchor *et al.* (2008, 2010) and Gentry (2009). These authors demonstrated the possibility of performing both addition and multiplication with the same system, paving the way for applications involving polynomial computations on encrypted data. As we will see in this chapter, schemes of this type are costly to implement, but sufficient progress has been made in recent years so that applicative proofs of the concept are now available. Subsequent schemes are expensive, but the progress made since then is such that the first applicative proofs of concept have already emerged.

The aim of this chapter is to present the current state of the art of these techniques, which show great promise in terms of long-term applications. Research in this field is extremely dynamic, and each year sees the introduction of new techniques and significant improvements. This state of the art will continue to evolve. Nevertheless, we shall describe a number of component elements that will remain relevant and essential, even in new, as-yet unpublished systems. The practical use of homomorphic systems raises a number of questions. Our objective is threefold: (1) to present the current state of the art in a synthetic manner (section 6.2); (2) to provide points of reference relating to these questions and the choices that must be made with respect to their practical implementation (section 6.3), and finally (3) to present current experimental results demonstrating the real applicative potential of these systems (section 6.4).

6.2. Different classes of homomorphic encryption systems

As we saw briefly in section 6.1, there are several different classes of homomorphic encryption systems. In this section, we shall describe a selection of the most widespread examples, used in the experiments presented later. First, it is important to note that all of these schemes result in an increase in data size: encrypted data are larger than clear data. This is due to the fact that, for security reasons, these schemes are all probabilistic (the same clear data element can correspond to several encrypted elements, but evidently these encrypted elements are all decrypted in the same way). In other terms, these approaches introduce noise into encrypted messages. Further details concerning the security aspect are given in section 6.3.4.

6.2.1. *Partial solutions in classic cryptography*

The oldest homomorphic encryption techniques permit either addition or multiplication, but it is not possible to combine these operations. The best-known examples are Paillier's scheme (Paillier 1999) for additions, and ElGamal's scheme (ElGamal 1985) for multiplications[3]. For more details on versions of these classic, single-operation schemes, see Fontaine and Galand (2007).

---

3 The basic RSA scheme is homomorphic, but is not considered a good encryption scheme as such, because it is not semantically secure; the OAEP version, which is semantically secure, is no longer homomorphic.

The first scheme to allow a combination of an arbitrary number of additions and a single multiplication operation was BGN, published in Boneh *et al.* (2005), based on pairing techniques.

Catalano and Fiore (2015) proposed an iterative construction approach that can be applied to this kind of scheme to permit an additional level of multiplication. The Paillier cryptosystem, for example, can thus be extended to evaluate quadratic functions. It is important to note, however, that this construction induces a higher cost for additions of second-degree monomials than for additions of first-degree monomials.

Although the use of this technique is not without effects in terms of performance, it enables the calculation of classic distances, such as Hamming, Euclidean or Mahalanobis distances, in the context of clear versus encrypted vectors. Note that these distances can also be evaluated with an additive system, but this results in a quadratic increase of the communication cost. The expression to evaluate is linear in xx^T (the tensor product of the encrypted vector with itself). These remarks are important in the sense that many applications of homomorphic encryption involve evaluating distances. Catalano and Fiore's technique was also used in Herbert *et al.* (2019) to construct a scheme allowing an arbitrary number of additions and two levels of multiplications, thus permitting the evaluation of fourth-degree polynomials.

These schemes are sufficient for certain applications, and their security properties are clearly understood since they rely on well-known mathematical problems. However, they lack flexibility, insofar as an application cannot be adjusted after implementation to take the calculations of unexpected complexity into account. Moreover, they are potentially vulnerable to attacks using the computing capabilities of quantum computers.

We shall now provide a brief overview of Paillier's cryptosystem (Paillier 1999), which will be used in some of the examples of applications presented in this chapter. Let p and q be two large prime numbers and $n = pq$. The clear domain of the Paillier cryptosystem is the ring of integers modulo n, $\mathbb{Z}_n$, and its encrypted domain is the ring of integers modulo n^2, $\mathbb{Z}_{n^2}$. Values $\lambda = \mathrm{lcm}(p-1, q-1)$ and $g < n^2$ must also be selected such that:

$$\gcd(L(g^\lambda \mod n^2), n) = 1, \text{ with } L(u) = \frac{u-1}{n}$$

The (public) encryption key is then given by n and g. The (private) decryption key is formed from p and q or the equivalent λ.

The encryption function corresponds to:

$$c = \mathrm{HomEnc}(m) = g^m r^n \mod n^2 \qquad [6.1]$$

where $m < n$ is the message and r is uniformly drawn from $\mathbb{Z}_n$.

Taking $D = L(g^\lambda \mod n^2)$ and D^{-1} as its multiplicative inverse in $\mathbb{Z}_n$, the decryption function requires us to evaluate:

$$m = \text{HomDec}(c) = L(c^\lambda \mod n^2) \times D^{-1} \mod n$$

This cryptosystem has the following homomorphic properties:

1) $\text{HomDec}(\text{HomEnc}(m_1) \cdot \text{HomEnc}(m_2) \mod n^2) = m_1 + m_2 \mod n$ (addition of two encrypted messages);

2) $\text{HomDec}(\text{HomEnc}(m) \cdot g^k \mod n^2) = m + k \mod n$, for $k \in \mathbb{Z}_n$ (addition of a clear integer to an encrypted message);

3) $\text{HomDec}(\text{HomEnc}(m)^k \mod n^2) = km \mod n$, for $k \in \mathbb{Z}_n$ (multiplication of an encrypted message by a clear integer).

In terms of concrete dimensioning, using a 2048 bit modulus provides relatively good medium-term security (for example, the RGS ANSSI[4] recommends this as the minimum modulus length for confidentiality requirements up to 2030).

6.2.2. *Complete solutions in cryptography using Euclidean networks*

Gentry (2009) proposed the first credible construction of a fully homomorphic encryption system in terms of security and (theoretical) efficiency. Gentry drew on previous work, notably Aguilar-Melchor et al. (2008, 2010) and Boneh et al. (2005); his main contribution lies in the development of a de-noising technique, bootstrapping, which essentially consists of performing a reencryption operation in a homomorphic way (i.e. the homomorphic equivalent of decryption followed by a re-encryption, without the data ever appearing in the clear during the operation). Encrypted elements contain a certain amount of noise due to the probabilistic aspect of encryption, and the application of operations to these elements increases the amount of noise in the resulting encrypted message. If measures are not taken to control the noise and it exceeds a certain threshold, then decryption will no longer operate correctly and it will be impossible to retrieve the original message. Gentry used bootstrapping to control this noise, thus extending the limits of homomorphic encryption much further than previously imagined. In theory, this technique means that polynomials of any degree can be evaluated; in practice, however, the computation and storage/transmission costs remain prohibitive.

Considerable developments have occurred in the intervening period. Current solutions permit the evaluation of general polynomials of higher degrees than in the

---

4 Available at: https://www.ssi.gouv.fr/administration/guide/cryptographie-les-regles-du-rgs/.

early examples cited above, allowing for more complex applications. All of these solutions are based on the mathematical structure of Euclidean networks, and offer the advantage of post-quantum security, that is, resistance to known cryptanalysis attacks using quantum computers. This is a significant advantage, but, in the context of homomorphic encryption, comes at the cost of a large increase in encrypted file size, high computational cost and, for now, difficulties in the accurate derivation of security parameters. Nevertheless, the progress made in this field in recent years is impressive, and there is no doubt that future developments will enable more and more practical applications.

In this chapter, a distinction shall be made between two main families of schemes: *somewhat homomorphic encryption* (SHE) and *fully homomorphic encryption* (FHE). These will be presented from the simplest/fastest/cheapest/most limited to the most complex/slowest/most costly/most flexible.

6.2.2.1. *Fixed or leveled SHE schemes*

SHE schemes can only evaluate polynomials of a limited degree; this limit is fixed and cannot be parameterized. They are relatively cheap in terms of time and memory, but are not flexible. These solutions offer a broader range of potential applications than Paillier's system, for example, but are more costly than the earlier system and present a similar level of rigidity.

Leveled SHE schemes are an alternative that may be used to evaluate a polynomial of limited degree; the upper bound of the degree can be chosen, but must be defined before the application is implemented.

These schemes are more flexible than fixed SHEs; applications may evolve following the initial implementation, as long as the degree of polynomials to evaluate remains below the predefined threshold.

Many examples of this type exist, and while the field was initially subject to much confusion, matters are now much clearer. There are three schemes which appear to be gaining in popularity: BFV (Fan and Vercauteren 2012), CKKS (Cheon *et al.* 2017, 2018) and TFHE (Chillotti *et al.* 2016, 2017, 2020). Only the first of these examples will be described in detail here, based on the fact that this approach is the simplest to explain.

BFV is a leveled, almost FHE scheme developed by Fan and Vercauteren (2012), drawing on Brakerski's initial SHE scheme (Brakerski 2012). Further details can be found in the corresponding articles.

Let q and t be two security parameters (q for key size and t for message size) and let $\Delta = \lfloor q/t \rfloor$. A distribution χ over the ring R of polynomials is required. The secret key s is an element in $\mathcal{R}$. The associated public key requires that we first select an element a from the polynomial ring with a value in $\mathbb{Z}_q$ and an element e selected according to the distribution χ, before calculating $A = [-(as.e)]_q$. The couple (A, a) is used as the public key to encrypt a message m. More precisely, for a message in the ring of polynomials with values in $\mathbb{Z}_t$, this encryption process involves the following steps:

– take u uniformly from the ring of polynomials with values in $\mathbb{Z}_2$, and take e_1, e_2 according to the distribution χ;

– calculate $c_0 = [Au + e_1 + \Delta m]_q$ and $c_1 = [p_1 u + e_2]_q$ and generate the encrypted value $c = (c_0, c_1)$.

Decryption is then carried out by calculating:

$$\left[\left[\frac{t[c_0 + c_1 s]_q}{q}\right]\right]_t$$

This scheme possesses the two necessary homomorphic properties:

– addition: by simply adding two encrypted values $c = (c_0, c_1)$ and $\tilde{c} = (\tilde{c}_0, \tilde{c}_1)$, with messages m and $\tilde{m}$, respectively, component by component, we obtain a new encrypted value $c' = (c'_0, c'_1) = ([c_0 + \tilde{c}_0]_q, [c_1 + \tilde{c}_1]_q)$ corresponding to the encrypted value of $m + \tilde{m}$;

– multiplication: this operation is more complicated. Given two encrypted values $c = (c_0, c_1)$ and $\tilde{c} = (\tilde{c}_0, \tilde{c}_1)$ of messages m and $\tilde{m}$, respectively, we can calculate:

$$d_0 = \left[\left[\frac{t(c_0 + \tilde{c}_0)}{q}\right]\right]_q$$

$$d_1 = \left[\left[\frac{t(c_0 \cdot \tilde{c}_1 + c_1 \cdot \tilde{c}_0)}{q}\right]\right]_q$$

$$d_2 = \left[\left[\frac{t(c_1 + \tilde{c}_1)}{q}\right]\right]_q$$

However, in this format, the output is not compatible with a new multiplication operation. A *relinearization* method must then be applied in order to obtain an encrypted value in the initial form, enabling further multiplications in the encrypted domain. This step involves the generation of a relinearization key (k_0, k_1) and the following formulas (where the values $d_2[i]$ correspond to the components of d_2 in a base T associated with relinearization):

$$c'_0 = \left[d_0 + \sum_{i=0}^{\ell} k_0[i] \cdot d_2[i]\right]_q \text{ and } c'_1 = \left[d_1 + \sum_{i=0}^{\ell} k_1[i] \cdot d_2[i]\right]_q$$

The encrypted message $c' = (c'_0, c'_1)$ then corresponds to an encryption of $m \times \tilde{m}$.

6.2.2.2. *FHE schemes*

FHE schemes have the capacity, in the strict sense, to evaluate polynomials of any degree (to an extent which is limited by computation time constraints and the factors of expansion accepted by the target application). A major advantage of these approaches is that the degree of polynomials does not need to be bounded prior to programming and implementation; however, this flexibility comes at a cost, in terms of both time and memory.

Many leveled approaches can be transformed into FHE approaches using the bootstrapping technique introduced by Gentry (2009), which we shall not describe in detail here. One notable example is the BFV approach presented above. This bootstrapping approach is costly, but a number of techniques have been developed to reduce its impact.

6.3. From theory to practice

Now, let us consider the practical implementation of these schemes. The first step is to consider the representation of the processing or calculation to apply to the data. From a programming perspective, this is coded at a more or less high level (such as C or C++); however, in this case, we shall consider representations in the form of Boolean or arithmetic circuits, depending on the required level of granularity. The case of a Boolean circuit is illustrated in Figure 6.2, but the same process may be transposed to an arithmetic circuit. Consider the normal circuit used to process plaintext data. This same circuit is then transformed by replacing the AND, XOR and NOT gates by their counterparts $f_\times$ and f_+ (the NOT gate is replaced by an addition of a plaintext value 1), so that the associated computations can be applied to the encrypted values. Using versions of the original data encrypted using the homomorphic scheme as input, the circuit then provides the results of the calculation in a form which is also encrypted by the homomorphic scheme.

There are several questions to address here, many of which are not easy to answer, particularly in light of constant developments in the state of the art and in practical implementations of these schemes. Some authors have proposed comparisons of the most promising schemes, but extracting generic rules which remain stable over time has proven difficult; in practice, method choice is generally guided by the constraints of the target applications. Nevertheless, in this section, we shall propose a number of elements that may guide developers in selecting appropriate solutions for use in applications drawing on this technology.

– *Choosing a scheme*: this choice may be influenced by the available libraries, the degree of polynomials to evaluate, potential evolutions (flexibility: is the calculation likely to evolve over time?), the way in which the characteristics of the scheme correspond to the target application, and the desired security level (post-quantum or otherwise).

– *Choice of parameters*: this question is tricky, as it has a significant bearing on both security and flexibility (dimensions of the circuit to evaluate), and has a major impact on cost in terms of space and time.

– *Encoding information*: the choice of an encoding approach is linked to the chosen scheme, which imposes a specific algebraic structure. The choice of scheme may be guided by the chosen encoding approach, or vice-versa, depending on the constraints associated with the data. Furthermore, several data elements may be grouped into a single structure in order to process them in one go (parallel processing).

– *Limiting costs in terms of time and space*: time and cost savings can be made by carefully choosing the circuit to evaluate, by hybridization with standard encryption approaches, selecting appropriate parameters and hardware and software acceleration (parallelization).

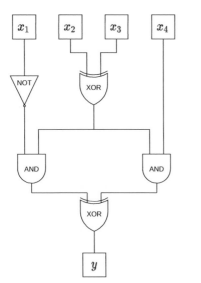
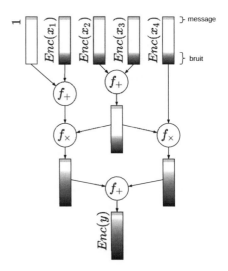

a) Function evaluated for plaintext
messages: $y = P(x_1, x_2, x_3, x_4)$

b) Function evaluated for encrypted
messages: Enc $(y) =$
f_P (Enc (x_1), Enc (x_2), Enc (x_3), Enc (x_4))

Figure 6.2. *Computation expressed for plaintext*
data in the form of a circuit (Boolean)

COMMENT ON FIGURE 6.2.– *The same circuit is used for calculations on encrypted data, replacing the AND and XOR gates with ad hoc operators as a function of the chosen encryption scheme. The result obtained in this way is encrypted, and can only be decrypted using the appropriate key. For simplicity's sake, the notation Enc() is used here, replacing the more explicit HomEnc() used elsewhere in this chapter.*

6.3.1. *Algorithmics*

In developing an application, the classic approach is to choose the algorithm with the lowest possible complexity to solve each problem. The average complexity value is usually considered. However, in our case, even if the application has branching conditions depending on certain data elements, the underlying circuit that will be evaluated in homomorphism will be evaluated in its entirety; in other words, all branches will be evaluated, whatever the data. This is essential for privacy reasons, and implies that the worst-case complexity measure always applies. Thus, algorithms must be chosen with a view to minimizing the worst case, rather than average, complexity.

6.3.2. *Implementation and optimization*

In this section, we shall describe several essential elements used to make homomorphic encryption systems more cost-effective. For reasons of space, we cannot provide all of the details here; readers may wish to consult the articles in the references. Further details can also be found in our case studies.

6.3.2.1. *Data encoding*

There are several ways of encoding plaintext data, depending on the chosen homomorphic scheme. SHE schemes of BFV type (described in section 6.2.2.1) and BGV type (Brakerski *et al.* 2012) define clear messages as polynomials of a degree less than n (size of the Euclidean lattice) with integer coefficients modulo p (a power of a prime number). Using only the zero-degree coefficient to encode data makes applications easier, as homomorphic operations then correspond to additions and multiplications on scalars modulo p. Boolean circuits can be executed in the case where $p = 2$. Nevertheless, a number of methods have been proposed in the literature for optimizing this polynomial space. Chen *et al.* (2018), for example, introduced a method for encoding a number modulo p^n in a single encrypted element, while Yasuda *et al.* (2015) described a way of obtaining the scalar products of two vectors by encoding each vector as a single encrypted element.

The CKKS scheme features an additional operation, division by a constant, which cannot be found in the BFV and BGV schemes. With this operation, fixed-point real numbers can be encoded with a predefined precision. Many more practical applications use arithmetic on real numbers, rather than modulo p arithmetic. SHE schemes using polynomial rings can be used to encode vectors (of size n for BFV/BGV and size $n/2$ for CKKS) into a single encrypted element. Homomorphic operations become term-to-term operations in this case (the equivalent of the SIMD notion in processors). This technique is called *batching* and will be discussed briefly in section 6.3.3.

Fast bootstrapping FHE schemes, such as TFHE and FHEW (Ducas and Micciancio 2015; Bonnoron *et al.* 2018), on the other hand, are a special case in terms of encoding. Their message space is strictly Boolean (only one Boolean value is encoded per element, and there is no notion of batching). However, they natively support more homomorphic operations than SHE schemes. In TFHE and FHEW, more complex generic binary gates (such as thresholds) can be implemented directly. Thus, more complex operations can be performed at the individual gate level than in schemes, which rely on basic logic gates alone; this means that shallower circuits can be used.

The Chimera framework (Boura *et al.* 2018) introduces a hybrid solution that combines three homomorphic schemes (BFV, TFHE and CKKS) in a single application, in order to enjoy the advantages of each approach, according to the operations to be performed. The authors present a common algebraic structure for the clear message spaces and propose efficient algorithms for passing between these spaces. Chimera allows arithmetic and Boolean computations to be combined in the same homomorphic application, something which is difficult to achieve using a single homomorphic scheme. One example of an application is presented in Carpov *et al.* (2019). These authors used the TFHE scheme to train a logistic regression model, before using the CKKS scheme to find all of the features in a numerical database, which may be used to improve the quality of the initial model.

6.3.2.2. *Circuit optimization*

Multiplicative depth is the maximum number of consecutive multiplications in the arithmetic circuit that describes the homomorphic calculation. It is therefore related to the degree of the polynomial corresponding to the calculation to perform. Minimizing this depth is a key aim in improving the performance of fixed or leveled SHE schemes. The size of encrypted elements and the speed of execution of homomorphic operations are highly dependent on this depth, as multiplication has the greatest impact on cost in terms of both time and space. Multiplicative depth minimization can be performed manually when designing homomorphic applications. The design flow that we used to develop a homomorphic application with reduced multiplicative depth is presented in section 6.4.3. Several approaches have been presented in the literature, such as shallow circuits for sorting (Çetin *et al.* 2015) and Levenshtein distance for genomic similarity (Cheon *et al.* 2015).

In this context, automatic multiplicative depth optimization of Boolean circuits was first discussed in Carpov *et al.* (2017) and later in other studies (Aubry *et al.* 2020; Häner and Soeken 2020; Lee *et al.* 2020). These works are not limited to Boolean circuits, and the approaches presented can also be used to optimize arithmetic circuits. Several rules are proposed for the local rewriting of Boolean circuits. By applying these rules to critical parts of the circuit (notably the paths of maximum depth), the multiplicative depth can be reduced. The cited works differ in terms of the rewriting rules that they use, and the way in which these rules are applied. With respect to the performance of automatic methods, for example, the method published in Aubry *et al.* (2020) was able to transform a carry-propagating (128-bit) binary adder (depth 255) into an equivalent carry-forward binary adder with a multiplicative depth of 9.

Operations supported by fast bootstrapping FHE schemes, such as TFHE or FHEW, all have the same computational complexity. Computation time can be reduced by minimizing the number of logic gates to execute in the Boolean circuit. The body of literature on the subject of logical synthesis is vast, and many different optimization methods can be applied directly in order to reduce the size of Boolean circuits.

The optimization methods defined above change the Boolean circuit in order to minimize the complexity and/or number of homomorphic operations to perform. A further complementary approach concerns the optimal scheduling of relinearization (Chen 2017) and bootstrapping operations (Paindavoine and Vialla 2015; Benhamouda *et al.* 2017). In this case, the aim is to order homomorphic operations (relinearization in SHE schemes, bootstrapping in FHE) in such a way that the total execution time is minimized.

6.3.2.3. *Software implementation*

At first, implementations of SHE and FHE were not systematically published with each new scheme, but this practice became increasingly regular over time and is now universal. Only public, maintained examples will be cited here. Certain libraries focus on one or two schemes, while others are veritable experimental platforms including multiple schemes.

HElib[5], launched by Halevi and Shoup in 2014 and maintained by IBM, offers an implementation of BGV (Brakerski *et al.* 2012) and CKKS (Cheon *et al.* 2017, 2018). It is intended to provide support for concept proofs rather than for production purposes.

---

5 Available at: https://github.com/homenc/HElib.

The SEAL library[6] was launched in 2015 by Laine *et al.* and is maintained by Microsoft. It currently implements BFV (Fan and Vercauteren 2012) and CKKS, and also targets at production applications.

Several implementations of BFV exist, such as FV-NFLlib[7], which uses the NFLlib library[8]. Further implementations can be found in the PALISADE and CINGULATA libraries.

The TFHE library[9] was created in 2016, and is run by a group of researchers who were involved in designing the eponymous scheme (Chillotti *et al.* 2016).

The HEAAN library[10], launched in 2017, offers an implementation of the CKKS scheme, designed for fixed point number encryption.

The PALISADE project[11] offers implementations of BGV, BFV, CKKS, FHEW (Ducas and Micciancio 2015) and a variant of TFHE.

The final platform for discussion, launched in 2012, differs from the others in the fact that it includes a compilation and circuit optimization engine, in addition to executing computations. This case is described in greater detail below.

6.3.2.4. *Cingulata: a special case*

Homomorphic encryption systems allow low-level arithmetic operations (such as addition and multiplication in binary space) to be performed directly on encrypted data. To facilitate the use of these libraries, compilation tools are needed to transform applications written in high-level programming languages into executables using a homomorphic encryption library. Cingulata, formerly known as Armadillo (Aguilar-Melchor *et al.* 2013; Carpov *et al.* 2015), is the first compilation and execution tool dedicated to homomorphic encryption. Cingulata combines a compiler chain with an execution environment, allowing developers to write the application and underlying algorithms in C++ without needing to take the inherent homomorphic encryption scheme or homomorphic operations into account. Applications are thus programmed in the same way as for non-encrypted data. Cingulata then couples the program with the chosen encryption scheme, and automatically recodes it to permit execution on encrypted input.

---

6 Available at: https://www.microsoft.com/en-us/research/project/microsoft-seal/ and https://github. com/Mi-crosoft/SEAL.

7 Available at: https://github.com/CryptoExperts/FV-NFLlib.

8 Available at: https://github.com/quarkslab/NFLlib.

9 Available at: https://github.com/tfhe/tfhe.

10 Available at: https://github.com/snucrypto/HEAAN.

11 Available at: https://palisade-crypto.org/.

High-level abstractions and tools are provided to facilitate the implementation and execution of privacy-preserving applications. Cingulata is openly distributed as open source and is available from GitHub[12].

Instrumented C++ types, such as the CiInt type for integers and CiBit type for Booleans, are used to denote encrypted (confidential) variables. The Cingulata environment tracks each bit of these variables independently. Operations on integers are performed using Boolean circuits. For example, a carry propagation adder is used to perform addition between two integers. The generation of Boolean circuits corresponding to integer operations is automatic, and two circuit generators are available, allowing users to minimize either the size or the multiplicative depth of the circuit. Users also have the option to implement their own circuit generators or combine existing generators.

Each bit, represented by a CiBit object, may be in a clear or encrypted state. Operations between clear and encrypted elements are optimized automatically. Operations between encrypted bits are executed by an object which implements the IBitExec interface. This object may either encapsulate a homomorphic library, track each bit in the BitTracker application, or carry out clear bit-to-bit execution for debugging purposes.

The use of the BitTracker object makes it possible to construct a representation of the application in the form of a Boolean circuit. The Cingulata chain can then minimize the size or multiplicative depth of the Boolean circuit using specialized optimization modules.

The ABC toolchain[13], generally used for hardware synthesis, is used to minimize the size of the Boolean circuits, and Cingulata modules implement heuristics to minimize the multiplicative depth of the circuit (Carpov *et al.* 2017; Aubry *et al.* 2020).

The optimized Boolean circuit is then executed using the Cingulata parallel execution environment. The execution environment is generic, that is, it uses an object encapsulating a homomorphic library (TfheBitExec, BfvBitExec), to execute the Boolean gates of the circuit. The parallel scheduler is designed to take full advantage of multicore processors. A set of utility applications is provided for parameter generation (with a target security level), key generation, data encryption and decryption. These applications are also generic, in the same way as the runtime environment.

---

12 Available at: https://github.com/CEA-LIST/Cingulata.

13 Available at: http://www.eecs.berkeley.edu/ãlanmi/abc/.

6.3.2.5. *Hardware optimization*

A first means of speeding up computation time is to deport part of the processing onto suitable hardware implementations. This is particularly critical for schemes using Euclidean networks, which are the most memory intensive and computationally intensive (handling polynomial multipliers of degree $n \in [4,096, 32,768]$ with coefficients of a size of $\log_2 q \in [125, 1,228]$ bits). One approach, which is relatively economical in terms of investment, is to use GPU cards. Nevertheless, the gains to be made in this case are highly dependent on the homomorphic scheme, since some are less suited to this treatment than others. Much better results can be obtained using specialized hardware components, such as FPGAs or ASICs. However, it is important to understand the expected benefits before implementing these hardware solutions. It is not reasonable to deport everything; a compromise must be found in order to maximize overall gains, offsetting accelerations in terms of calculation time against the time taken to transfer potentially voluminous data. Only the most time-consuming operations, notably multiplications, are deported to hardware.

Several approaches have already been explored. Most hardware implementations of multipliers rely on the use of the NTT (Number Theoretic Transform, a Fourier transform on finite fields). This can result in a very significant acceleration, but requires particular parameters, which can sometimes be over-dimensioned. Given that, in this case, n must be a power of 2, if the required value of n exceeds 2^p then $n = 2^{p+1}$, which is much larger, must be taken. This means that the body of data will be much larger, and calculations will be more costly. Moreover, the batching techniques that are usually used to reduce data size and parallelize computations are not natively compatible with this approach. Typical examples of NTT use include (Doröz *et al.* 2013; Pöppelmann *et al.* 2015; Sinha Roy *et al.* 2015).

Recent work has focused on designing accelerators for polynomial multiplication for SHEs, working on several RNS channels simultaneously in order to avoid explicit manipulation of large integers (Cathébras *et al.* 2018). These developments draw on work carried out by the signal processing community on the hardware implementation of the FFT, notably using the Spiral modulo tool for adaptations; in addition to finite field operations, and in contrast with the case of FFT, the coefficients of the transform change constantly. Thus, the development of a hardware module to generate these coefficients on-the-fly, coupled with the circuits produced by the Spiral tool, enables a potential acceleration with a factor of between 5 and 15 for multiplications of encrypted numbers (the main bottleneck in terms of SHE performance).

Another strategy may be used to avoid over-dimensioning parameters and facilitate the natural grouping of data via batching techniques: for example, the Karatsuba algorithm may be used for multiplication, as proposed in Migliore *et al.* (2017, 2018). Excellent results can be obtained in this case, notably by optimizing the co-design of the remaining software computation and the operations that are deported onto the hardware (Migliore *et al.* 2018).

Once again, there is a trade-off to be made, guided by the specificities of the target application. Is it better to use an algorithm such as NTT, which provides high acceleration but may use over-dimensioned parameters, or an algorithm such as Karatsuba, which offers lower acceleration for the same parameters but ensures that these parameters will be a better fit (leading to reduced computation cost and smaller encrypted elements)? There is no one-size-fits-all answer in this case, as the solution depends on application-specific constraints in terms of time/memory, parameter size and choice of encryption scheme.

6.3.3. *Managing and reducing the size of encrypted elements*

The size of the encrypted elements involved in computations performed with homomorphic encryption systems is a real problem, especially for schemes based on Euclidean networks, which result in significant inflations in message size. The scale of inflation ranges from a factor of 2 for Paillier to several (tens/hundreds of) thousands for the most greedy FHE. The first point to keep in mind is that this expansion factor strongly depends on the security parameters, as well as on the chosen system; as a general rule, the more flexible the scheme, the higher the inflation factor. However, there are certain techniques that can be applied to all schemes to generate significant space savings. Two complementary approaches are discussed below.

6.3.3.1. *Encoding and batching*

The first key point is to choose the right encoding approach for the data. Raw data must first be transformed into words in the clear message space of the chosen encryption scheme. In the case of the Paillier scheme, this space is the set of integers modulo n; for schemes based on Euclidean lattice structures, it is a polynomial of degree n (note that the value of n is very different in both cases, and the coefficients of the polynomials belong to large algebraic structures). This encoding can be done in a naive manner, but it is also possible to reduce data size at this stage by grouping several data elements into the same structure. This is only possible for certain algebraic structures, such as polynomials on rings; in this case, several data elements can be encoded in the coefficients of the polynomial, which will constitute the clear message. This technique, called batching, means that multiple data elements can be processed simultaneously. It thus constitutes a form of parallelization applied directly at the data encoding level: several data elements will be processed by processing a single clear message.

6.3.3.2. *Transcryption*

Another process which is extremely useful for reducing the data load on both client and server is illustrated in Figure 6.3. This process, known as transcryption, was presented in Naehrig *et al.* (2011). Data are initially encrypted using a classical symmetric encryption system, noted SymEnc, rather than with a homomorphic system, noted HomEnc; thus, the size of the data is not increased. The encrypted data $\text{SymEnc}_{SymKey}(m)$ is sent to the server with no added cost, and will then be transcrypted by the server itself to produce a version as encrypted by the homomorphic system HomEnc(m). Without going into too much detail, note that this transcryption approach is possible for algebraic reasons (homomorphy), and that the key of the symmetric encryption system encrypted using the homomorphic system, that is, HomEnc($SymKey$), needs to be sent alongside $\text{SymEnc}_{SymKey}(m)$. Using these two data elements, the server can calculate the HomEnc(m) cipher without passing through m. The whole problem is thus deported onto the server. This comes at a cost, but offers a solution for a large number of otherwise impossible problems. Nevertheless, great care must be taken when choosing the symmetric encryption system, since the transcryption process requires the SymDec process to be evaluated in a homomorphic manner (in the encrypted domain of the homomorphic scheme). We must therefore choose a scheme for which SymDec gives rise to a circuit of which the homomorphic evaluation is as reasonable as possible, notably in terms of multiplicative depth.

Evidently, the first works focused on existing symmetric encryption schemes, initially on AES, which turned out to be much too costly (Gentry *et al.* 2012; Cheon *et al.* 2013; Doröz *et al.* 2016); the focus then shifted onto lighter encryption schemes such as Simon and Prince, designed for constrained environments, but these also proved to be too costly (Doröz *et al.* 2014; Lepoint and Naehrig 2014) (the relevant constraints here are not the same as those taken into account when designing these schemes). Given the unsuitable nature of existing schemes, several groups have worked on designing new schemes specific to this context. The first example is Low MC (Albrecht *et al.* 2015b); the initial version was attacked (Dinur *et al.* 2015), and then patched (Rechberger 2016). However, these schemes have a flaw linked to their block cipher structure. Canteaut *et al.* (2016, 2018) proposed a new approach based on stream cipher designs, and this appears to be much better suited to the context in terms of both performance and security. This approach notably allows part of the computation process to be carried out offline, facilitating the later online phase. Efficient solutions to this issue are now available. Two stream cipher schemes have been proposed: Kreyvium (Canteaut *et al.* 2016, 2018), based on the Trivium scheme, the security of which has been widely tested and recognized over the past decade; and FLIP (Méaux *et al.* 2016), the security of which is less certain (Duval *et al.* 2016). These solutions have been implemented and tested experimentally. Another more innovative solution was proposed in (Fouque *et al.* 2016), but this is less advanced from an experimental perspective.

It should be noted, however, that the transcryption process currently only applies to data transfers from the client to a homomorphic computer, and not to the transfer of computation results to the holder of the secret decryption keys, which are currently transferred in FHE encrypted form. Several solutions to this problem have been explored (Carpov and Sirdey 2016; Kuaté 2018), notably decomposing multislot homomorphic ciphertexts (before computation) and then recomposing them (after computation). However, these solutions are not fully satisfactory, either for performance reasons or because the homomorphic properties of the resulting ciphers are not preserved. Minimizing the bandwidth increase linked to the transfer of homomorphic computations to the client is an important question for current and future research.

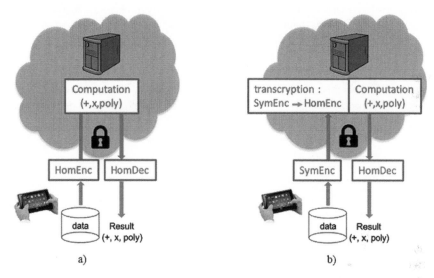

Figure 6.3. *Use of a transcryption system to lighten the data load sent to the server: a) classic approach and b) transcryption architecture*

6.3.4. *Security*

Evidently, since these schemes are designed to ensure data confidentiality, security is of paramount importance. As always, this question must be addressed both from a theoretical point of view (what security reductions can be proved between mathematical problems that are known to be difficult and the problems related to the security of the schemes to be evaluated) and from a practical standpoint (in concrete terms, what is the best known attack). We shall begin with some general remarks, valid for all homomorphic systems. The best security level reached by current homomorphic schemes is IND-CPA[14], and we know that, inherently, no homomorphic scheme will be able to reach the IND-CCA2 security level due to the property of homomorphy itself. The question of whether a homomorphic scheme may reach IND-CCA1 remains open.

6.3.4.1. *Schemes based on elliptic curves and pairings*

Notable examples of schemes belonging to this category include Paillier (1999), ElGamal (1985) and BGN (Boneh *et al.* 2005; Herbert *et al.* 2019). Their theoretical security involves mathematical problems whose difficulty has been extensively studied (calculations of discrete logarithms in large groups, factorization of large integers, etc.). This means that we are on familiar ground, although further developments are possible. This familiarity is a significant advantage; nevertheless, these techniques will cease to be functional with the advent of quantum computers, which have the capacity to solve such problems in an efficient and effective manner. The best way of choosing appropriate parameters is to consult the article presenting the scheme in question in order to identify the mathematical problem, and then consult official documents such as those issued by the ANSSI[15] or listed on the BlueKrypt[16] website in order to select parameters in accordance with the desired security level.

6.3.4.2. *Schemes based on Euclidean networks*

The security of schemes based on Euclidean network structures involves different mathematical problems, such as the Bounded Distance Decoding Problem (BDD), the Shortest Vector Problem (SVP) or the resolution of linear systems of equations with errors (learning with errors (LWE)), in its original version or on rings (R-LWE). This family of mathematical problems differs from the previous group (factorization or discrete logarithm calculation) insofar as there are currently no known algorithms with the capacity to solve these problems in a much more efficient way on a quantum computer. For this reason, security schemes using these problems may be referred to as *post-quantum*: in the current state of the art, they are considered to be as resistant to quantum cryptanalysis as to classical cryptanalysis. This is a significant advantage in the long term, but comes at a high cost in terms of computation and data size, as we have seen.

The sticking point in this case is that these schemes are still relatively new, and the associated problems have received much less attention than their classic counterparts. This implies a less thorough understanding of their security. This consideration is particularly true for concrete security estimations, which go beyond reduction proofs

---

14 It is assumed that the reader is familiar with cryptographic security notions (semantic security, IND-CPA, IND-CCA, etc.). Further details and explanations may be found in Fontaine and Galand (2007).

15 Available at: www.ssi.gouv.fr/administration/guide/cryptographie-les-regles-du-rgs/.

16 Available at: www.keylength.com.

and seek to find the best cryptanalysis strategies. From these cryptanalyses, relations between the parameters and the security level of the scheme can be deduced. This point is crucial, since the desired level of security and the duration of this security must be taken into account when deploying an application. The lack of stability in concrete security analysis also affects the choice of parameters; over-dimensioning is not an option, as the additional costs in terms of calculation and data size are not acceptable. This consideration does not preclude the use of these solutions, but is an important factor to bear in mind. Current research efforts are focused on analyzing the concrete deployment of these schemes, notably on the question of parameter choice and security. Increasing work is also being carried out in the field of cryptanalysis in order to develop understanding. Notable examples include some previous studies (Albrecht *et al.* 2015a, 2016; Peikert 2016; Bai *et al.* 2018; Albrecht *et al.* 2019; Bai *et al.* 2019; Espitau and Joux 2020) and the Martin Albrecht's estimator[17], which is updated as new developments occur, and is extremely useful for choosing parameters.

6.4. Proofs of concept and applications

Several applications have been explored in recent years, combining academic knowledge and industrial skill. We have worked on a number of cases, described below. Other works of interest include some previous studies (Pedrouzo-Ulloa *et al.* 2016; Bouslimi *et al.* 2016; Bourse *et al.* 2018). The cases considered here are presented in order of increasing multiplicative depth, and thus complexity.

6.4.1. *Facial recognition*

In this section, we present a proof of concept performed on a facial recognition application for biometric authentication. Details of this work can be found in Bouzerna *et al.* (2016). For further information on biometric techniques in general and facial recognition in particular, see Chapter 1.

6.4.1.1. *Principle and system architecture*

Consider a case in which an employer wishes to implement a facial recognition authentication system at a company site, alongside the existing badge authentication strategy. To do this, the biometric credentials of a number of employees must be stored (and processed) on a server. Our aim is to reinforce the confidentiality of these credentials using a three-party system architecture: the employer, the employee (using an off-site enrollment procedure) and a third party, responsible for key management. This architecture is interesting in that responsibility for the confidentiality of the credentials is shared between the employer (who holds the

---

17 Available at: https://lwe-estimator.readthedocs.io/en/latest/.

encrypted credentials but does not have access to the decryption key) and the third party (who possesses the encryption and decryption keys but does not have access to the encrypted credentials). Evidently, our model is not resistant to collusion between the employer and the third party; nevertheless, it remains relatively acceptable, particularly if the third party is an IS security agency or a provider offering turnkey authentication solutions to multiple companies.

A high-level view of the system architecture is shown in Figure 6.4, with Dilbert and Dogbert in the roles of employee and third party, respectively.

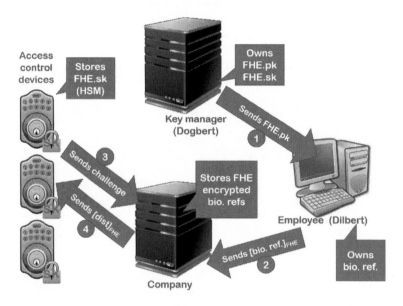

Figure 6.4. *Facial recognition: synthetic view of the global system architecture*

The principle here is to use homomorphic encryption so that the employer's server can process biometric references directly in the encrypted domain. The architecture guarantees the following properties:

– the third-party key manager (Dogbert) possesses both the public and secret keys, pk and sk, of the homomorphic encryption system; however, they do not have access to the reference data;

– the access control devices (Device) know the sk and have access to computation results (a distance to compare to a threshold), but not to the reference data;

– the employer does not have the sk, and thus cannot access the reference data or the (encrypted) results of computations;

– the employee (Dilbert) must be confident that the third-party key manager (Dogbert) will not collude with the employer.

6.4.1.2. *The face-matching algorithm*

The face-matching algorithm used in this case is the OpenIMAJ[18] implementation of the LTP (*Local Ternary Patterns*) algorithm (Tan and Triggs 2007). OpenIMAJ is one of the reference libraries for multimedia data processing, and the algorithm in question is known to give good results, particularly in suboptimal lighting conditions.

First, enrollment is carried out using one or more photographs of an individual's face. This phase relies on advanced image processing techniques, and produces a reference made up of 118 distance maps, $M^{(0)}, ..., M^{(117)}$, each corresponding to an 80×80 matrix of values in $[0, 1]$. The authentication process also requires one or more photographs of the individual, and generates 118 sets of coefficient coordinates $S^{(0)}, ..., S^{(117)}$. A detailed description of the operation of the algorithm lies outside the scope of this work; instead, we shall focus on the passage into the encrypted domain. Further details can be found in Tan and Triggs (2007).

The matching part of the algorithm is most relevant for our purposes, in terms of execution in the encrypted domain. Matching relies on the following calculation:

$$\ell = \sum_{i=k}^{117} \sum_{(i,j) \in S^{(k)}} M_{ij}^{(k)} \qquad\qquad [6.2]$$

Given a threshold T, authentication will be successful if $\ell \geq T$, and fail otherwise. Typically, on an empirical base, a threshold value of $T = 92$ is appropriate.

6.4.1.3. *Converting the algorithm to the encrypted domain*

With respect to the system architecture presented above, equation [6.2] must be evaluated in the encrypted domain. Helpfully, this can be carried out using an additive encryption system, with the hypothesis that the authentication request (coordinate subsets) is sent in unencrypted form[19].

Table 6.1 presents a summary of the results obtained when the Paillier cryptosystem is used for homomorphic evaluation (using GMP for the modular arithmetic and OpenMP for parallelization). The evaluation step notably takes less

---

18 Available at: www.openimaj.org.

19 If this is not the case, a homomorphic cryptosystem with the capacity to evaluate a single level of multiplication will suffice (Bouzerna *et al.* 2016).

than 2 seconds using an 8-core processor, and can easily be shortened to less than 1 second by using a more powerful machine. The online execution time is thus eminently reasonable. Note, too, that similar execution times can be obtained using an SHE such as BGV, optimized for additive function and using batching capacities. Performance is therefore a relatively unimportant factor in the choice of approach.

Step	When?	Where?	Duration
Precomputation	Offline	Dogbert	$\approx$ 30 mins
Encryption	Enrollment	Dilbert	21 secs
Evaluation	Authentication	Company	< 2 secs
Decryption	Authentication	Device	ε

Table 6.1. *Facial recognition: summary of performance*

6.4.2. *Classification*

6.4.2.1. *Elementary medical diagnostics*

Healthcare data are inherently highly personal in nature. The confidentiality of this data is a priority for both storage and processing solutions. Its sensitive nature means that medical diagnosis is a prime domain for the application of computation techniques using encrypted data. In this section, which draws on the work of (Carpov *et al.* 2016), we describe a medical diagnosis application used to evaluate an individual's risk of cardiovascular disease. In this context, homomorphic encryption is used to ensure that the patient's health data remains confidential.

The implemented algorithm evaluates a set of rules which, when activated, correspond to cardiovascular risk factors. The set of 11 rules is shown in Figure 6.5. The result of the algorithm is an integer between 0 and 9; a higher value denotes a higher risk of cardiovascular disease. The algorithm was implemented in C++ and compiled using the Cingulata compilation chain (see section 6.3.2.4). The highlighted terms in Figure 6.5 were processed in encrypted form. Although the algorithm is relatively simple in terms of computation requirements, it represents a certain reality in the context of online medical diagnostics, as an example of a relatively simple algorithm handling intrinsically personal, sensitive data.

Figure 6.6 gives a schematic overview of this application in a cloud implementation. The patient fills out a form (using an Android tablet), providing their medical data, and the cardiovascular risk assessment application is executed in the cloud. Transcryption is used in order to limit the volume of transmitted data (see section 6.3.3.2), and Kreyvium symmetric stream cipher is used to encrypt medical data sent to the cloud. The Kreyvium encryption key, $SymKey$, is in the tablet.

1: +1 if <u>male</u> and <u>aged</u> > 50
2: +1 if <u>female</u> and <u>aged</u> > 60
3: +1 if <u>there is a family history of cardiovascular disease</u>
4: +1 if a <u>smoker</u>
5: +1 if <u>diabetic</u>
6: +1 if <u>high blood pressure</u>
7: +1 if <u>HDL cholesterol</u> is < 40
8: +1 if <u>weight</u> > <u>height</u> - 90 cm
9: +1 if <u>daily physical activity</u> is < 30 minutes
10: +1 if <u>male</u> and <u>alcohol consumption</u> is > 3 glasses per day
11: +1 if <u>female</u> and <u>alcohol consumption</u> is > 2 glasses per day

Figure 6.5. *Set of rules used in the cardiovascular risk evaluation algorithm*

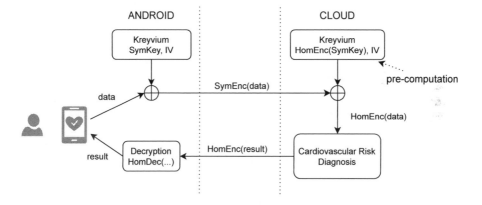

Figure 6.6. *Homomorphic computation process
for the cardiovascular risk evaluation*

It is interesting to note that the transcryption key HomEnc($SymKey$) is only sent to the cloud once, when the user registers. A public initialization vector IV, common to both parties, is used to synchronize the two streams in the transcryption process. The homomorphic execution of Kreyvium decryption, used to prepare the stream used for the transcryption operation, can be carried out offline by the cloud, in advance of the transaction itself, to minimize transaction length. This is one of the main advantages of this stream cipher-based transcryption solution.

Now, consider what happens online at the moment of transaction. Once the user's data, encrypted using Kreyvium, is received by the cloud, the homomorphically encrypted Kreyvium stream (prepared in advance offline) is used for transcryption (a simple additive operation). In this way, the Cloud obtains the user's medical data in a homomorphically encrypted form. The data then serve as input for the cardiovascular risk calculation algorithm, executed by the Cingulata environment in homomorphic form. The result of the calculation (the risk factor) is represented by four homomorphic numbers, one for each bit of the result. These ciphertexts are grouped into a single ciphertext using batching. The resulting ciphertext is sent back to the user's tablet, which decrypts it using the secret key of the homomorphic scheme sk; the risk factor is then reconstructed from its binary form and displayed on the patient's tablet.

6.4.2.1.1. Third-party recipients

In the case described above, the owner of the medical data is also the recipient of the result of the diagnostic algorithm. In other cases, however, the final recipient of the result may not be the owner of the input data, for example if a medical professional wishes to receive the results of the computation carried out using the patient's data. Our architecture can easily be adapted to this case: only the initialization phase needs to be modified.

The patient, instead of sending their symmetric Kreyvium key encrypted homomorphically using their own public key pk-patient to the cloud, will send the symmetric Kreyvium key encrypted using the doctor's homomorphic public key, pk-doctor. The decryption process then transforms the patient's data into the doctor's pre-authorized homomorphic domain. This process may be seen as the patient authorizing the doctor to access the result of the algorithm applied to their data. In the security model for this case of use, the cloud and the doctor must not collude, or patient data may be decrypted using the doctor's homomorphic secret key.

6.4.2.1.2. Implementation and performance

The Android application on the patient side was developed in Java. Figure 6.7 shows a screenshot from the application, specifically the form into which the patient inserts their data. The BFV homomorphic encryption scheme (Fan and Vercauteren 2012), parameterized using 128 security bits, was used for homomorphic computations. The Kreyvium cryptosystem used in transcryption has a key length of 128 bits. Thus, in this configuration, the cloud diagnosis service offers end-to-end security of 128 bits. In terms of multiplicative depth, the Kreyvium algorithm has a depth of 12 and the risk calculation algorithm has a depth of 8. The leveled SHE library used here was then dimensioned to take a total multiplicative depth of 20 into account, in order to ensure error-free execution. Each homomorphic ciphertext has a size of around 250 kb.

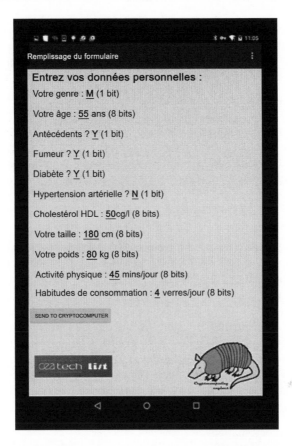

Figure 6.7. *Android application for calculating cardiovascular risk. Users fill in personal details and give information on their current health, diet and lifestyle following the guidelines given in Figure 6.5*

During the first interaction between the patient and the cloud, the patient sends the transcryption key $\text{HomEnc}(SymKey)$. This corresponds to 128 homomorphic ciphertexts (one per bit in the Kreyvium key). Hence, a total of $\sim$32 Mb are sent to the cloud during this phase.

Since Kreyvium is used to send medical data to the cloud, the size of the encrypted payload transmitted over the network to the server is the same as that of the clear payload. The only additional element is the symmetric key encrypted using the homomorphic system: this is relatively small. Once the homomorphic calculation has been carried out, the patient or doctor receives a single ciphertext ($\sim$250 Kb) containing the encrypted result of the calculation. The total response time between the moment when the tablet sends the data and the moment the result of the calculation is received is less than 4 seconds, of which ~3.2 seconds are taken up by the homomorphic execution of the diagnostic algorithm.. The homomorphic execution of the Kreyvium decryption algorithm prior to transcryption takes around 8 minutes: this is why this step should be carried out in advance, offline.

6.4.2.2. *Medical diagnostics using artificial neural networks*

Cardiac arrhythmia corresponds to a set of conditions which causes an irregular heartbeat. While some of these conditions are relatively benign, others cause more or less problematic symptoms. For certain chronic patients, electrocardiogram (EKG) monitoring is crucial for identifying arrhythmia as soon as it occurs to prevent their state from worsening.

6.4.2.2.1. Context

Services now exist for collecting patient EKG data via specific portable devices, analyzing these data to detect arrhythmia and transmitting the results to a medical professional, who then produces a report. In this case, arrhythmia is detected via algorithms based on neural networks (NNs). Nevertheless, outsourcing the analysis of a patient's EKG to a service that is not necessarily trusted clearly raises issues concerning the confidentiality of health data, which are particularly important since recent data protection regulations (such as the GDPR) impose strict analysis constraints for so-called special categories of data (Article 9). Thus, the option to perform this analysis on encrypted data, such that only the healthcare professional ultimately obtains the patients' health information, is an important goal in this context.

6.4.2.2.2. Neural networks

The idea, developed in greater detail in Azraoui *et al.* (2019), is to create a simple NN compatible with the use of encrypted data. Learning is carried out using clear data taken from the PhysioBank database[20].

A NN consists of a certain number of interconnected nodes, or neurones, with a layered structure. Each node carries out an operation according to the type of layer to which it belongs:

– convolution layer (optional): generally used in image recognition, in order to obtain information about the similarity between the part of the original image covered by a filter and the filter itself. This layer is not used in our case;

– activation layer: used to determine whether the filter pattern is truly present at a given position. The most well-known activation function types include the sigmoid (σ), hyperbolic tangent (tanh) and rectified linear unit (ReLU);

---

20 Available at: https//www.physionet.org/physiobank/database/mitdb.

– pooling operations consist of reducing the spatial size of the input in order to make it more manageable. This layer is not used in our case;

– the fully connected layer correlates the output from the previous layer with the characteristics of each class.

Some of these layers require costly calculations, meaning that it may be difficult (if not impossible) to execute them directly on encrypted data. The idea is thus to approximate these functions in order to increase the efficiency of execution in the encrypted domain, without sacrificing the precision of the chosen model:

– approximation of pooling functions: since the pooling function is nonlinear, it is often approximated by summing all values or calculating their mean;

– approximation of the activation function: there are several ways of executing the activation function. The most effective (in terms of efficiency and prediction precision) consists of using the square function, which directly calculates x^2 for any input x.

The NN in our study consists of two fully connected layers and an activation layer using x^2 with an input vector of size 180, 40 hidden neurones and an output vector of size 16. A model of this type gives a precision of 96.34%.

6.4.2.2.3. Homomorphic encryption

In terms of homomorphic encryption, we have chosen to use the CKKS scheme implemented by Microsoft in SEAL 3.1. The CKKS scheme allows calculations to be carried out directly on floating point numbers. We set a precision of 15 bits after the point to ensure that the precision of the encrypted version is as good as if the same evaluation had been carried out on the unencrypted version. Network weights are not encrypted. Thus, operations are primarily carried out between clear and encrypted data elements, rather than between two encrypted elements; this results in a significant increase in performance. We selected $m = 4\,096$ and $q = 2\,116$ as parameters for the CKKS scheme, resulting in 128-bit security.

6.4.2.2.4. Experimental tests

Experimental tests were performed on a computer with six Intel Core i7-7800X processors at 4.0 GHz, 128 GB of RAM, and a 1 TB SSD. The results are summarized in Table 6.2. We performed two different tests for the NN models: one classifying a single heartbeat and the other classifying packets of 2,048 heartbeats.

6.4.3. *RLE and image compression*

Compression is a major, widely used step in the field of multimedia. Video compression processes typically aim to avoid transmitting redundant information (while coding the remaining information as efficiently as possible), in order to reduce

	Computational cost (ms)	Spatial cost (Mb)
1 heartbeat	1 253	0.0018
2,048 heartbeats	1 253	3.69

Table 6.2. *Performance evaluation for EKG classification using homomorphic encryption*

bandwidth requirements. More precisely, the compression of a video sequence consists schematically of exploiting the spatial, temporal and spatio-temporal redundancies that naturally appear in a video stream destined for interpretation by the human visual system (HVS). The vast majority of modern video compression schemes encode the residual information in a non-conservative way, meaning that the output image of the decompressor is different from the input image of the compressor. This loss is rendered unnoticeable or minimal by exploiting the fact that the HVS is more sensitive to some types of information than others.

In this context, we will now focus on the RLE algorithm, which is probably the most basic compression algorithm currently available. This algorithm is used in several image formats, for example the BMP format, as well as in the coding of quantized DCT in H264. The idea is to see what can still be done when the image is encrypted. First, we shall study the complexity of implementation. Further details can be found in Canard *et al.* (2017).

6.4.3.1. *Compression using a homomorphic machine*

Our aim in this section is to understand the implications of the characteristics of homomorphic approaches in terms of the implementation of data compression algorithms. In concrete terms, the characteristics of the homomorphic machine impose, by construction, that the quantities of input and output data of a program are bounded (if not known) or, more generally, independent of the data of the encrypted domain. It is not, therefore, possible to directly implement a variable output rate algorithm; unfortunately, most of the usual compression algorithms fall into this category.

6.4.3.2. *Study of the RLE algorithm*

Given a sequence of input symbols $e_1, e_2, \ldots$, the RLE algorithm consists simply of producing a sequence of {counter, symbol} pairs to compress repetitions. For example, the sequence of input symbols

$$0, 0, 2, 3, 3, 3, 4, 0, 0, 0, 0$$

gives the following sequence of {counter, symbol} pairs:

$$\{2,0\}, \{1,2\}, \{3,3\}, \{1,4\}, \{4,0\}$$

```
 1: procedure RLE(())
 2:     int n_chars;
 3:     char *input;
 4:     cin≫n_chars;
 5:     input=new char[n_chars];
 6:     assert(input);
 7:     for (int i = 0; i <n_chars; i + +) do cin≫input[i];
 8:     end for
 9:     for (int i = 0; i <n_chars) do
10:         int j = 0;
11:         while (i + j <n_chars && input[i + j] ==input[i]) do j + +;
12:         end while
13:         cout≪ j ≪" "≪ input[i] ≪endl;
14:         i+ = j;
15:     end for
16: end procedure
```

Figure 6.8. *Pseudo-code of the classic version of the RLE algorithm*

Despite its simplicity, this algorithm cannot be implemented directly in a homomorphic context: the reason for this, and possibilities for an implementation in principle, will be explained below. As a starting point, the pseudo-code of the algorithm in its usual form is shown in Figure 6.8. As we have just indicated, this algorithm does not conform to the constraints of the homomorphic machine: the loop in line 9 advances by variable increments depending on the number of iterations of the loop in line 11, and the stop loop criterion depends on the encrypted data (input). We will progressively regularize this algorithm below.

– The first step is to eliminate the variable increment of the loop index i (line 9). This is done by internalizing the output of the symbol counter j (and the associated symbol) in an if of which the condition depends on the encrypted data (either the symbol changes, and in this case the counter and symbol are printed, or the symbol remains the same, and the counter is simply incremented). The assignment of the symbol counter j (line 11) can be regularized using a conditional assignment, as we have just seen.

– The real difficulty lies in the test $input[i + j] == input[i]$ in line 11. As we have seen, a condition may be regularized (schematically) by executing both branches then recombining their effects according to the numerical result of the condition evaluation. This notably implies that the passage to either clause of an if

must be indistinguishable in terms of effect. The effect of the if in question is to print something when the condition is satisfied and do nothing otherwise (different effects). For the effect to be identical whatever branch of the if is executed, we must either systematically do nothing (which is unhelpful), or print a certain symbol which gives no indication as to whether or not there is something to print. This is known as indistinguishability.

The latter property is ensured by the semantic security of the underlying cryptosystem. For example, we could print a zero counter value (encrypted) followed by an arbitrary symbol (encrypted) and the decompressor would work. The problem is that in this case there would be no compression at all, since the output stream would systematically be twice as big as the input stream. For compression to be possible, the algorithm must be made to work at a constant compression rate. This implies relaxing the conservative compression characteristic of the algorithm. A constant compression rate can be achieved by working with a constant number of {counter, symbol} output pairs. Thus, the final algorithm (Figure 6.9) includes an additional parameter, n_pairs, which fixes the number of (encrypted) pairs, which will be systematically generated at output. Each of these pairs is initialized at 0 for the counter and an arbitrary symbol, in this case a, is used (lines 13–16 of the final algorithm). We then proceed to the compression phase (described below). The program then prints the set of n encrypted {counter, symbol} pairs. Whatever the input sequence, the algorithm always produces the same number of pairs as the output. From here, there are two possible cases:

1) the pre-defined number of pairs is sufficient to represent the input sequence, in which case the reconstruction produced by the decompressor will be correct; a certain number of pairs may remain unused (counter value of 0), meaning that compression is not optimal;

2) if the number of pairs is not sufficient, the decompressor will not be able to reconstruct the input sequence, and a form of padding will be needed to reconstruct a sequence of the correct length.

Compression will be applied when:

$$(\alpha + \beta) \times n\_pairs < \alpha \times n\_chars$$

where α and β are the numbers of bits required to represent the symbols and counters, respectively.

The compression step (lines 17–29 of the final algorithm) then proceeds as follows. The integer k is initialized at 0 (or, more precisely, an encryption of 0): this counter designates the current pair in the pair buffer. The loop is executed on symbols in the input sequence, line 18. The for loop in line 19 corresponds to the assignment operation in a table with an encrypted index (this is a loop since its complexity is linear, as we saw earlier in this chapter). In functional terms, this loop is equivalent to $output\_ctr[k] = j$ and $output[k] = input[i - 1]$, but with an encrypted k. Next, k (respectively, j) is incremented if the symbol changes (respectively, does not change) using a conditional assignment (lines 23 and 24). Finally, once the loop in line 18 is complete, the loop in line 26 corresponds to a new assignment of the pair buffer with encrypted k.

6.4.3.3. *Implementation and experimental results*

The HRLE algorithm (as shown in Figure 6.9) can be rewritten using Cingulata (section 6.3.2.4), which offers automatic multiplicative depth optimization. Using Cingulata, the subjacent circuit can be optimized simply and automatically, and the resulting efficiency level is close to that achieved through time-consuming manual optimizations.

Finally, a test run of HRLE was performed, with a compression ratio of 25% on a sequence of 64 values, representing a macroblock of size 8×8. We thus have an output budget of 16 bytes, corresponding to 8 {symbol, counter} pairs. The results of this execution are as follows. The initial circuit has an approximate depth of 70 with 12,000 AND gates; the output circuit has a depth of 23, but approximately 60,000 AND gates. The multiplicative depth has thus decreased, but at the cost of a fivefold increase in the number of AND gates. Overall, the result is still beneficial. Executing a circuit with a depth of 70 is not practically possible. The new circuit, with a depth of 23, executes in around 30 minutes (2,003 seconds) on a 48-core computer, taking into account the acceleration factor of 47.3 obtained by optimizing the circuit using Cingulata.

It is possible to go further. In Kuaté *et al.* (2018), the authors implemented H264 and HEVC pipelines, regularized for homomorphic execution, and were able to compress a 128×128 image in 244 seconds (H264) and 149 seconds (HEVC).

While these results are still limited, and the execution of a compression algorithm on homomorphically encrypted data still poses a number of significant problems, this approach clearly merits further investigation. If the transcription of streams in the encrypted domain were to become affordable, this technique would pave the way for a wide range of helpful applications.

```
1:  procedure HRLE(())
2:      int n_chars,n_pairs ;
3:      char *input, *output ;
4:      int *output_ctr ;
5:      cin»n_chars ;
6:      input=new char[n_chars] ;
7:      assert(input) ;
8:      for (int i=0 ;i<n_chars ;i++) do cin»input[i] ;
9:      end for
10:     cin»n_pairs ;
11:     output=new char[n_pairs] ;
12:     output_ctr=new int[n_pairs] ;
13:     for (int i=0 ;i<n_pairs ;i++) do
14:         output_chr[i]='a' ;
15:         output_ctr[i]=0 ;
16:     end for
17:     int i,j=1,k=0 ;
18:     for (i=1 ;i<n_chars ;i++) do
19:         for (int l=0 ;l<n_pairs ;l++) do
20:             output_ctr[l]=l !=k ?output_ctr[l]=j ;
21:             output_chr[l]=l !=k ?output_chr[l] :input[i-1] ;
22:         end for
23:         k=input[i] !=input[i-1] ?k+1 :k ;
24:         j=input[i] !=input[i-1] ?1 :j+1 ;
25:     end for
26:     for (int l=0 ;l<n_pairs ;l++) do
27:         output_ctr[l]=l !=k ?output_ctr[l]=j ;
28:         output_chr[l]=l !=k ?output_chr[l] :input[i-1] ;
29:     end for
30:     for (int l=0 ;l<n_pairs ;l++) do
31:         cout«output_ctr[i]«" "«output_chr[i]«endl ;
32:     end for
33: end procedure
```

Figure 6.9. *Pseudo-code of the homomorphic version of the RLE algorithm*

6.5. Conclusion

As we have seen in this chapter, homomorphic encryption systems offer a range of attractive prospects in terms of functionality. While their use is still hampered by significant computational and storage costs, progress has been made to the extent that we may begin to consider deployment in certain realistic applications. Huge efforts are currently being made to ensure the usability of these solutions, first in applications such as those presented in this chapter, then in more demanding, currently unattainable contexts. Academic work is focused on reducing computation time and ciphertext size, and on understanding the security aspect of the schemes in question. Standardization is a further key aim, providing a solid point of reference for industrial use, and represents an important step toward the adoption and official acceptance of this technology.

A consortium of academic researchers, industrial players and government bodies[21] has been working on standardization for homomorphic encryption since 2007, with the aim of further developing secure computation techniques. An ISO/IEC work group began to look at a draft version of a homomorphic encryption standard in early 2020. The aim of this standard is to standardize and simplify the APIs of homomorphic libraries, train developers in their use, and facilitate understanding of the security of homomorphic schemes.

6.6. Acknowledgments

We wish to thank all of our co-authors with whom we have worked on this topic, notably Carlos Aguilar-Melchor, Pascal Aubry, Monir Azraoui, Muhammad Barham, Bhaskar Biswas, Guillaume Bonnoron, Nabil Bouzerna, Beyza Bozdemir, Anne Canteaut, Joël Carthébras, Eleonora Ciceri, Paul Dubrulle, Orhan Ermis, Simon Fau, Fabien Galand, Nicolas Gama, Mariya Georgieva, Guy Gogniat, Vincent Herbert, Vianney Lapôtre, Ramy Masalha, Vincent Migliore, Marco Mosconi, María Naya-Plasencia, Thanh-Hai Nguyen, Donald Nokam Kuaté, Melek Onen, Pascal Paillier, Marie Paindavoine, Adeline Roux-Langlois, Boris Rozenberg, Cédric Seguin, Oana Stan, Arnaud Tisserand, Bastien Vialla, Sauro Vicini, and Philippe Wolf.

6.7. References

Aguilar-Melchor, C., Gaborit, P., Herranz, J. (2008). Additively homomorphic encryption with d-operand multiplications. Report, Cryptology ePrint Archive [Online]. Available at: http://eprint.iacr.org/2008/378.

---

21 Microsoft Research, IBM, Intel, Alibaba, Inpher, CryptoExperts, CEA, NIST, EPFL and MIT, among others: a full list can be found at https://homomorphicencryption.org/participants.

Aguilar-Melchor, C., Gaborit, P., Herranz, J. (2010). Additively homomorphic encryption with d-operand multiplications. In *CRYPTO 2010*. IACR, Santa Barbara.

Aguilar-Melchor, C., Fau, S., Fontaine, C., Gogniat, G., Sirdey, R. (2013). Recent advances in homomorphic encryption: A possible future for signal processing in the encrypted domain. *IEEE Signal Processing Magazine*, 30(2), 108–117.

Albrecht, M.R., Player, R., Scott, S. (2015a). On the concrete hardness of learning with errors. *Journal of Mathematical Cryptology*, 9(3), 169–203.

Albrecht, M.R., Rechberger, C., Schneider, T., Tiessen, T., Zohner, M. (2015b). Ciphers for MPC and FHE. In *EUROCRYPT 2015*. IACR, Sofia.

Albrecht, M.R., Bai, S., Ducas, L. (2016). A subfield lattice attack on overstretched NTRU assumptions: Cryptanalysis of some of FHE and graded encoding schemes. Report, Cryptology ePrint Archive.

Albrecht, M.R., Ducas, L., Herold, G., Kirshanova, E., Postlethwaite, E.W., Stevens, M. (2019). The general sieve kernel and new records in lattice reduction. In *EUROCRYPT 2019 – 38th Annual International Conference on the Theory and Applications of Cryptographic Techniques*. IACR, Darmstadt.

Aubry, P., Carpov, S., Sirdey, R. (2020). Faster homomorphic encryption is not enough: Improved heuristic for multiplicative depth minimization of Boolean circuits. In *Cryptographers' Track at the RSA Conference*. RSA, San Francisco.

Azraoui, M., Barham, M., Bozdemir, B., Canard, S., Ciceri, E., Ermis, O., Masalha, R., Mosconi, M., Önen, M., Paindavoine, M., Rozenberg, B., Vialla, B., Vicini, S. (2019). Sok: Cryptography for neural networks. In *Privacy and Identity Management. Data for Better Living: AI and Privacy*. IFIP, Windisch.

Bai, S., Stehlé, D., Wen, W. (2018). Measuring, simulating and exploiting the head concavity phenomenon in BKZ. In *24th International Conference on the Theory and Application of Cryptology and Information Security*. ASIACRYPT, Brisbane.

Bai, S., Miller, S., Wen, W. (2019). A refined analysis of the cost for solving LWE via uSVP. In *11th International Conference on Cryptology in Africa*. AFRICACRYPT, Rabat.

Benhamouda, F., Lepoint, T., Mathieu, C., Zhou, H. (2017). Optimization of bootstrapping in circuits. In *28th Annual ACM-SIAM Symposium on Discrete Algorithms*. SIAM, Barcelona.

Boneh, D., Goh, E., Nissim, K. (2005). Evaluating 2-DNF formulas on Ciphertexts. In *2nd Annual Theory of Cryptography Conference*. TCC, Cambridge.

Bonnoron, G., Ducas, L., Fillinger, M. (2018). Large FHE gates from tensored homomorphic accumulator. In *10th International Conference on Cryptology in Africa*. AFRICACRYPT, Marrakech.

Boura, C., Gama, N., Georgieva, M., Jetchev, D. (2018). Chimera: Combining ring-LWE-based fully homomorphic encryption schemes. Report, Cryptology ePrint Archive [Online]. Available at: https://eprint.iacr.org/2018/758.

Bourse, F., Minelli, M., Minihold, M., Paillier, P. (2018). Fast homomorphic evaluation of deep discretized neural networks. In *38th Annual International Cryptology Conference*. CRYPTO, Santa Barbara.

Bouslimi, D., Bellafqira, R., Coatrieux, G. (2016). Data hiding in homomorphically encrypted medical images for verifying their reliability in both encrypted and spatial domains. In *38th Annual International Conference of the IEEE Engineering in Medicine and Biology Society*. IEEE, Orlando.

Bouzerna, N., Sirdey, R., Stan, O., Nguyen, T.H., Wolf, P. (2016). An architecture for practical confidentiality-strengthened face authentication embedding homomorphic cryptography. In *International Conference on Cloud Computing Technology and Science*. IEEE, Luxembourg.

Brakerski, Z. (2012). Fully homomorphic encryption without modulus switching from classical GapSVP. In *32nd Annual Cryptology Conference*. CRYPTO, Santa Barbara.

Brakerski, Z., Gentry, C., Vaikuntanathan, V. (2012). (Leveled) fully homomorphic encryption without bootstrapping. In *3rd Innovations in Theoretical Computer Science Conference*. ACM, Cambridge.

Canard, S., Carpov, S., Kuaté, D.N., Sirdey, R. (2017). Running compression algorithms in the encrypted domain: A case-study on the homomorphic execution of RLE. In *15th Annual Conference on Privacy, Security and Trust*. IEEE, Calgary.

Canteaut, A., Carpov, S., Fontaine, C., Lepoint, T., Naya-Plasencia, M., Paillier, P., Sirdey, R. (2016). Stream ciphers: A practical solution for efficient homomorphic-ciphertext compression. In *Fast Software Encryption*. IACR, Bochum.

Canteaut, A., Carpov, S., Fontaine, C., Lepoint, T., Naya-Plasencia, M., Paillier, P., Sirdey, R. (2018). Stream ciphers: A practical solution for efficient homomorphic-ciphertext compression. *Journal of Cryptology*, 31(3), 885–916.

Carpov, S. and Sirdey, R. (2016). Another compression method for homomorphic ciphertexts. In *4th ACM International Workshop on Security in Cloud Computing*. ACM, Xi'an.

Carpov, S., Dubrulle, P., Sirdey, R. (2015). Armadillo: A compilation chain for privacy preserving applications. In *3rd International Workshop on Security in Cloud Computing*. ACM, Singapore.

Carpov, S., Nguyen, T.H., Sirdey, R., Constantino, G., Martinelli, F. (2016). Practical privacy-preserving medical diagnosis using homomorphic encryption. In *9th International Conference on Cloud Computing (CLOUD)*. IEEE, San Francisco.

Carpov, S., Aubry, P., Sirdey, R. (2017). A multi-start heuristic for multiplicative depth minimization of Boolean circuits. In *International Workshop on Combinatorial Algorithms*. IWOCA, Newcastle.

Carpov, S., Gama, N., Georgieva, M., Troncoso-Pastoriza, J.R. (2019). Privacy-preserving semi-parallel logistic regression training with fully homomorphic encryption. *IACR Cryptol. ePrint Arch.*, 101.

Catalano, D. and Fiore, D. (2015). Using linearly-homomorphic encryption to evaluate degree-2 functions on encrypted data. In *22nd ACM SIGSAC Conference on Computer and Communications Security*. ACM, Denver.

Cathébras, J., Carbon, A., Milder, P., Sirdey, R., Ventroux, N. (2018). Data flow oriented hardware design of RNS-based polynomial multiplication for SHE acceleration. *IACR Transactions on Cryptographic Hardware and Embedded Systems*, 3, 69–88.

Çetin, G.S., Doröz, Y., Sunar, B., Savaş, E. (2015). Depth optimized efficient homomorphic sorting. In *International Conference on Cryptology and Information Security in Latin America*. LATINCRYPT, Guadalajara.

Chen, H. (2017). Optimizing relinearization in circuits for homomorphic encryption [Online]. Available at: https://arxiv.org/abs/1711.06319.

Chen, H., Laine, K., Player, R., Xia, Y. (2018). High-precision arithmetic in homomorphic encryption. In *Cryptographers Track at the RSA Conference*. RSA, San Francisco.

Cheon, J.H., Coron, J., Kim, J., Lee, M.S., Lepoint, T., Tibouchi, M., Yun, A. (2013). Batch fully homomorphic encryption over the integers. In *EUROCRYPT*. IACR, Athens.

Cheon, J.H., Kim, M., Lauter, K. (2015). Homomorphic computation of edit distance. In *International Conference on Financial Cryptography and Data Security*. FC, San Juan.

Cheon, J.H., Kim, A., Kim, M., Song, Y. (2017). Homomorphic encryption for arithmetic of approximate numbers. In *ASIACRYPT*. IACR, Hong Kong.

Cheon, J.H., Han, K., Kim, A., Kim, M., Song, Y. (2018). Bootstrapping for approximate homomorphic encryption. In *Eurocrypt*. IACR, Tel Aviv.

Chillotti, I., Gama, N., Georgieva, M., Izabachène, M. (2016). Faster fully homomorphic encryption: Bootstrapping in less than 0.1 seconds. In *22nd International Conference on the Theory and Application of Cryptology and Information Security*. IACR, Hanoi.

Chillotti, I., Gama, N., Georgieva, M., Izabachène, M. (2017). Faster packed homomorphic operations and efficient circuit bootstrapping for TFHE. In *23rd International Conference on the Theory and Applications of Cryptology and Information Security*. IACR, Hong Kong.

Chillotti, I., Gama, N., Georgieva, M., Izabachène, M. (2020). TFHE: Fast fully homomorphic encryption over the torus. *Journal of Cryptology*, 33(1), 34–91.

Dinur, I., Liu, Y., Meier, W., Wang, Q. (2015). Optimized interpolation attacks on LowMC. *IACR, Cryptology ePrint Archive*, 418 [Online]. Available at: https://eprint.iacr.org/2015/418.

Doröz, Y., Ozturk, E., Sunar, B. (2013). Evaluating the hardware performance of a million-bit multiplier. In *Euromicro Conference on Digital System Design*. IEEE, Los Alamitos.

Doröz, Y., Shahverdi, A., Eisenbarth, T., Sunar, B. (2014). Toward practical homomorphic evaluation of block ciphers using prince. In *International Conference on Financial Cryptography and Data Security*. WAHC, Christ Church.

Doröz, Y., Hu, Y., Sunar, B. (2016). Homomorphic AES evaluation using the modified LTV scheme. *Designs, Codes and Cryptology*, 80, 333–358 [Online]. Available at: https://doi.org/10.1007/s10623-015-0095-1.

Ducas, L. and Micciancio, D. (2015). FHEW: Bootstrapping homomorphic encryption in less than a second. In *34th Annual International Conference on the Theory and Applications of Cryptographic Techniques*. IACR, Sofia.

Duval, S., Lallemand, V., Rotella, Y. (2016). Cryptanalysis of the FLIP family of stream ciphers. In *36th Annual International Cryptology Conference*. IACR, Santa Barbara.

ElGamal, T. (1985). A public key cryptosystem and a signature scheme based on discrete logarithms. *IEEE Transactions on Information Theory*, 31(4), 469–472 [Online]. Available at: http://www.ams.org/mathscinet-getitem?mr=86j.

Espitau, T. and Joux, A. (2020). Certified lattice reduction. *Advances in Mathematics of Communications*, 14(1), 137–159.

Fan, J. and Vercauteren, F. (2012). Somewhat practical fully homomorphic encryption. Report, Cryptology ePrint Archive [Online]. Available at: http://eprint.iacr.org/2012/144.

Fontaine, C. and Galand, F. (2007). A survey of homomorphic encryption for nonspecialists 3. *EURASIP Journal on Information Security*, 1, 1–15.

Fouque, P.-A., Hadjibeyli, B., Kirchner, P. (2016). Homomorphic evaluation of lattice-based symmetric encryption schemes. In *International Computing and Combinatorics Conference*. COCOON, Ho Chi Minh City.

Gentry, C. (2009). A fully homomorphic encryption scheme. PhD Thesis, Stanford University, Stanford.

Gentry, C., Halevi, S., Smart, N.P. (2012). Homomorphic evaluation of the AES circuit. In *32nd International Cryptology Conference*. IACR, Santa Barbara.

Häner, T. and Soeken, M. (2020). Lowering the t-depth of quantum circuits by reducing the multiplicative depth of logic networks [Online]. Available at: https://arxiv.org/abs/2006.03845.

Herbert, V., Biswas, B., Fontaine, C. (2019). Design and implementation of low-depth pairing-based homomorphic encryption scheme. *Journal of Cryptographic Engineering*, 9, 185–201.

Kuaté, D.N. (2018). Cryptographie homomorphe et transcodage d'image/video dans le domaine chiffré. (Homomorphic encryption and image/video transcoding in the encrypted domain). PhD Thesis, Université Paris Saclay, Paris.

Kuaté, D.N., Canard, S., Sirdey, R. (2018). Towards video compression in the encrypted domain: A case-study on the H264 and HEVC macroblock processing pipeline. In *17th International Conference in Cryptology and Network Security*. CANS, Naples.

Lee, D., Lee, W., Oh, H., Yi, K. (2020). Optimizing homomorphic evaluation circuits by program synthesis and term rewriting. In *41st ACM SIGPLAN Conference on Programming Language Design and Implementation*. ACM, London.

Lepoint, T. and Naehrig, M. (2014). A comparison of the homomorphic encryption schemes FV and YASHE. In *AFRICACRYPT*. IACR, Marrakech.

Méaux, P., Journault, A., Standaert, F.-X., Carlet, C. (2016). Towards stream ciphers for efficient FHE with low-noise ciphertexts. In *Annual International Conference on the Theory and Applications of Cryptographic Techniques*. IACR, Vienna.

Migliore, V., Seguin, C., Mendez Real, M., Lapotre, V., Tisserand, A., Fontaine, C., Gogniat, G., Tessier, R. (2017). A high-speed accelerator for homomorphic encryption using the Karatsuba algorithm. *ACM Trans. Embedded Comput. Syst.*, 16(5), 138:1–138:17.

Migliore, V., Mendez Real, M., Lapotre, V., Tisserand, A., Fontaine, C., Gogniat, G. (2018). Hardware/software co-design of an accelerator for FV homomorphic encryption scheme using Karatsuba algorithm. *IEEE Transactions on Computers*, 67(3), 335–347.

Naehrig, M., Lauter, K.E., Vaikuntanathan, V. (2011). Can homomorphic encryption be practical? In *Conference on Computer and Communications Security*. ACM, Chicago, 113–124.

Paillier, P. (1999). Public-key cryptosystems based on composite degree residuosity classes. In *International Conference on the Theory and Applications of Cryptographic Techniques*. IACR, Prague.

Paindavoine, M. and Vialla, B. (2015). Minimizing the number of bootstrappings in fully homomorphic encryption. In *International Conference on Selected Areas in Cryptography*. SAC, New Brunswick.

Pedrouzo-Ulloa, A., Troncoso-Pastoriza, J.R., Pérez-González, F. (2016). Image denoising in the encrypted domain. In *International Workshop on Information Forensics and Security (WIFS)*. IEEE, Abu Dhabi.

Peikert, C. (2016). How (not) to instantiate Ring-LWE. In *International Conference on Security and Cryptography for Networks*. SCN, Amalfi.

Pöppelmann, T., Naehrig, M., Putnam, A., Macias, A. (2015). Accelerating homomorphic evaluation on reconfigurable hardware. In *Cryptographic Hardware and Embedded Systems*. IACR, Saint-Malo.

Rechberger, C. (2016). The FHEMPCZK-cipher zoo. *FSE Rump Session*, 22 March.

Rivest, R.L., Adleman, L., Dertouzos, M.L. (1978). On data banks and privacy homomorphisms. In *Foundations of Secure Computation*, DeMillo, R.A. (ed.). Academia Press, New York.

Sinha Roy, S., Järvinen, K., Vercauteren, F., Dimitrov, V., Verbauwhede, I. (2015). Modular hardware architecture for somewhat homomorphic function evaluation. In *Cryptographic Hardware and Embedded Systems*. IACR, Saint-Malo.

Tan, X. and Triggs, B. (2007). Enhanced local texture feature sets for face recognition under difficult lighting conditions. In *Analysis and Modeling of Faces and Gestures*, Zhou, S.K., Zhao, W., Tang, X., Gong, S. (eds). Springer, Berlin/Heidelberg.

Yasuda, M., Shimoyama, T., Kogure, J., Yokoyama, K., Koshiba, T. (2015). New packing method in somewhat homomorphic encryption and its applications. *Security and Communication Networks*, 8(13), 2194–2213.

7

Data Hiding in the Encrypted Domain

Pauline PUTEAUX and William PUECH
LIRMM, Université de Montpellier, CNRS, France

In recent years, the development of cloud computing has meant that more and more users are uploading their personal data to remote servers. However, this can result in major security breaches that pose a constant risk in terms of confidentiality, authentication and integrity. To mitigate these problems, multimedia data may be encrypted prior to transmission and storage. In this chapter, we focus on the problem of processing this encrypted multimedia data, specifically on data hiding in the encrypted domain.

7.1. Introduction: processing multimedia data in the encrypted domain

For security reasons, more and more digital data are encrypted before being transferred or archived. During the transmission or archiving process, these data often need to be analyzed or processed directly in the encrypted domain, without knowing its original, clear content (Erkin *et al.* 2007). Figure 7.1 shows some of the main applications for multimedia data processing in the encrypted domain: sharing visual secrecy between multiple people; data hiding in encrypted multimedia data (so that the person inserting or extracting data does not have access to its original content); recompression of crypto-compressed images or videos (for secure transmission over

---

For a color version of all figures in this chapter, see www.iste.co.uk/puech/multimedia2.zip.

low-speed networks); indexing and searching for multimedia content in encrypted databases; and the correction of noisy encrypted images. Note that the processing of encrypted multimedia data in the context of homomorphic encryption is discussed in Chapter 6, and, as such, these specific applications will not be presented again here.

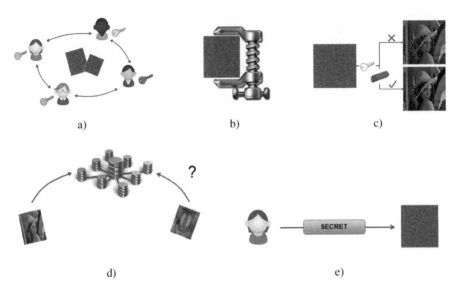

a)   b)   c)

d)   e)

Figure 7.1. *Target applications for multimedia data processing in the encrypted domain: a) visual secret sharing; b) recompression of crypto-compressed images; c) correction of noisy encrypted images; d) searching and indexing in encrypted databases; and e) data hiding in the encrypted domain*

In this section, we describe three of these applications: visual secret sharing (section 7.1.1), indexing and searching for multimedia content in encrypted databases (section 7.1.2) and data hiding in the encrypted domain (section 7.1.3).

The recompression of crypto-compressed images is discussed in detail in Chapter 4, and the notion of visual secret sharing is covered in Chapter 8.

7.1.1. *Applications: visual secret sharing*

There are two categories of methods that may be used to share visual secrets: visual cryptography, as proposed by Naor and Shamir (1994), and secret image sharing, as proposed by Thien and Lin (2002). Visual cryptography consists of sharing visual information (text or image) between several individuals in a secure manner. In the approach described in Naor and Shamir (1994), developed for binary images, two images known as shares are generated after sharing. In these images, the black pixels of the secret image are protected, while the white pixels are randomized. The secret image is then reconstructed using an exclusive-or between the two shares. Secret image sharing draws on secret sharing methods developed independently by both Blakley (1979) and Shamir (1979). The method, broadly based on the concept of polynomial interpolation, enables an image to be shared between n users in a secure manner (Thien and Lin 2002). Each user receives a personal share in the form of an image. This share is unique and in visual terms appears to have been generated randomly. The original image can only be reconstructed by assembling at least k shares, with $k \leq n$. Thus, with $k - 1$ shares, no information can be retrieved concerning the original content of the image. The parameter k may be higher or lower depending on the level of trust within the sharing group. Note that the reconstructed secret image I' is very similar to the original secret image I, and may even be strictly identical when using a "perfect" method. Figure 7.2 shows an illustration of the secret sharing process.

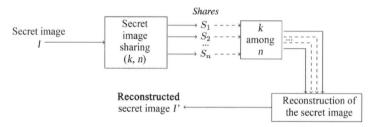

Figure 7.2. *Illustration of the secret image sharing process*

7.1.2. *Applications: searching and indexing in encrypted image databases*

Searchable encryption allows a database to be stored in a secure manner on an unreliable server while maintaining content search and indexing functionalities. With the development of cloud computing, efficient searchable encryption approaches are now of crucial importance. The methods used must ensure that the stored data are secure without increasing their size. Furthermore, the computational cost of search and indexing operations must be low. While most existing methods have been developed for textual document retrieval, image retrieval methods based on content analysis are also valuable for many applications. In the medical field, for example, doctors may use these techniques to match medical images of patients with similar symptoms to help establish a diagnosis (Pavlopoulou *et al.* 2003). Law enforcement agencies may also use these approaches to compare evidence from crime scenes with records in their archives (Jain *et al.* 2009). Lu *et al.* (2009a) were the first to propose a search system for images in the encrypted domain based on content analysis, preserving the visual privacy of the original images. Their approach used the reverse index and the secure min-Hash. Elsewhere, the same authors presented a study of three different techniques for protecting the features of an image: randomizing, projection and random encoding of their bitplanes (Lu *et al*. 2009b). They showed that features encrypted by bitplane randomization or by random coding can be used to compute a Hamming distance in the encrypted domain. Furthermore, features encrypted by bitplane randomization can be used to compute an L1 distance in the encrypted domain. Hsu *et al*. (2012) proposed a method based on homomorphic encryption, where the use of the Scale-Invariant Feature Transform (SIFT) to extract features from the image does not compromise the confidentiality of the original content. Ferreira *et al*. (2015) described a new image encryption method that permits retrieval in the encrypted domain. In this case, texture and color information are separated then encrypted independently. Texture information is encrypted using a probabilistic cryptosystem to protect the image content, while color information is encrypted by a deterministic cryptosystem to enable searching based on color characteristics. Finally, Xia *et al*. (2016) recently found that none of the state-of-the-art methods took account of the idea that users could perform dishonest searches and illegally distribute the retrieved images. The authors proposed a solution to this problem using a protocol based on data hiding.

7.1.3. *Applications: data hiding in the encrypted domain*

Methods for data hiding in the encrypted domain are used to conceal secret messages in the encrypted domain without access to the key used to encrypt multimedia data, or to the original clear content. These approaches are mostly used to annotate multimedia data, or for authentication purposes. The secret message that is inserted can thus be a label, timestamp data, or information about the origin of the data, such as EXIF data for images. In this type of approach, the owner of the multimedia data and the person inserting the secret message may be different people. For example, if images are stored on a cloud platform, encryption is performed by the image owner to protect the original content, and then the resulting encrypted image is stored on the cloud server. The server manager has no access to the original content of the image. However, they can still insert a secret message directly in the encrypted domain. In this particular application, the labels inserted into encrypted images may permit better management of the cloud server by administrators (Qian *et al*. 2018). During the decryption phase, the secret message should be extracted without error. In addition, if an authorized user downloads the marked encrypted image from the cloud server, they should be able to retrieve the original image content without loss after the decryption operation. Data hiding methods thus provide an alternative to traditional file management systems, providing additional information inside the encrypted multimedia data itself, instead of using an auxiliary metadata file. To this end, many methods have been proposed since 2008, aiming to achieve the best trade-off between the payload (i.e. the amount of data embedded), the bit error rate in the secret message and the quality of the reconstructed media data compared to the expected original data.

In the remainder of this chapter, we focus on data hiding (DH) methods in the encrypted domain. Section 7.2 presents the main aims of DH methods. Section 7.3 provides a more detailed description of different classes and characteristics. The main state-of-the-art methods are described in section 7.4 and compared in section 7.5. In section 7.6, we describe a high-capacity DH method based on MSB prediction, which achieves very good results. We conclude our discussion in section 7.7.

7.2. Main aims

Data hiding is an approach used to conceal secret data inside a signal (such as an image). After extracting these data, it must be possible to reconstruct the original image without alteration. Furthermore, for confidentiality reasons, it may be necessary to make an image illegible using encryption methods. Encryption and data hiding can be carried out simultaneously. Puech *et al.* (2008) described one of the very first methods for data hiding in the encrypted domain in 2008. Several different methods have since been developed. As can be seen from Figure 7.3, there were 40 times more publications on this subject in 2019 than in 2009. Target applications for hiding data in the encrypted domain include digital rights management (buyer–vendor protocol), cloud storage, patient confidentiality (medical field), classified data management (military), journalism, video surveillance and data analysis.

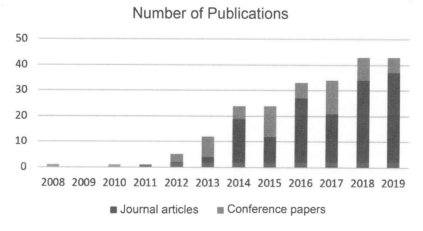

Figure 7.3. *Evolution of publications on data hiding in the encrypted domain (2008–2019)*

7.2.1. *Digital rights management*

Before selling multimedia data, distributors encrypt these data to ensure its visual privacy. Furthermore, to prevent illegal distribution, the distributor watermarks the data with information about the buyer. When media data are purchased, each copy sold is therefore unique. This is particularly useful for tracking and tracing purposes, making it possible to identify a customer when a suspicious copy is found.

However, since the distributor knows the watermark, dishonest clients may claim that illegal copies are in fact being distributed by the distributor. Conversely, it is also possible for the distributor to "frame" an honest customer as dishonest by inserting their personal watermark into the media data and distributing copies. Solutions have been proposed to prevent this based on ensuring that the distributor does not know the final form of the watermark (Poh 2009).

7.2.2. *Cloud storage*

Users may encrypt personal multimedia data before storing it on a cloud platform in order to preserve their privacy. To facilitate server management, the cloud platform administrator embeds data required for indexing purposes, for example, directly into the encrypted domain (Qian *et al.* 2014).

7.2.3. *Preserving patient confidentiality*

In hospitals, medical images of patients are encrypted to preserve their privacy (Bouslimi *et al.* 2012). In addition, patient information is embedded into the resulting encrypted images for ease of identification. A nurse or administrative worker handling the data may extract this information without viewing the original. Authorized physicians, on the other hand, may access both the patient's identification information and the clear images.

7.2.4. *Classified data*

In the military field, low-ranking officers (e.g. a lieutenant) may extract the label inserted into encrypted multimedia data for administrative purposes (e.g. copying, archiving or transferring) without being able to access the original content. A higher ranking officer (such as a general) may be able to decrypt the data, giving them access to both the inserted label and the original clear data (Cao *et al.* 2016).

7.2.5. *Journalism*

Journalists may encrypt multimedia data before sending it to the company for which they are working, so that only authorized persons may access the content. This guarantees exclusive coverage of an incident or event, preventing competitors from accessing the information. Details such as the sender's identity or the GPS coordinates of a field report may be inserted for authentication purposes (Wong and Tanaka 2014) to prevent content counterfeiting.

7.2.6. *Video surveillance*

Video recordings from surveillance cameras are selectively encrypted (masking regions of interest, such as faces, for example) to protect people's privacy (Dufaux and Ebrahimi 2008). Information concerning image acquisition (camera ID, time and date) must be included in the recorded images for authentication purposes, notably if the video stream is used as proof in a legal context.

7.2.7. *Data analysis*

Huge amounts of data are now generated and collected every day (Hey *et al.* 2009). These data must be labeled, but also remain confidential.

7.3. Classes and characteristics

As we saw in section 7.2, many data hiding methods have been developed for digital images in recent years. Several different classes and characteristics can be defined. We shall begin by defining different properties used to categorize the state-of-the-art methods in section 7.3.1. In section 7.3.2, we shall describe classic approaches to image encryption in data hiding methods. Finally, in section 7.3.3, we detail the criteria used to evaluate the performance of these methods.

7.3.1. *Properties*

In this section, we describe the properties that define and categorize data hiding methods, namely the trade-off between embedding capacity and the quality of the reconstructed image, and approaches that can be used for the encoding and decoding phases.

7.3.1.1. *Capacity/quality trade-off*

In data hiding methods, there is a real trade-off between the number of secret bits inserted in the encrypted image and the quality of the reconstructed image obtained after decrypting the marked encrypted image. A distinction may be made between two types of methods, depending on the quantity of bits of a secret message that can be inserted. Data hiding methods with a payload of less than half a bit per pixel are said to be low capacity. Conversely, a method is said to be high capacity when the payload is close to or in excess of one bit per pixel. No state-of-the-art methods offered the capacity to insert more than one bit per pixel until 2018. Some methods allow the message to be kept secret when the clear image is decrypted: in these cases, it is essential for the reconstructed image to be similar to the original clear image. A method is said to be fully reversible when the original image can be reconstructed without loss after the message has been extracted. Finally, note that the higher the number of bits to insert in the secret message, the more likely it is that the reconstructed image produced during the decoding phase will be degraded.

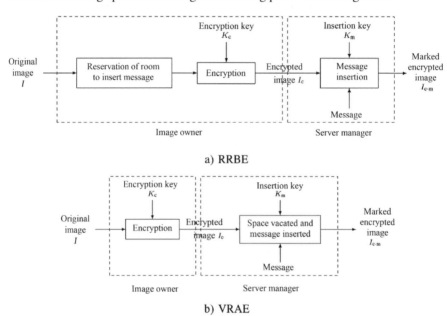

Figure 7.4. *Two possible encoding approaches: a) reserving room before encryption (RRBE) or b) vacating room after encryption (VRAE)*

7.3.1.2. *Two approaches to encoding*

In terms of encoding approaches, data hiding methods may be grouped into two categories: those in which space is freed up for message embedding before encryption (reserving room before encryption, RRBE) and those in which space is made available for the message after encryption (vacating room after encryption, VRAE). These two approaches are shown in Figure 7.4. In RRBE methods, the original image is pre-processed by the owner before encryption in order to leave space for the bits of a secret message. The image is then encrypted and another person – such as a cloud server manager – may insert the bits of a secret message into the specific positions reserved for this purpose (Ma *et al*. 2013; Cao *et al*. 2016; Zhang *et al*. 2016; Puteaux and Puech 2018a). In VRAE methods, the content of the original image is directly encrypted by the owner with no pre-processing. The cloud server manager then modifies the encrypted data in order to embed the bits of the secret message (Puech *et al*. 2008; Hong *et al*. 2012; Zhang 2011, 2012; Qian *et al*. 2014). Both approaches are effective, but both present certain drawbacks. RRBE methods allow a larger number of bits to be embedded but require pre-processing before encryption. This may be difficult in practice if the owner of the image is not aware that the encrypted image needs to be analyzed or processed at a later stage. In VRAE methods, the person receiving the marked encrypted image must be able to predict the contents of the original image in order to reconstruct it. This means that the retrieved image is generally an estimation of the original, and perfect reversibility is not possible. Furthermore, the number of secret bits embedded must remain low in order to minimize distortion.

7.3.1.3. *Two approaches to decryption*

The extraction of a secret message and the reconstruction of the original image may be carried out jointly or separately during the decryption phase, as shown in Figure 7.5. In the joint case, the clear image cannot be obtained without knowing the data hiding key. Using the encryption key alone, it is only possible to obtain a degraded version of the original image (Puech *et al*. 2008). Furthermore, in certain methods, knowledge of the data hiding key alone is not sufficient to extract the message (Zhang 2011). In the case of separate operations, the message can be extracted and the original image can be reconstructed separately, i.e. by two different people. If a user only knows the encryption key, two cases are possible:

– a clear image, marked with the secret message but very similar to the original, may be obtained (Zhang 2012);

– the original image may be reconstructed perfectly, without being marked by the secret message (Puteaux and Puech 2018a).

Using the data hiding key alone, users may extract the secret message directly from the encrypted image. Note that the message can also be extracted in the clear domain if the chosen method allows this message to be preserved within the clear image.

7.3.2. *Classic approaches to encryption*

Stream-based encryption methods are generally used to preserve the confidentiality of original data in data hiding methods; however, in some cases, block encryption may be used, for example using the AES algorithm (Daemen and Rijmen 1999), or a public key cryptosystem such as Paillier's approach may be preferred (Paillier 1999).

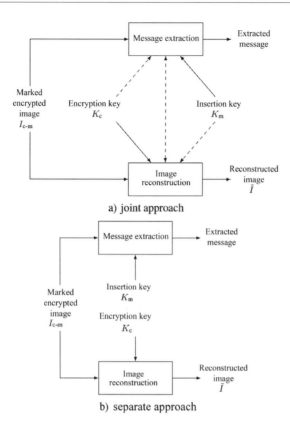

Figure 7.5. *Two possible decryption approaches. The embedded data are extracted and the original image is reconstructed: a) jointly and b) separately*

7.3.2.1. *Stream encryption*

In most state-of-the-art methods (Zhang 2011), the original image I is stream encrypted. As we see from Figure 7.6, an encryption key K_e is used as the seed for a pseudo-random number generator (PRNG). This PRNG is used to obtain a sequence of pseudo-random bytes $s(i, j)$. The encrypted pixels $p_e(i, j)$ are then calculated using an exclusive-or with the values of $s(i, j)$:

$$p_e(i, j) = s(i, j) \oplus p(i, j) \qquad [7.1]$$

As the encryption operation is fully reversible and causes no overflow, the original image I can be retrieved from the encrypted image I_e with no alterations. Note that the pseudo-random sequence may be generated using a cryptographically secure pseudo-random number generator (CSPRNG), a chaotic generator (Li *et al.* 2005), or even the AES algorithm (Daemen and Rijmen 1999) in OFB mode.

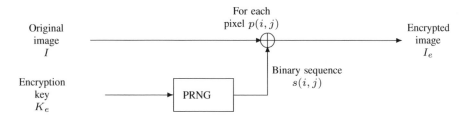

Figure 7.6. *Stream encryption*

7.3.2.2. *Symmetrical block encryption*

Certain methods in the state of the art exploit the correlation within the pixel blocks of images in the clear domain (Puech *et al.* 2008). They thus use symmetrical block encryption to preserve the block structure of pixels in the encrypted image. The most commonly used method is the Advanced Encryption Standard (AES) (Daemen and Rijmen 1999). Designed in 1999 by Joan Daemen and Vincent Rijmen, AES is composed of a set of operations, repeated over several repetition cycles, or rounds. The number of rounds depends on the size of the encryption key: 10 cycles for 128-bit keys, 12 cycles for 192-bit keys or 14 cycles for 256-bit keys. The first stage in encrypting a 128-bit sequence is to apply the *AddRoundKey* operation. Each byte in the sequence is combined with an associated block in the round key using an exclusive-or operation. Next, four different operations are performed during each round: *SubBytes*, *ShiftRows*, *MixColumns* and *AddRoundKey*. The *SubBytes* operation is a nonlinear substitution step where each byte is substituted with another according to a conventionally defined table. The *ShiftRows* operation is a transposition step where the last three lines of the block undergo a cyclical shift. *MixColumns* is a linear shuffle operation that operates on the columns of the block, combining the four bytes of each column. The last round consists of the same operations with the exception of *MixColumns*. The AES algorithm has the capacity to support different encryption modes, such as ECB (*Electronic Code Book*), CBC (*Cipher Block Chaining*), CFB (*Cipher Feedback*), OFB (*Output Feedback*) or CTR (*Counter*), for example.

7.3.2.3. *Public key encryption*

Many data hiding methods that draw on the probabilistic and homomorphic properties of public key cryptosystems use Paillier's cryptosystem to encrypt the original image. Paillier's system, introduced in 1999 (Paillier 1999), involves the following steps. First, to generate the public and private keys, two prime numbers p and q are chosen such that:

$$\gcd(pq,\ (p-1)(q-1)) = 1 \qquad\qquad [7.2]$$

Values n and λ are then calculated:

$$n = pq \text{ et } \lambda = \text{lcm}((p-1),(q-1)) \qquad\qquad [7.3]$$

A number $g \in (\mathbb{Z}/n^2\mathbb{Z})^*$ is selected such that:

$$\exists\, \mu \mid \mu = (L(g^\lambda \bmod (n^2)))^{-1} \bmod (n) \qquad\qquad [7.4]$$

where $L(\cdot)$ is the application defined by:

$$L(x) = \frac{x-1}{n}, \text{ where } x \in \mathbb{N}^* \qquad\qquad [7.5]$$

The public key is thus (n, g) and the private key is (λ, μ). Given a message to encrypt m, with $0 \leq m < n$, in the case of image encryption, m generally corresponds to a pixel block. To encrypt this message, a random number r is generated, with $r \in (\mathbb{Z}/n\mathbb{Z})^*$. Note that choosing r in this way guarantees that the Paillier cryptosystem will be non-deterministic.

The final step is to calculate the encrypted message c:

$$c = \mathcal{E}(m) = g^m \times r^n \bmod (n^2) \qquad\qquad [7.6]$$

where $\mathcal{E}(\cdot)$ is the encryption function of the Paillier ecosystem.

Note here that squaring n results in an inflation of the size of the encrypted message in relation to the clear message.

The original clear message m can then be reconstructed from the encrypted message c:

$$m = \mathcal{D}(c) = L(c^\lambda \bmod (n^2)) \times \mu \bmod (n) \qquad\qquad [7.7]$$

where $\mathcal{D}(\cdot)$ is the encryption function of the Paillier cryptosystem.

Furthermore, Paillier's cryptosystem possesses a homomorphic property in that decrypting the product of two encrypted messages corresponds to summing the two corresponding messages m_1 and m_2 in the clear domain:

$$\mathcal{D}(\mathcal{E}(m_1) \times \mathcal{E}(m_2) \bmod (n^2)) = m_1 + m_2 \bmod (n) \qquad\qquad [7.8]$$

7.3.3. *Evaluation criteria*

Data hiding methods are evaluated based on the quantity of bits embedded in terms of payload, the bit error rate during message extraction, and the visual quality after reconstruction compared to the original clear image. In addition, the visual security level of the marked encrypted image can also be assessed by in-depth statistical analysis.

7.3.3.1. *Quantity of embedded bits*

The quantity of bits embedded in a message is expressed in bits per pixel. For an image with pixels encoded over 256 levels of gray, this quantity is thus between 0 and 8 bpp. A distinction can be made between embedding capacity and payload. Embedding capacity relates to the total number of bits that can be inserted into an image by applying the data hiding method. The payload denotes the total number of bits in a message that can be inserted into the image. Thus, the payload may be significantly lower than the embedding capacity, notably when the chosen data hiding method requires some of the capacity to be sacrificed to leave space for additional information, for example for overflow management (Huang *et al.* 2016) or for pixels that are hard to predict (Puteaux and Puech 2018a).

7.3.3.2. *Bit error rate*

When extracting the message from the marked encrypted image (or the marked decrypted image, where applicable), the bit error rate is calculated by dividing the number of erroneously reconstructed bits by the total number of bits in the secret message. The resulting number of bits must be as low as possible to ensure proper transmission of the secret data inserted into the encrypted image. In most of the state-of-the-art methods, the bit error rate is zero, indicating that the secret message is extracted without error.

7.3.3.3. *Visual quality*

The visual quality of the image that is reconstructed by decrypting the marked encrypted image compared to the original clear image can be evaluated using two different metrics, both widely used in image coding and compression. Note that the quality of the reconstructed image can be evaluated both before and after message extraction. If the chosen data hiding method allows the secret message to be retained in the decoded image, we may evaluate the distortion resulting from message insertion in the original image. However, it is important to realize that some methods are irreversible, and the original image cannot be recovered without alteration after the message has been extracted.

7.3.3.3.1. Peak signal-to-noise ratio

Peak signal-to-noise ratio (PSNR) is used to measure the quality of a reconstructed image with respect to the original image. The following formula is used:

$$\text{PSNR} = 10 \cdot \log_{10} \frac{255^2}{\frac{1}{m \times n} \sum_{i=0}^{m-1} \sum_{j=0}^{n-1} (p(i,j) - p'(i,j))^2} \qquad [7.9]$$

where $p(i,j)$, with $0 \leq i < m$, $0 \leq j < n$, is a pixel in the original image and $p'(i,j)$ is the corresponding pixel in the reconstructed image, both of size $m \times n$ pixels coded on 255 levels of gray.

PSNR is measured in decibels (dB). The PSNR between two images with entirely different content is around 10 dB. For two images which are similar but affected by noise, it is around 15 dB. If the two images are very similar, the value is above 30 dB. Finally, in cases of perfect reconstruction, that is, when the two images are strictly identical, the value of the PSNR tends toward $+ \infty$. Note that many data hiding methods that are considered reversible have a PSNR value of around 50 dB. The major drawback of PSNR is that it fails to take account of the visual quality of the reconstructed image; as such, it cannot be considered to be fully objective. For this reason, another metric – structural similarity (SSIM) – is also used.

7.3.3.3.2. Structural similarity

SSIM is used to evaluate the similarity between the structures of two images, rather than between corresponding pixels, as in the case of PSNR (Wang *et al.* 2004). The underlying hypothesis is that the human visual system is more sensitive to changes in the structure of an image. The formula used is as follows:

$$\text{SSIM}(x,y) = \frac{(2E(x)E(y) + \gamma_1)(2Cov(x,y) + \gamma_2)}{(E(x)^2 + E(y)^2 + \gamma_1)(V(x)^2 + V(y)^2 + \gamma_2)} \qquad [7.10]$$

where x and y are windows in the two images, $E(x)$ is the mean of the set x, $V(x)$ is its variance, $Cov(x,y)$ is the covariance between sets x and y, $\gamma_1 = (0.01 \times 255)^2$ and $\gamma_2 = (0.03 \times 255)^2$.

This formula is applied to different windows in the two images to be compared. The average between the different values obtained is then calculated to obtain the global SSIM value. This value is between 0 and 1; a value of 1 indicates that the two images are strictly identical. Note that it is often necessary to observe at least three decimal places for the SSIM value to be significant.

7.3.3.4. *Visual security level*

No metric has yet been defined specifically to evaluate the visual security level of marked encrypted images. As such, we shall draw on the work of Preishuber *et al.* (2018) to describe the metrics used by many authors to experimentally demonstrate the visual security of image encryption methods. We conclude that a good level of visual security is achieved in the marked encrypted image when the message embedding phase does not affect the security level of the encryption method. On the other hand, if the embedded message is itself encrypted, embedding this message into an encrypted image amounts to hiding "noise in noise"; thus, the encrypted message cannot, *a priori*, be detected in the encrypted domain.

7.3.3.4.1. Correlation coefficient

One classic approach is to observe the correlation between pixels in horizontal, vertical and diagonal directions. M pairs of neighboring pixels (x_i, y_i) are chosen in all three directions, with $x_i \in x$ and $y_i \in y$, in order to calculate the correlation coefficient:

$$corr_{x,\,y} = \frac{\frac{1}{M}\sum_{i=1}^{M}(x_i - E(x)) \times (y_i - E(y))}{\sqrt{\frac{1}{M}\sum_{i=1}^{M}(x_i - E(x))^2}\sqrt{\frac{1}{M}\sum_{i=1}^{M}(y_i - E(y))^2}} \qquad [7.11]$$

where $E(x)$ is the mean of set x.

The value of this correlation coefficient falls between -1 and 1, with -1 and 1 indicating strong correlation and 0 an absence of correlation. As the values of neighboring pixels in the clear domain are strongly correlated, $corr_{x,\,y}$ is generally high for the original image. However, it should be close to zero in the encrypted domain.

7.3.3.4.2. Shannon entropy

Shannon entropy is a measure of the quantity of information used to evaluate the randomness of the distribution of pixels in a marked encrypted image (Shannon 1948):

$$H(I) = -\sum_{k=0}^{N-1} P(\alpha_k) \log_2(P(\alpha_k)) \qquad [7.12]$$

where I is an image of $m \times n$ pixels coded on N values α_k ($0 \le k < N$) and $P(\alpha_k)$ is the probability associated with α_k.

The entropy value is expressed in bits per pixel (bpp) and falls between 0 bpp and $\log_2(N)$ bpp, when the pixel distribution is perfectly uniform. Generally speaking, grayscale images are coded on 256 values. In this case, the maximum entropy is $\log_2(256) = 8$ bpp. The entropy value of a marked encrypted image should be very close to the maximum entropy value.

7.3.3.4.3. χ^2 test

The uniformity of the pixel distribution in a marked encrypted image can also be evaluated using the chi-square test, defined as:

$$\chi^2 = N \sum_{k=0}^{N-1} \left(P(\alpha_k) - \frac{1}{N} \right)^2 \tag{7.13}$$

where the pixels in the image are coded on N values α_k $(0 \leq k < N)$ and $P(\alpha_k)$ is the probability associated with α_k.

The lower the value obtained, the closer the pixel distribution of the marked encrypted image is to a uniform distribution, indicating a higher level of visual security. Note that the square root of the χ^2 value is often used.

7.3.3.4.4. Number of changing pixel rate

The number of changing pixel rate (NPCR) between two images of size $m \times n$ pixels, $p(i,j)$ and $p'(i,j)$ $(0 \leq i < m, 0 \leq j < n)$ is given by Wu *et al.* (2011):

$$\text{NPCR} = \frac{\sum_{i=0}^{m-1} \sum_{j=0}^{n-1} d(i,j)}{m \times n} \times 100 \tag{7.14}$$

where $d(i,j)$ is defined by:

$$d(i,j) = \begin{cases} 1, \text{ if } p(i,j) = p'(i,j) \\ 0, \text{ otherwise.} \end{cases} \tag{7.15}$$

This value is expressed in % and is used to determine the extent to which an encrypted (or marked encrypted) image differs from the original. Thus, the closer the value is to 100%, the larger the difference between the two images, and the higher the level of visual security.

7.3.3.4.5. Unified averaged changed intensity

Unified averaged changed intensity (UACI) is also used to measure the difference between two images of $m \times n$ pixels, of which pixels $p(i,j)$ and $p'(i,j)$ $(0 \leq i < m, 0 \leq j < n)$ are coded on 256 grayscale values (Wu *et al.* 2011):

$$\text{UACI} = \frac{100}{m \times n} \sum_{i=0}^{m-1} \sum_{j=0}^{n-1} \frac{|p(i,j) - p'(i,j)|}{255} \tag{7.16}$$

This value is also expressed as a percentage. The higher the value, the higher the visual security level. Note that the ideal value depends on the range of tones used in the image. This metric can be used to test the sensitivity of the encryption key. The original image is encrypted using two keys with only one different bit, and the resulting images are then compared. In this case, the optimum value of the UACI is 33.33% (Preishuber *et al.* 2018). However, the UACI value is often lower when used to compare an original clear image and its marked encrypted counterpart. Note that there is no statistical decision criterion for this test; optimal values are determined on a purely experimental basis.

7.4. Principal methods

In this section, we shall describe data hiding methods that we consider to be particularly representative of the current state of the art. These are grouped according to key concepts: image partitioning (section 7.4.1), histogram shifting (section 7.4.2), encoding (section 7.4.3), prediction (section 7.4.4) or public key encryption (section 7.4.5). The criteria and characteristics defined in section 7.3 will also be discussed.

7.4.1. *Image partitioning*

In several data hiding methods, the pixels in an image are divided into two groups. Those in the first group are used to embed a secret message, while those in the second group are not marked and are used to reconstruct the original, clear image. Partitioning can be performed before or after encryption, depending on the chosen methods. Some authors have applied this partition in a pseudo-random way by using the data hiding key (Zhang 2011); more sophisticated techniques rely on an analysis of the properties of the clear pixels (Ma *et al.* 2013).

7.4.1.1. *Use of the data hiding key*

In one of the very first data hiding methods, Zhang (2011) proposed a stream-based approach to encrypting the original image. The encrypted image is then divided into blocks of $s \times s$ pixels, with the aim of hiding one bit of the secret message in each block. The pixels in each block are then partitioned into two groups, S_0 and S_1, using the data hiding key. If the bit of the secret message to be inserted is 0 (respectively, 1), the three least significant bits (LSB) of each pixel in S_0 (respectively, S_1) are inverted. During the decoding phase, the marked encrypted image is decrypted in order to obtain an approximation of the original image. The five most significant bit (MSB) planes are perfectly reconstructed, and only the LSB may be altered. A fluctuation function is then used to evaluate the irregularities in the S_0 and S_1 groups of reconstructed pixels. The bits of the secret message can then be extracted and the original configuration of each block can be recovered. However, while the chances of perfectly reconstructing the original image can be improved by increasing the size of the blocks, Zhang's method is not reversible as perfect reconstruction is not guaranteed. Moreover, the payload is low (less than 0.1 bpp) since only one bit is inserted per block. Improvements to this method have been proposed in the literature (Zhang 2011; Hong *et al.* 2012).

7.4.1.2. *Use of a fluctuation function*

Ma *et al.* (2013) were the first to propose a RRBE approach, in a radical break from existing methods. The authors began by dividing the original image into blocks. The correlation between pixels in each block was evaluated using a fluctuation function. The blocks were then partitioned into two groups, A and B: A is composed of textured blocks and B of relatively homogeneous blocks. Blocks from group A are placed at the beginning of the image and blocks from group B are placed at the end. To free up space for a secret message, the bits of the LSB planes of A are inserted, by histogram shifting, into the clear domain in the group B pixels. The resulting image is then stream-encrypted and the number of pixels that can be marked is stored in the LSB of the first pixels of A. Using this information, a secret message can be embedded by simply substituting the LSBs of the other pixels of A. Note that the first three LSB planes of each pixel can be used. The total payload of the marked encrypted image can thus reach 0.5 bpp: a payload 10 times higher than that offered by previous state-of-the-art methods. Finally, in the reconstruction phase, message extraction and original image reconstruction can be performed separately.

7.4.2. *Histogram shifting*

Histogram shifting techniques have been used in many data hiding methods, due to their simplicity and capacity to produce very high quality images after decrypting the marked encrypted image. Clear, natural images present high levels of correlation between neighboring pixels. Thus, the distribution of differences between pixels is modeled by a Laplacian centered about zero. This statistical data can then be used to embed data using histogram shifting methods (Huang *et al.* 2016; Xiao *et al.* 2017; Ge *et al.* 2019).

7.4.2.1. *Pixel difference or prediction error histograms*

Huang *et al.* (2016) noted that existing data hiding algorithms designed for the clear domain cannot be applied in the encrypted domain. This is due to the fact that classical encryption methods are unable to maintain the correlation between neighboring pixels without creating a security risk. The authors thus developed a new strategy for image encryption that is robust with respect to the application of classic data hiding methods in the clear domain. First, the original image is divided into non-overlapping blocks. All pixels in each block are encrypted by applying an exclusive-or with the same pseudo-randomly generated byte. Next, the blocks in the resulting image are pseudo-randomly swapped. Note that pixels within the same block are not swapped: only the order of the blocks changes. Using this encryption method, the statistical properties of the clear image, notably pixel difference or prediction error histograms, are preserved. This means that existing data hiding algorithms designed for the clear domain can now be applied directly in the encrypted domain. However, embedding capacity is limited by the need to manage overflow problems.

7.4.2.2. *Homomorphism and pixel value ordering*

Xiao *et al.* (2017) proposed an adaptation of the pixel value ordering concept, defined for the clear domain by Li *et al.* (2013), for the homomorphic encrypted domain. The authors began by noting that, by adapting the encryption method, it was possible to obtain a histogram of pixel differences with a zero-centered Laplacian distribution, identical to that of the clear domain, in the encrypted domain. After encryption, the image is divided into non-overlapping blocks of 2×2 pixels. The four pixels in each block are then rearranged into ascending order, noted $\{p_{e1}, p_{e2}, p_{e3}, p_{e4}\}$, with $p_{e1} \leq p_{e2} \leq p_{e3} \leq p_{e4}$. The pixel with the highest value (p_{e4}) is then selected for data hiding. This operation is carried out by calculating the difference d between p_{e4} and p_{e3}. A bit $b \in \{0, 1\}$ is then inserted into p_{e4} as a function of the value of d, resulting in a marked version p_{e-m4} such that:

$$p_{e-m4} = \begin{cases} p_{e4} + b \text{ if } d = 1 \\ p_{e4} + 1 \text{ if } d > 1 \\ p_{e4} + b \text{ if } d = 0 \\ p_{e4} + 1 \text{ if } d < 0 \end{cases} \qquad [7.17]$$

Note that a similar operation can also be applied to embed a bit in the pixel with the lowest value p_{e1}. In this method, the order of the pixels remains unchanged after the data hiding. In terms of the histogram, this operation is equivalent to expanding the bins associated with the difference values of 0 and 1, and shifting the other bins. This method offers a solution to the data expansion problem encountered with many similar methods in the encrypted domain. Nevertheless, the embedding capacity is limited: 0.2 bpp. This is due to the fact that the marked encrypted image needs to store a location map of blocks that are prone to overflow, resulting in a significant payload reduction.

7.4.2.3. *Pixel value histogram*

Ge *et al.* (2019) recently proposed a data hiding method based on a shift in the pixel value histogram. Instead of using the pixel difference or prediction error histogram, as in Huang *et al.* (2016), the authors suggest modifying pixel values directly within a block. Unlike Xiao *et al.* (2017), the pixels used for data hiding are not necessarily those with the highest, or lowest, value in the block. Two reference pixels, p_{ei} and p_{ej}, with $p_{ei} < p_{ej}$, are selected in a pseudo-random manner using a data hiding key. All other pixels p_{ek} in the block are then modified to p_{e-mk} in order to embed a bit b of the secret message:

$$p_{e-mk} = \begin{cases} p_{ek} - 1 \text{ if } p_{ek} < p_{ei} \\ p_{ek} - b \text{ if } p_{ek} = p_{ei} \\ p_{ek} \quad \text{ if } p_{ei} < p_{ek} < p_{ej} \\ p_{ek} + b \text{ if } p_{ek} = p_{ej} \\ p_{ek} + 1 \text{ if } p_{ek} < p_{ej} \end{cases} \qquad [7.18]$$

This operation is applied to all blocks in the image. Furthermore, secret data can be embedded several times throughout the image: this has the effect of increasing the embedding capacity. With a single pass over the image, the Ge *et al.* (2019) method embeds half of the payload obtained in the Xiao *et al.* (2017) approach, since the size of the location map for blocks subject to overflow problems is larger. If several passes are performed, on the other hand, a payload of 0.8 bpp can be reached if a degradation in the quality of the original image is acceptable.

7.4.3. *Encoding*

Some of the methods in the state of the art apply encoding to the image data – before or after encryption – in order to optimize the number of bits needed to represent these data. This compression phase vacates memory space that can then be used to embed bits of a secret message. There are many available algorithms that can be used for this encoding. The Qian and Zhang (2016) method, based on distributed source coding, and the Cao *et al.* (2016) method, based on sparse coding, have shown particularly interesting performances.

7.4.3.1. *Distributed source encoding*

Qian and Zhang (2016) proposed the use of distributed source encoding in a data hiding method. During the encoding phase, the original image is first encrypted using a stream approach. The encrypted image I_e with pixels $p_e(i, j)$, with $0 \le i < m$ and

$0 \leq j < n$, is then split into four sub-images $I_e^{(k)}$ ($1 \leq k \leq 4$), of which the pixels $p_e^{(k)}(i,j)$, with $0 \leq i < \frac{m}{2}$ and $0 \leq j < \frac{n}{2}$, are such that:

$$\begin{cases} p_e^{(1)}(i,j) = p_e(2i-1, 2j-1) \\ p_e^{(2)}(i,j) = p_e(2i-1, 2j) \\ p_e^{(3)}(i,j) = p_e(2i, 2j-1) \\ p_e^{(4)}(i,j) = p_e(2i, 2j) \end{cases} \qquad [7.19]$$

Note that the decryption of each of the sub-images $I_e^{(k)}$ produces a miniature copy of the original image. Once the sub-images $I_e^{(k)}$ have been obtained, bits from the three MSB planes of $I_e^{(2)}$, $I_e^{(3)}$ and $I_e^{(4)}$ are permutated and compressed using LDPC codes (Slepian and Wolf 1973). This compression vacates space to embed a secret message. The decoding phase is fully separable. The unmodified sub-image $I_e^{(1)}$ is decrypted then oversampled by bilinear interpolation in order to obtain a reference image to reconstruct the clear version of the marked image. For reconstruction purposes, LDPC codes are decoded using a sum-product algorithm (Liu *et al.* 2009).

7.4.3.2. *Sparse coding*

Cao *et al.* (2016) developed a data hiding method using sparse coding with the aim of permitting a high payload. A three-step RRBE encoding approach is used. First, the original image is divided into patches. These patches are then represented using a redundant dictionary with sparse coding. Next, the most homogeneous patches with the smallest residual errors are selected as the location for secret message insertion and are represented using sparse coefficients. The residual errors are encoded and embedded in patches that are not selected for data hiding, using a classic data hiding algorithm for clear images. Finally, stream encryption is used to protect the clear data. Once the image has been encrypted, bits of a secret message can be inserted into the designated space. In this case, the decoding phase is separative and reversible. The original image can be losslessly reconstructed, using the residual errors extracted from the unmarked patches. This means that the secret message can also be found.

7.4.4. *Prediction*

In some state-of-the-art methods, the bits of certain pixels in the encrypted image are replaced by the bits of a secret message during the encoding phase. Their original value is therefore lost and must be predicted during decoding in order to produce a high-quality reconstruction of the original clear image. Prediction may be carried out based on the differences between clear pixel blocks and their encrypted counterparts (Puech *et al.* 2008), or by exploiting the high levels of correlation between neighboring pixels in the clear domain (Wu and Sun 2014).

7.4.4.1. *Prediction based on local standard deviation*

Puech *et al.* (2008) proposed one of the very first data hiding methods in an article published in 2008. This method uses a VRAE approach for encoding. The original image is encrypted in blocks of 16 pixels in grayscale (128 bits) using the AES algorithm in ECB mode. One bit of the secret message is then embedded in each block of the encrypted image, corresponding to an embedding capacity of 0.0625 bpp. Note that a data hiding key is used as the seed for a pseudo-random generator to identify the pixel to mark and the location of the bit to replace with a bit from the secret message. The marked encrypted image is obtained once all blocks have been traversed. During the decoding phase, the message is extracted by using the data hiding key to read the bits of the pixels that have been marked. However, after extraction, the pixels are still marked by the message bits, which makes the image difficult to decode. To overcome this problem, local analysis of the standard deviation in each block is performed. For each block of the marked encrypted image, the marked bit is located using the data hiding key, then replaced by the two possible values of the substituted original bit (0 and 1). This gives us two decrypted configurations: one corresponds to the original clear image block, while the other is erroneous and looks like a fully encrypted block. The hypothesis that the standard deviation in an encrypted (wrongly decrypted) block is greater than that in a clear (correctly decrypted) block is then used. The standard deviation associated with the two decrypted configurations is calculated and the pattern with the lower standard deviation value is selected as the clear block. Note that, as the data hiding key is required to reconstruct the original image, extraction and decoding must be carried out jointly.

7.4.4.2. *Prediction by interpolation*

Wu and Sun (2014) developed a data hiding method in two different forms: a joint approach and a separative approach. In both cases, the first step is a stream encryption of the original image. A subset of pixels is then selected, as a function of the data hiding key, to insert a hidden message. Note that the neighbors of the selected pixels will be used to predict these pixels during decoding. In the joint approach, to insert a hidden bit, the LSB of the selected pixels are inverted if the message bit is equal to 1, or left unchanged if the message bit is 0. During decoding, unmarked neighboring pixels are interpolated to predict the original value of each marked pixel and the value of the inserted bit. In the separative approach, the LSB of the selected pixels are replaced by the value of a bit in the secret message. An approximation of the original image is reconstructed during decoding using a median filter. Improvements to these approaches have since been proposed (Dragoi *et al.* 2017; Dragoi and Coltuc 2018).

7.4.5. *Public key encryption*

Data hiding methods using the homomorphic properties of public key cryptosystems can be grouped into two categories depending on the chosen encryption approach. A distinction is made between methods based on Paillier's cryptosystem (Chen *et al.* 2014) and those that use learning with errors (LWE) (Ke *et al.* 2016).

7.4.5.1. *Methods based on Pailler's cryptosystem*

Chen *et al.* (2014) proposed the first data hiding method based on the use of the Paillier cryptosystem. Each pixel in the original image is split into two distinct parts: an even integer, made up of the seven MSB, and the LSB. Each part is encrypted independently, and a bit from the message is embedded into each pair of neighboring pixels. During decoding, all of the pairs of decrypted pixels are compared in order to reconstruct the whole of the secret message and the original clear image. The main drawback in this approach is the fact that overflow problems are not managed. Shiu *et al.* (2015) proposed a solution to this problem, applying the concept of difference expansion to the homomorphic encrypted domain. Note that both of these methods rely on an RRBE approach. Methods using the Paillier cryptosystem with VRAE have since been proposed by Wu *et al.* (2016) and Zhang *et al.* (2016).

7.4.5.2. *Methods based on LWE encryption*

The first data hiding method using LWE encryption was proposed by Ke *et al.* (2016). The authors indicate that the use of an LWE algorithm offers a high level of security, simple and fast implementation, and controllable redundancy for hidden data insertion. They established parameters for the LWE encryption and described their multi-level data hiding approach, based on recoding the redundancy in the encrypted domain using homomorphic operations. The main drawback of this approach is that it is not fully separative.

7.5. Comparison and discussion

A comparison between the different state-of-the-art methods described in section 7.4 is shown in Table 7.1. Methods are classed by year (from 2008 to 2019), encoding approach (RRBE or VRAE), decoding type (joint or separative), reversability and payload.

The most obvious feature of this table is that the earliest methods in the state of the art all present the same characteristics: space is created for message insertion after encryption, the original image cannot be reconstructed without error, and the payload is very low (< 0.1 bpp). The first separative method was described by Zhang (2012). Note that this property is important in terms of the practical usability of data hiding methods. After 2013, following the publication of Ma *et al.*'s method (Ma *et al.* 2013), VRAE began to be used in an increasing number of approaches. This resulted in increased payloads compared to earlier methods (> 0.1 bpp), although the value remained relatively low (< 0.5 bpp). Over the following years, several different models were developed that offer full reversability in reconstructing the original image. However, none of these approaches offer high capacity, that is, a payload close to or in excess of one bit per pixel. Methods based on public key encryption, indicated by an asterisk (∗) in Table 7.1, have a payload expressed in bits per bit of the encrypted image (bpb) rather than bits per pixel (bpp). It is important to note that the use of the Paillier or LWE public key cryptosystems results in an increase in the size of the image after encryption. Depending on the method, if the pixels in the original image are coded on 8 bits, almost 2048 bits may be required in the encrypted domain, as shown by Ke *et al.* (2018). A comparison of the payload in bpp for the marked encrypted image is therefore not appropriate and would result in a false interpretation of the results.

Year	Method	Encoding	Decoding	Reversibility	Payload
2008	Puech *et al.* (2008)	VRAE	Joint	No	< 0.1 bpp
2011	Zhang (2011)	VRAE	Joint	No	< 0.1 bpp
2012	Hong *et al.* (2012)	VRAE	Joint	No	< 0.1 bpp
	Zhang (2012)	CLEI	Separative	No	< 0.1 bpp
2013	Ma *et al.* (2013)	RRBE	Separative	Yes	< 0.5 bpp
	Chen *et al.* (2014)	RRBE	Joint	No	< 0.001 bpb*
2014	Wu and Sun (2014) (1)	RRBE	Joint	No	< 0.5 bpp
	Wu and Sun (2014) (2)	RRBE	Separative	No	< 0.5 bpp
2015	Shiu *et al.* (2015)	RRBE	Joint	Yes	< 0.001 bpb*
	Cao *et al.* (2016)	RRBE	Separative	Yes	< 1 bpp
	Huang *et al.* (2016)	RRBE	Separative	Yes	< 0.1 bpp
	Wu *et al.* (2016) (1)	VRAE	Separative	No	< 0.5 bpb*
	Wu *et al.* (2016) (2)	VRAE	Joint	Yes	< 0.01 bpb*
	Qian and Zhang (2016)	VRAE	Separative	No	< 0.5 bpp
2016	Zhang *et al.* (2016) (1)	VRAE	Joint	Yes	< 0.001 bpb*
	Zhang *et al.* (2016) (2)	RRBE	Separative	No	< 0.001 bpb*
	Ke *et al.* (2016)	VRAE	Joint	Yes	< 0.5 bpb*
	Xiao *et al.* (2017)	RRBE	Separative	Yes	< 0.5 bpp
2017	Dragoi *et al.* (2017) (1)	RRBE	Joint	Yes	< 0.1 bpp
	Dragoi *et al.* (2017) (2)	RRBE	Separative	Yes	< 0.1 bpp
2018	Dragoi and Coltuc (2018) (1)	RRBE	Joint	Yes	< 0.1 bpp
	Dragoi and Coltuc (2018) (2)	RRBE	Separative	Yes	< 0.1 bpp
2019	Ge *et al.* (2019)	VRAE	Separative	Yes	< 1 bpp

Table 7.1. *Comparison of key methods in the state of the art*

COMMENT ON TABLE 7.1.– *Comparison of methods by encoding approach (RRBE or VRAE), decoding type (joint or separative), reversibility (in the strict sense of the* *term, i.e. PSNR→ ∞), and payload (in bpp, bits-per-pixel, or in bpb, bits-per-bit, for models marked with a *).*

7.6. A high-capacity data hiding approach based on MSB prediction

None of the methods presented above combine a high payload (greater than or equal to 1 bpp) and high visual quality (greater than 50 dB). In most cases, the values of the least significant bits (LSBs) are replaced to insert the bits of a secret message. However, when an image is encrypted, it is difficult to detect whether or not it contains a secret message. This is due to the fact that the pixel values of an encrypted image are generated pseudo-randomly. Thus, the correlation between a pixel and its neighbors is very low. For this reason, Puteaux and Puech (2018a) propose using the most significant bit (MSB) values instead of the LSB to embed the secret message, taking the opposite approach to previous state-of-the-art methods. We note that confidentiality in the encrypted domain remains the same and that, during the decoding phase, MSB values are simpler to predict than LSB values.

In this section, we shall begin by introducing the general scheme of this data hiding method. Unlike previous methods, the secret message is embedded by replacing the values of the MSBs. Since the values of the replaced MSBs are lost during the message insertion phase, we must be able to predict them without error during the decoding phase. Next, we provide a detailed presentation of two possible approaches, according to the most desirable characteristic: strict reversibility (PSNR → +∞) or maximum payload (1 bpp). The first approach is not perfectly reversible but allows the insertion of one bit of the secret message per pixel: this approach is known as CPE-HCRDH, high-capacity reversible data hiding approach with correction of prediction errors. The second approach, in which the original image is perfectly reconstructed but the inserted message must be adapted, is called EPE-HCRDH: high-capacity reversible data hiding approach with embedded prediction errors.

7.6.1. *General description of the method*

7.6.1.1. *Encoding*

The encoding phase consists of three steps: detection of prediction errors in the MSBs, accounting for prediction errors combined with image encryption, and embedding of the secret message by replacing the MSBs. An outline diagram of the encoding method is shown in Figure 7.7.

In this method, since the secret message is embedded by MSB substitution, the original MSB values are lost after the secret message is embedded. Thus, it is important to be able to predict these values without error during the decoding phase.

To recover the original image, the previously reconstructed pixels are used to predict the current pixel value. The first step is thus to analyze the content of the original image to detect any prediction errors:

– consider the current pixel $p(i, j)$, with $0 \leq i < m$ and $0 \leq j < n$, and its inverse value, $inv(i, j) = (p(i, j) + 128) \mod 256$. As the difference between these two values is 128, the inverse value corresponds to the original value of $p(i, j)$ but with an inversed MSB;

– using the values of the neighbors of $p(i, j)$, we calculate the value $pred(i, j)$, regarded as a predictor in the decoding phase;

– we calculate the absolute difference between $pred(i, j)$ and $p(i, j)$ and between $pred(i, j)$ and $inv(i, j)$. The resulting values are noted Δ and Δ^{inv} and are such that:

$$\begin{cases} \Delta = |pred(i, j) - p(i, j)| \\ \Delta^{inv} = |pred(i, j) - inv(i, j)| \end{cases} \qquad [7.20]$$

– we then compare the values of Δ and Δ^{inv}. If $\Delta < \Delta^{inv}$, then there is no prediction error, since the original value of $p(i, j)$ is closer to the predictor than the inverse value. Otherwise, an error is identified and its location will be specified in a binary error location map, as shown in Figure 7.7.

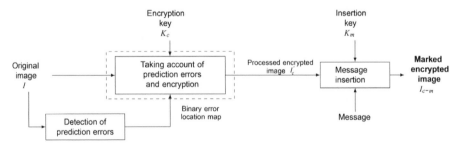

Figure 7.7. *General scheme of the encoding method*

Depending on the chosen approach, the binary error location map may be used in one of two ways. The original image may be pre-processed to correct prediction errors, resulting in an image I', which is very similar to the original. The other option is to indicate the location of prediction errors in the encrypted domain after encrypting the original image, instead of correcting them.

In both cases, the clear image is encrypted using a stream approach, as described in section 7.3.2. This results in the encrypted pixels $p_e(i, j)$:

$$p_e(i, j) = s(i, j) \oplus p(i, j) \qquad [7.21]$$

where $s(i, j)$ is the byte corresponding to $p(i, j)$ in a pseudo-random binary sequence and $\oplus$ is the exclusive-or operation.

Note that in the case of the error signaling approach, the encrypted image will be modified.

During the message insertion phase, using the data hiding key K_m, the secret message is encrypted to prevent it from being detected in the marked encrypted image. Next, the pixels in the encrypted image are passed through in scanline order (left to right and top to bottom), and the MSB of each available pixel is replaced with a bit b_k, with $0 \leq k < m \times n$, from the secret message in order to obtain the corresponding pixel $p_{e-m}(i, j)$:

$$p_{e-m}(i, j) = b_k \times 128 + (p_e(i, j) \bmod 128) \qquad [7.22]$$

Note that only the first pixel cannot be marked, since its value cannot be predicted: this pixel is therefore left unchanged.

7.6.1.2. Decoding

Since the method is separable, the secret message can be extracted and the original clear image $\tilde{I}$ can be reconstructed independently during the decoding phase. $\tilde{I}$ is strictly identical to the original image I or to the pre-processed image I', which is very similar to the original image, depending on the chosen approach. There are then three possible scenarios for the recipient of the data:

1) the recipient only has the data hiding key K_m;

2) the recipient only has the encryption key K_e;

3) the recipient has both keys.

A general outline of the decoding phase is shown in Figure 7.8.

If the recipient of the data only has the data hiding key K_m, the pixels in the marked encrypted image will be read in scanline order and the MSB of each pixel will be extracted to obtain the bits of the encrypted secret message:

$$b_k = p_{e-m}(i, j)/128 \qquad [7.23]$$

where $0 \leq k < m \times n$ and relates to the index of the extracted message bit.

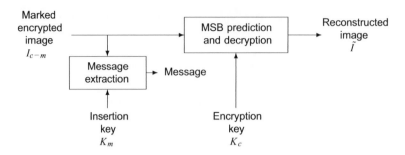

Figure 7.8. *General outline of the decoding method*

The corresponding clear version of the secret message is then obtained using the data hiding key.

In the second case, if the recipient of the data holds only the encryption key K_e, image $\tilde{I}$ can be reconstructed in the form it had prior to message insertion and encryption:

1) the encryption key K_e is used to generate a pseudo-random binary sequence of $m \times n$ bytes $s(i, j)$;

2) the pixels in the marked encrypted image are read in scanline order, and the seven LSB of each pixel are reconstructed by applying an exclusive-or between the marked encrypted value $p_{e-m}(i, j)$ and the corresponding byte $s(i, j)$ in the pseudo-random binary sequence:

$$\tilde{p}(i, j) = s(i, j) \oplus p_{e-m}(i, j) \tag{7.24}$$

where $\oplus$ is the exclusive-or operation;

3) the value of the MSB is predicted in the following manner:

- the value of the predictor $pred(i, j)$ is calculated using the values of neighboring pixels that have already been reconstructed;

- the two possible values of the original pixel are generated, with MSB $= 0$ and MSB $= 1$. The differences between these two values and $pred(i, j)$ are calculated and noted Δ^0 and Δ^1:

$$\begin{cases} \Delta^0 = \left| pred(i, j) - \tilde{p}(i, j)^{MSB=0} \right| \\ \Delta^1 = \left| pred(i, j) - \tilde{p}(i, j)^{MSB=1} \right| \end{cases} \tag{7.25}$$

- the lowest value from Δ^0 and Δ^1 gives us the desired value of the original pixel:

$$\tilde{p}(i,j) = \begin{cases} \tilde{p}(i,j)^{\mathrm{MSB}=0}, \text{ if } \Delta^0 < \Delta^1 \\ \tilde{p}(i,j)^{\mathrm{MSB}=1}, \text{ otherwise} \end{cases} \qquad [7.26]$$

7.6.2. *The CPE-HCRDH approach*

In the CPE-HCRDH approach, shown in Figure 7.9, the first step is to pre-process the original image to eliminate any prediction errors, enabling a high-quality reconstruction of the original image during the decoding phase. The pre-processed image is then encrypted. During the data hiding phase, each pixel in the encrypted image is marked with one bit of the message. Using this approach, a maximum payload of 1 bpp can be attained.

7.6.2.1. *Choice of predictor*

As we saw in section 7.6.1.1, the value of the current pixel is predicted using those of the previous pixels. In this approach, the mean value of the pixel to the left and the pixel above the current pixel is used as the predictor $pred(i,j)$:

$$pred(i,j) = \frac{p(i-1,j) + p(i,j-1)}{2} \qquad [7.27]$$

Note that a specific treatment is used for pixels in the first line and the first column.

Using the mean value as a predictor minimized the modification in the value of the current pixel in cases of error, notably when the difference between the value of the current pixel and that of one of its neighbors is large.

7.6.2.2. *Image pre-processing*

Once prediction errors have been detected, the original image I is pre-processed to generate an image I' free from prediction errors. The value of the prediction error is observed for all pixels concerned, then the minimum modification required to correct the error in the current pixel is calculated. The modification used to eliminate all errors during the decoding phase is given in equation [7.28]:

$$|pred(i,j) - p(i,j)| < 64 \qquad [7.28]$$

The pre-processing steps applied to the original image to correct all prediction errors are shown in Algorithm 7.1.

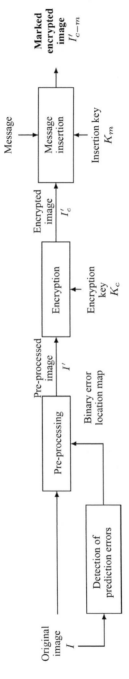

Figure 7.9. *Encoding using the CPE-HCRDH approach*

Algorithm 7.1. Pre-processing algorithm

Require: Original image I of size $m \times n$ pixels
Ensure: Preprocessed image I' of size $m \times n$ pixels
  for $i \leftarrow 0$ **to** m **do**
    for $j \leftarrow 0$ **to** n **do**
      $inv(i,j) \leftarrow (p(i,j) + 128) \bmod 256$;
      if $i = 0$ **or** $j = 0$ **then**
        specific treatment;
      else
        $pred(i,j) \leftarrow \frac{p(i-1,j)+p(i,j-1)}{2}$;
      end if
      $\Delta \leftarrow |pred(i,j) - p(i,j)|$;
      $\Delta^{inv} \leftarrow |pred(i,j) - inv(i,j)|$;
      if $\Delta \geq \Delta^{inv}$ **then**
        if $p(i,j) < 128$ **then**
          $p'(i,j) \leftarrow pred(i,j) - 63$;
        else
          $p'(i,j) \leftarrow pred(i,j) + 63$;
        end if
      else
        $p'(i,j) \leftarrow p(i,j)$;
      end if
    end for
  end for

The predicted image I' is then encrypted. The secret message is inserted by replacing the MSB of each pixel in the encrypted image I'_e with a message bit, following equation [7.22]. Finally, the marked encrypted image I'_{e-m} is obtained, with a maximum payload of 1 bpp.

7.6.2.3. *Message extraction and image reconstruction*

During decoding, to extract the secret message, the marked encrypted image I'_{e-m} is read and the MSB for each pixel is simply extracted using equation [7.23]. The original preprocessed image I' can also be reconstructed without loss. To do this, the marked encrypted image I'_{e-m} is decrypted to give the seven LSB of each pixel (equation [7.24]), then the value of the MSB is predicted by applying equations [7.25] and [7.26]. Note that the reconstructed image is very similar to the original image.

7.6.3. *The EPE-HCRDH approach*

In the IEPE-HCRDH approach, the main aim is to ensure perfect reconstruction of the original image. In this case, the payload may be significantly lower as the location of prediction errors must be indicated. The embedded message is modified in order to take account of the error location map, constructed during the error prediction detection phase. The original image is then encrypted without pre-processing, then the location of the prediction errors is inserted into the encrypted image. Bits of the secret message can then only be inserted into available pixels. At the end of the decoding process, the original image is reconstructed without loss due to the fact that prediction errors have been signaled: this results in a PSNR value which tends toward $+\infty$. A general overview of this approach is presented in Figure 7.10.

7.6.3.1. *Predictor choice*

For each pixel, two neighboring pixels may be used as predictors: the pixel on the left $p(i, j - 1)$ and the pixel directly above $p(i - 1, j)$. To identify which of these pixels to use as the predictor, the absolute value of their difference with the current pixel $p(i, j)$ is calculated and the nearest value is selected:

$$\text{If} \quad |p(i - 1, j) - p(i, j)| < |p(i, j - 1) - p(i, j)|$$

$$\text{then,} \qquad pred(i, j) = p(i - 1, j) \qquad\qquad [7.29]$$

$$\text{otherwise,} \qquad pred(i, j) = p(i, j - 1)$$

In certain cases, the other value may be used to predict the inverse of the pixel $inv(i, j)$ during error prediction, but the result remains the same. Note that the mean of the left and upper pixel may also be used as the predictor, as in the CPE-HCRDH approach, but the results obtained experimentally in this case were not as good.

7.6.3.2. *Signaling the location of errors*

During the prediction error detection stage, the locations of errors are indicated in a binary error location map, as described in section 7.6.1.1. Next, the original image I is encrypted, and the encrypted image I_e is adapted prior to data hiding in order to eliminate prediction errors. The image is divided into blocks of 8 pixels then read in scanline order. If there is at least one prediction error in a block, according to the binary error location map, the current block is flagged on both sides by replacing the MSB of each pixel in the previous and following blocks with a 1. In the current block, the MSB is replaced by a value of 1 if there is a prediction error and by 0 otherwise, as shown in Figure 7.11. If there are no errors in the current block and if it is not used for flagging purposes, then all eight pixels in this block will be used for message embedding, as described in section 7.6.1.1. If errors are found in two adjacent blocks, the flag indicating the end of the error is shifted to the next error-free block. This reduces the payload loss since flags may be used for more than one prediction error. Note that smaller blocks may be used, but the statistical risk of part of the secret message being identified as a flag is increased. Using blocks of eight pixels gives a

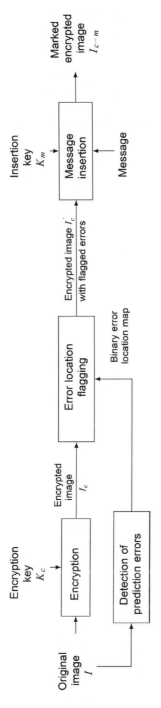

Figure 7.10. *Encoding using the EPE-HCRDH approach*

good tradeoff between payload loss and the risk of false alarms. Few pixels cannot be marked with bits of the secret message, and the probability of part of the message being mistaken for a flag is very low ($\frac{1}{2^8}$).

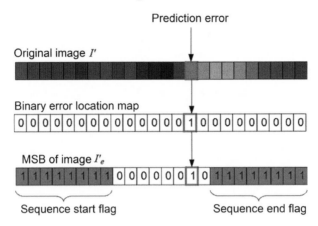

Figure 7.11. *Signaling prediction errors*

This method produces an encrypted image I_e' with embedded prediction errors. With this type of processing, during the insertion phase, the MSB values of each pixel can be extracted and the error location information can be used to detect which pixels can be marked with secret message bits (i.e. in all blocks where there are no prediction errors and that are not used as flags). All available pixels are then marked to obtain the encrypted marked image I_{e-m}, using equation [7.22].

7.6.3.3. *Message extraction and image reconstruction*

The secret message can be extracted during the decoding process using the following steps:

– the pixels of the marked encrypted image I_{e-m} are read and the MSB value for each pixel is extracted, following equation [7.23], and stored. All bits extracted up until the first sequence of 8 bits equal to 1 are considered to belong to the secret message;

– a sequence of 8 bits equal to 1 indicates the start of a sequence that includes prediction errors. Given that the following pixels were not marked during the message insertion phase, pixels will be skipped over up until the next sequence of eight MSBs equal to 1, which indicates the end of the error sequence;

– this process is repeated throughout the whole image.

Furthermore, since this method is entirely reversible, the original image I is perfectly reconstructed. The marked encrypted image I_{e-m} is first decrypted to obtain the seven LSBs for each pixel using equation [7.24]. The values of the MSB of each pixel are then predicted using equations [7.25] and [7.26].

7.6.4. *Experimental results for both approaches*

The two approaches were applied to the same original image of 512×512 pixels, shown in Figure 7.12, taken from the BOWS-2 database (Bas and Furon 2008).

Figure 7.12. *Original image I taken from the BOWS-2 database (Bas and Furon 2008)*

Figure 7.13 shows the results obtained using the CPE-HCRDH approach, while Figure 7.14 shows the results obtained using the EPE-HCRDH approach. The location of pixels concerned by an MSB prediction error is shown in white in Figures 7.13(a) and 7.14(a). We see that the number and location of prediction errors differ, since the predictors used in each case are not the same, as we saw in sections 7.6.2.1 and 7.6.3.1; nevertheless, they are of a similar order of magnitude.

In the CPE-HCRDH approach (Figure 7.13(a)), the MSB of certain pixels in the original image are wrongly predicted if pixel values are not adjusted during the pre-processing phase. In the EPE-HCRDH approach (Figure 7.14(a)), the pixels concerned by prediction errors (in white) cannot be marked. Furthermore, the pixels in gray cannot be marked either as they are used as flags or form part of a sequence containing one or more errors. Note that prediction errors are often encountered on contours; moreover, a single block can sometimes contain multiple errors. In this case, the payload reduction is lower. The histogram in Figure 7.13(b) shows the distribution of prediction errors when the CPE-HDRDH approach is used, alongside the modifications that must be applied to the pixels in order to remove these errors. Figure 7.13(c) shows the same image after pre-processing using Algorithm 7.1. We see that the pre-processed image is very similar to the original image: the PSNR value is 46.87 dB, with an SSIM of 0.9997. Figure 7.13(d) shows the pre-processed image after stream encryption using the encryption key. Figure 7.14(b) shows the encrypted image obtained using the EPE-HCRDH approach, and Figure 7.14(c) corresponds to this image after prediction errors have been flagged. The content of the original image and the locations of the prediction error are visually confidential. Figures 7.13(e) and 7.14(d) show the marked encrypted images obtained at the end of the encoding phase, after embedding a secret message. In the CPE-HCRDH approach, each pixel in the pre-processed image is used to embed one bit of the secret message (payload = 1 bpp). In the EPE-HCRDH approach, pixels are marked to signal prediction errors and although the payload is lower, it is still high, with a value of 0.9220 bpp. Figures 7.13(f) and 7.14(e) show the reconstructed images after data extraction. Figure 7.13(f) is identical to the pre-processed image (PSNR = 46.87 dB), while the original image is perfectly reconstructed in the case of EPE-HCRDH, resulting in a PSNR which tends toward $+\infty$ and an SSIM of 1 (Figure 7.14(e)). Finally, note that the secret message is extracted without error in both cases.

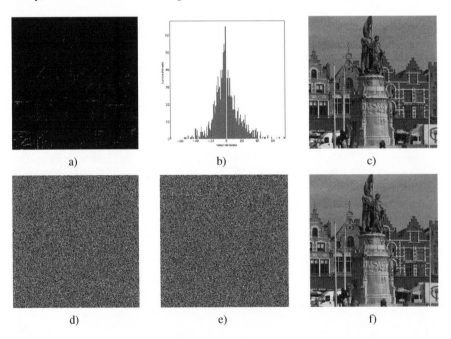

Figure 7.13. *Experimental results obtained using the CPE-HCRDH approach, with a payload of 1 bpp: a) location of errors, number of errors = 1 242 (0.47 %); b) histogram of prediction errors, c) pre-processed image I', PSNR = 46.87 dB; d) encrypted image I'_c; e) marked encrypted image I'_{e-m}, f) reconstructed image I', PSNR = 46.87 dB, SSIM = 0.9997*

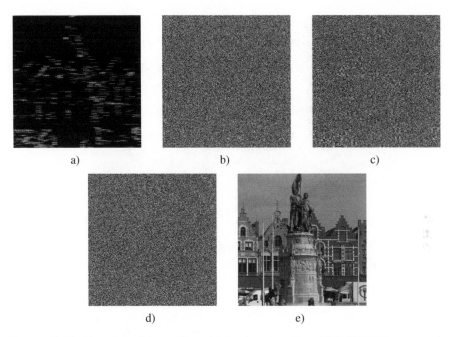

Figure 7.14. *Experimental results obtained using the EPE-HCRDH approach: a) location of unmarked pixels (errors and flags), number of errors = 1 225 (0.46 %); b) encrypted image I_e; c) encrypted image I'_e with flagged errors; d) marked encrypted image I_{e-m} with payload = 0.9220 bpp; e) reconstructed image I, PSNR → +∞, SSIM = 1*

The two proposed approaches were also applied to 10,000 grayscale images of size 512×512 pixels, taken from the BOWS-2 database (Bas and Furon 2008). Note that these images present high statistical variability in terms of content. The results obtained for this image database are shown in Table 7.2. In 6.3% of cases, when there is no prediction error (i.e. all differences between the original pixels and their predictors are less than or equal to 64), both approaches are fully reversible. In this case, the original images are reconstructed without error, giving a PSNR which tends toward $+\infty$ and an SSIM equal to 1. Moreover, all of the pixels in the images can be marked in this case, giving a maximum payload of 1 bpp. In other cases, for the CPE-HCRDH approach, the payload value is unchanged, but the original images cannot be reconstructed without loss because a certain number of pixels have to be modified in order to correct prediction errors. Nevertheless, for low contrast images, the quality of the reconstructed images is high, with an average PSNR of 57.4 dB and SSIM of almost 1 (0.9998). Moreover, the PSNR is higher than 40 dB in 98.64% of cases, indicating very good image quality. The EPE-HCRDH approach, on the other hand, is fully reversible for all images, with a PSNR tending to $+\infty$ and a SSIM of 1. Even if the presence of prediction errors means that not all pixels are labeled (especially in the worst case scenario), the payload remains high, with an average value of 0.9681 bpp. The payload exceeds 0.9 bpp in 92.19% of cases.

		Best case (6.3%)	Worst case	Average
CPE-HCRDH	**Percentage of prediction errors in the original image**	0%	4.9%	0.2%
	Payload (bpp)	1	1	1
	PSNR (dB)	$+\infty$	29.0	57.4
	SSIM	1	0.9872	0.9998
EPE-HCRDH	**Percentage of prediction errors in the original image**	0%	5.3%	0.2%
	Payload (bpp)	1	0.3805	0.9681
	PSNR (dB)	$+\infty$	$+\infty$	$+\infty$
	SSIM	1	1	1

Table 7.2. *Performance of the two approaches using the BOWS-2 database (10,000 images) (Bas and Furon 2008)*

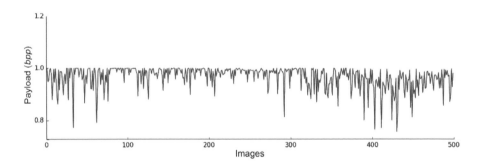

Figure 7.15. *Payload measures for the EPE-HCRDH approach, obtained for 500 images in the BOWS-2 database (Bas and Furon 2008)*

For ease of visualization, Figure 7.15 shows the payload results obtained using the EPE-HCRDH approach for 500 of the 10,000 images in the BOWS-2 (Bas and Furon 2008) database, selected at random.

7.7. Conclusion

In this chapter, we presented the challenges involved in hiding data within encrypted images. Following a description of different applications for analytical and processing purposes in the encrypted domain, we examined the reasons and applicative contexts for data hiding methods, before presenting the main classes and characteristics of the existing methods. We then presented the state of the art in this domain, showing, via a comparative table of methods, that none of the existing approaches combine a large payload with perfect reconstruction of the original image. Finally, we gave a detailed description of the method designed by Puteaux and Puech (2018a), where a very good compromise between these two criteria is obtained. Both proposed approaches offer a payload of the order of 1 bpp and very high quality image reconstruction.

This method takes a different approach to other state-of-the-art methods, achieving very good results. As a result, a large number of new "high-capacity" methods have built on this technique to offer even greater increases in payload (Puyang et al. 2018). Some authors have notably suggested a recursive reading and treatment of all of the binary planes in an image, starting from the MSB plane (Puteaux and Puech 2018b, 2020; Yin et al. 2019). In this way, the strong correlation between pixels in the clear domain is fully exploited, and a payload of over 2.4 bpp can be achieved (Puteaux and Puech 2020). Current research work is focused on developing high-capacity data hiding methods which exploit the homomorphic properties of public key encryption approaches.

In this chapter, we chose to consider data hiding methods applied to non-compressed digital images. It is important to note that extensions have been proposed for JPEG images (Qian et al. 2014), videos (Xu et al. 2013) and 3D objects (Jiang et al. 2017).

7.8. References

Bas, P. and Furon, T. (2008). Image database of BOWS-2 [Online]. Available at: http://bows2.ec-lille.fr/.

Blakley, G.R. (1979). Safeguarding cryptographic keys. *Proceedings of the National Computer Conference*. AFIPS, New York, USA.

Bouslimi, D., Coatrieux, G., Cozic, M., Roux, C. (2012). A joint encryption/watermarking system for verifying the reliability of medical images. *IEEE Transactions on Information Technology in Biomedicine*, 16(5), 891–899.

Cao, X., Du, L., Wei, X., Meng, D., Guo, X. (2016). High capacity reversible data hiding in encrypted images by patch-level sparse representation. *IEEE Transactions on Cybernetics*, 46(5), 1132–1143.

Chen, Y.-C., Shiu, C.-W., Horng, G. (2014). Encrypted signal-based reversible data hiding with public key cryptosystem. *Journal of Visual Communication and Image Representation*, 25(5), 1164–1170.

Daemen, J. and Rijmen, V. (2002). *The Design of Rijndael: AES – The Advanced Encryption Standard*. Springer, Berlin, Germany.

Dragoi, I.C. and Coltuc, D. (2018). Reversible data hiding in encrypted images based on reserving room after encryption and multiple predictors. *Proceedings of the International Conference on Acoustics, Speech and Signal Processing (ICASSP)*. IEEE, Calgary, Canada.

Dragoi, I.C., Coanda, H.-G., Coltuc, D. (2017). Improved reversible data hiding in encrypted images based on reserving room after encryption and pixel prediction. *Proceedings of the 25th European Signal Processing Conference (EUSIPCO)*. EURASIP, Kos, Greece.

Dufaux, F. and Ebrahimi, T. (2008). Scrambling for privacy protection in video surveillance systems. *IEEE Transactions on Circuits and Systems for Video Technology*, 18(8), 1168–1174.

Erkin, Z., Piva, A., Katzenbeisser, S., Lagendijk, R.L., Shokrollahi, J., Neven, G., Barni, M. (2007). Protection and retrieval of encrypted multimedia content: When cryptography meets signal processing. *EURASIP Journal on Information Security*, 1–20.

Ferreira, B., Rodrigues, J., Leitao, J., Domingos, H. (2015). Privacy-preserving content-based image retrieval in the cloud. *Proceedings of the 34th Symposium on Reliable Distributed Systems (SRDS)*. IEEE, Montreal, Canada.

Ge, H., Chen, Y., Qian, Z., Wang, J. (2019). A high capacity multi-level approach for reversible data hiding in encrypted images. *IEEE Transactions on Circuits and Systems for Video Technology*, 29(8), 2285–2295.

Hey, T., Tansley, S., Tolle, K. (2009). *The Fourth Paradigm: Data-Intensive Scientific Discovery*. Microsoft Research, Redmond, USA.

Hong, W., Chen, T.-S., Wu, H.-Y. (2012). An improved reversible data hiding in encrypted images using side match. *IEEE Signal Processing Letters*, 19(4), 199–202.

Hsu, C.-Y., Lu, C.-S., Pei, S.-C. (2012). Image feature extraction in encrypted domain with privacy-preserving SIFT. *IEEE Transactions on Image Processing*, 21(11), 4593–4607.

Huang, F., Huang, J., Shi, Y.-Q. (2016). New framework for reversible data hiding in encrypted domain. *IEEE Transactions on Information Forensics and Security*, 11(12), 2777–2789.

Jain, A.K., Lee, J.-E., Jin, R., Gregg, N. (2009). Content-based image retrieval: An application to tattoo images. *Proceedings of the 16th International Conference on Image Processing (ICIP)*. IEEE, Cairo, Egypt.

Jiang, R., Zhou, H., Zhang, W., Yu, N. (2017). Reversible data hiding in encrypted three-dimensional mesh models. *IEEE Transactions on Multimedia*, 20(1), 55–67.

Ke, Y., Zhang, M., Liu, J. (2016). Separable multiple bits reversible data hiding in encrypted domain. *Proceedings of the International Workshop on Digital Watermarking*. IWDW, Beijing, China.

Ke, Y., Zhang, M., Liu, J., Su, T., Yang, X. (2018). A multilevel reversible data hiding scheme in encrypted domain based on LWE. *Journal of Visual Communication and Image Representation*, 54, 133–144.

Li, S., Chen, G., Mou, X. (2005). On the dynamical degradation of digital piecewise linear chaotic maps. *International Journal of Bifurcation and Chaos*, 15(10), 3119–3151.

Li, X., Li, J., Li, B., Yang, B. (2013). High-fidelity reversible data hiding scheme based on pixel-value-ordering and prediction-error expansion. *Signal Processing*, 93(1), 198–205.

Liu, W., Zeng, W., Dong, L., Yao, Q. (2009). Efficient compression of encrypted grayscale images. *IEEE Transactions on Image Processing*, 19(4), 1097–1102.

Lu, W., Swaminathan, A., Varna, A.L., Wu, M. (2009a). Enabling search over encrypted multimedia databases. *Proceedings of SPIE – Electronic Imaging*. International Society for Optics and Photonics, San Jose, USA.

Lu, W., Varna, A.L., Swaminathan, A., Wu, M. (2009b). Secure image retrieval through feature protection. *Proceedings of the International Conference on Acoustics, Speech and Signal Processing (ICASSP)*. IEEE, Taipei, Taiwan.

Ma, K., Zhang, W., Zhao, X., Yu, N., Li, F. (2013). Reversible data hiding in encrypted images by reserving room before encryption. *IEEE Transactions on Information Forensics and Security*, 8(3), 553–562.

Naor, M. and Shamir, A. (1994). Visual cryptography. *Proceedings of the Workshop on the Theory and Application of Cryptographic Techniques*. IACR, Perugia, Italy.

Paillier, P. (1999). Public-key cryptosystems based on composite degree residuosity classes. *Proceedings of the International Conference on the Theory and Applications of Cryptographic Techniques*. IACR, Prague, Czech Republic.

Pavlopoulou, C., Kak, A.C., Brodley, C.E. (2003). Content-based image retrieval for medical imagery. In *Medical Imaging 2003: PACS and Integrated Medical Information Systems: Design and Evaluation*, Huang, H.K., Ratib, O.M. (eds). International Society for Optics and Photonics, Bellingham, USA.

Poh, G.S. and Martin, K.M. (2009). An efficient buyer-seller watermarking protocol based on Chameleon encryption. *Proceedings of the 7th International Workshop on Digital Watermarking*. IWDW, Busan, South Korea.

Preishuber, M., Hütter, T., Katzenbeisser, S., Uhl, A. (2018). Depreciating motivation and empirical security analysis of chaos-based image and video encryption. *IEEE Transactions on Information Forensics and Security*, 13(9), 2137–2150.

Puech, W., Chaumont, M., Strauss, O. (2008). A reversible data hiding method for encrypted images. In *Security, Forensics, Steganography, and Watermarking of Multimedia Contents*, Delp III, E.J., Wong, P.W. (eds). International Society for Optics and Photonics, Bellingham, USA.

Puteaux, P. and Puech, W. (2018a). An efficient MSB prediction-based method for high-capacity reversible data hiding in encrypted images. *IEEE Transactions on Information Forensics and Security*, 13(7), 1670–1681.

Puteaux, P. and Puech, W. (2018b). EPE-based huge-capacity reversible data hiding in encrypted images. *Proceedings of the Workshop on Information Forensics and Security*. IEEE, Hong Kong, China.

Puteaux, P. and Puech, W. (2020). A recursive reversible data hiding in encrypted images method with a very high capacity. *IEEE Transactions on Multimedia*, 23, 636–650.

Puyang, Y., Yin, Z., Qian, Z. (2018). Reversible data hiding in encrypted images with two-MSB prediction. *Proceedings of the Workshop on Information Forensics and Security*. IEEE, Hong Kong, China.

Qian, Z. and Zhang, X. (2016). Reversible data hiding in encrypted images with distributed source encoding. *IEEE Transactions on Circuits and Systems for Video Technology*, 26(4), 636–646.

Qian, Z., Zhang, X., Wang, S. (2014). Reversible data hiding in encrypted JPEG bitstream. *IEEE Transactions on Multimedia*, 16(5), 1486–1491.

Qian, Z., Xu, H., Luo, X., Zhang, X. (2018). New framework of reversible data hiding in encrypted JPEG bitstreams. *IEEE Transactions on Circuits and Systems for Video Technology*, 29(2), 351–362.

Shamir, A. (1979). How to share a secret. *Communications of the ACM*, 22(11), 612–613.

Shannon, C.E. (1948). A mathematical theory of communication. *The Bell System Technical Journal*, 27, 379–423.

Shiu, C.-W., Chen, Y.-C., Hong, W. (2015). Encrypted image-based reversible data hiding with public key cryptography from difference expansion. *Signal Processing: Image Communication*, 39, 226–233.

Slepian, D. and Wolf, J. (1973). Noiseless coding of correlated information sources. *IEEE Transactions on Information Theory*, 19(4), 471–480.

Thien, C. and Lin, J. (2002). Secret image sharing. *Computers & Graphics*, 26(5), 765–770.

Wang, Z., Bovik, A.C., Sheikh, H.R., Simoncelli, E.P. (2004). Image quality assessment: From error visibility to structural similarity. *IEEE Transactions on Image Processing*, 13(4), 600–612.

Wong, K.S. and Tanaka, K. (2014). Data embedding for geo-tagging any contents in smart device. *Proceedings of the Region 10 Symposium*. IEEE, Kuala Lumpur, Malaysia.

Wu, X. and Sun, W. (2014). High-capacity reversible data hiding in encrypted images by prediction error. *Signal Processing*, 104, 387–400.

Wu, Y., Noonan, J.P., Agaian, S. (2011). NPCR and UACI randomness tests for image encryption. *Cyber Journals: Multidisciplinary Journals in Science and Technology, Journal of Selected Areas in Telecommunications*, 1(2), 31–38.

Wu, H.-T., Cheung, Y.-M., Huang, J. (2016). Reversible data hiding in Paillier cryptosystem. *Journal of Visual Communication and Image Representation*, 40, 765–771.

Xia, Z., Wang, X., Zhang, L., Qin, Z., Sun, X., Ren, K. (2016). A privacy-preserving and copy-deterrence content-based image retrieval scheme in cloud computing. *IEEE Transactions on Information Forensics and Security*, 11(11), 2594–2608.

Xiao, D., Xiang, Y., Zheng, H., Wang, Y. (2017). Separable reversible data hiding in encrypted image based on pixel value ordering and additive homomorphism. *Journal of Visual Communication and Image Representation*, 45, 1–10.

Xu, D., Wang, R., Shi, Y.Q. (2013). Reversible data hiding in encrypted H.264/avc video streams. *Proceedings of the International Workshop on Digital Watermarking*. IWDW, Auckland, New Zealand.

Yin, Z., Xiang, Y., Zhang, X. (2019). Reversible data hiding in encrypted images based on multi-MSB prediction and Huffman coding. *IEEE Transactions on Multimedia*, 22(4), 874–884.

Zhang, X. (2011). Reversible data hiding in encrypted image. *IEEE Signal Processing Letters*, 18(4), 255–258.

Zhang, X. (2012). Separable reversible data hiding in encrypted image. *IEEE Transactions on Information Forensics and Security*, 7(2), 826–832.

Zhang, X., Long, J., Wang, Z., Cheng, H. (2016). Lossless and reversible data hiding in encrypted images with public-key cryptography. *IEEE Transactions on Circuits and Systems for Video Technology*, 26(9), 1622–1631.

8

Sharing Secret Images and 3D Objects

Sébastien BEUGNON, Pauline PUTEAUX and William PUECH
LIRMM, Université de Montpellier, CNRS, France

Secret sharing was developed in 1979 by Blakley (1979) and (Shamir 1979) in response to problems associated with classic encryption methods. Unlike cryptographic systems, secret sharing does not rely on the use of a key, allowing secret data to be exchanged between several people. The scope of secret sharing was extended to new areas of security in the 1990s. With the evolution of encryption techniques, secret sharing began to be adapted for multimedia data, notably for images (Naor and Shamir 1994). Interest in secret image protection and sharing was revived in 2002, when Shamir's method (Shamir 1979) was applied without affecting image format (Thien and Lin 2002). Work on secret sharing for 3D objects began in 2010 (Elsheh and Hamza 2010).

8.1. Introduction

The concept of secret sharing was developed in the late 1970s by Blakley (1979). Shamir (1979) worked independently, to solve the problems associated with the classic encryption approaches described in Chapters 4, 6 and 7. A major drawback of these approaches is that they require a key, and that the secret is limited to a single container. The container may be lost, destroyed or tampered with during an attack, meaning that

---

For a color version of all figures in this chapter, see www.iste.co.uk/puech/multimedia2.zip.

the secret can no longer be retrieved. The applications of secret sharing have evolved since the 1980s. Nowadays, secret sharing offers a response to new problems such as secure multi-party computation, solving the Byzantine agreement problem, access control or attribute-based encryption (Beimel 2011). Secret sharing is presented as a keyless encryption approach, whereby a secret may be distributed to multiple users and reconstructed when a subset of these users collaborate to do so. The user who initially shares the secret is known as the dealer.

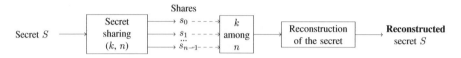

Figure 8.1. *Sharing and reconstruction of a secret S*

As we see from Figure 8.1, during the sharing phase, the dealer generates shares of the secret S denoted as s_i. Each share is assigned to a user among n such that $i \in [\![0 \, ; \, n[\![$. The shares are not disjointed parts of the secret S, but information computed from the secret S allowing it to be reconstructed. Taken individually, these shares do not provide any information about the secret S. To reconstruct the secret, at least k shares among those held by n users are needed. Any group of users with fewer than k of n members will be unable to reconstruct the secret.

This first approach to secret sharing is called the (k, n)-threshold method. This definition was extended and generalized by Ito *et al.* (1989), who defined a secret sharing method involving a secret, a set of users and a general access structure, that is, a collection of subsets with the capacity to reconstruct the secret. Note that this definition removes the minimum threshold principle, enabling generalization for user sets of different sizes.

The construction and/or the organization of their access structure means that some secret sharing methods have particularly interesting properties (Simmons 1988; Brickell 1989; Brickell and Davenport 1991; Brickell and Stinson 1992; Tassa 2004; Belenkiy 2008; Beimel 2011), insofar as they can be considered to be perfect, ideal, verifiable or clearly hierarchical.

A secret sharing method is said to be *perfect* when only a subset of the users can reconstruct the secret S and no information, in the theoretical sense, about S is revealed to other users. Methods such as those defined by Shamir (1979); Brickell and Stinson (1992); Lin *et al.* (2009) can be considered as *perfect*, while Blakley's method cannot (Blakley 1979).

Furthermore, a secret sharing method is said to be *ideal* when, for any secret S and any share generated from S, the shares are the same size (in bits) as the input secret (Brickell 1989). Shamir's method is one example of an *ideal* approach. The search for ideal secret sharing methods is an important subject for research. In contrast, other methods have focused on trying to reduce share size in order to optimize storage and transmission time (Krawczyk 1993).

Some secret sharing methods incorporate fault detection mechanisms with the ability to detect the provision of wrong shares by malicious users, aiming to prevent the reconstruction of the secret (Chor *et al.* 1985; Benaloh 1986; Zhao *et al.* 2007; Harn and Lin 2009). These mechanisms can be used to correct faults (Benaloh 1986) and identify users with ill intent (Harn and Lin 2009).

Finally, several secret sharing methods have proposed a hierarchization of users by groups or levels (Simmons 1988; Tassa 2004; Belenkiy 2008; Farràs *et al.* 2012; Nojoumian and Stinson 2015). In this type of approach, users have a different level of access to the secret; in classical thresholded methods, all users are at the same level. These methods can then be used as a basis for attribute-based encryption approaches. Simmons (1988) considers a system where users are divided into different groups, and each group is assigned a threshold that must be reached to allow the reconstruction of the secret by that group. Simmons also described two types of hierarchies for hierarchical secret sharing methods: multilevel sharing methods (multilevel threshold secret sharing scheme) and compartmentalized sharing methods (compartmented threshold secret sharing scheme).

While secret sharing methods were first developed for use with textual data, the increasing volume of multimedia data transiting over networks means that an adaptation of these methods for images and 3D objects is increasingly relevant. In section 8.2, we provide a brief introduction to classic secret sharing methods, along with the hierarchical aspects of some approaches. In section 8.3, we describe the principle of secret image sharing and the associated state-of-the-art methods. In section 8.4, we present work on the subject of secret 3D object sharing. Finally, in section 8.5, we describe an application of secret image sharing to social networks.

8.2. Secret sharing

We shall begin by presenting Shamir and Blakley's methods (Shamir 1979; Blakley 1979) in section 8.2.1. We then address the hierarchical property, introducing two hierarchical secret sharing methods based on Shamir's method, developed by Tassa (2007) and Belenkiy (2008).

8.2.1. *Classic methods*

8.2.1.1. *Shamir's method*

In Shamir's method, the secret S is considered as an element in a finite body (Shamir 1979). In this approach, the secret is protected by using polynomials over a finite body $\mathbb{F}_p$ such that $|\mathbb{F}_p| = p$ with $|.|$ as the cardinal of a finite body and p as a prime number, respecting the condition:

$$1 < k \leq n < p$$
$$0 \leq S < p \qquad\qquad [8.1]$$

with k as the minimum number of users required to reconstruct the secret and n as the maximum number of share holders.

Using parameters (k, n), this method distributes a set of shares for each of the n users, and allows the secret to be reconstructed when at least k of the n users pool their shares to solve a polynomial interpolation problem. No information concerning the secret will be revealed when using a subset of only $(k - 1)$ shares. During the sharing step, each user receives a unique identifier x_j, where $0 < x_j < p$ and $j \in [\![0 ; n[\![$. A polynomial of degree $(k - 1)$ is then constructed, such that $(k - 1)$ integers are randomly selected to form the set $\mathbf{a} = \{a_i \in \mathbb{F}_p\}$ with $i \in [\![1 ; k[\![$, $a_i < p$ and $a_0 = S$:

$$f(x) = \sum_{i=0}^{k-1} a_i \times x^i \qquad\qquad [8.2]$$

Thus, $f(0)$, which is equal to a_0, corresponds to the value of the secret S. Each of the n users receives an information pair $s_j = (x_j, y_j = f(x_j))$.

As we can see from Figure 8.2, the secret S can be reconstructed using a polynomial interpolation with at least k shares. These shares may be interpreted as points belonging to the selected polynomial. In Figure 8.2, for example, points $s_0 = (x_0, f(x_0))$ and $s_1 = (x_1, f(x_1))$ may be used to interpolate the polynomial of degree 1 $f(x)$ represented by the red line. The blue curve in Figure 8.2 represents a polynomial of degree 2, which can reconstruct the secret S when at least three points are used to interpolate the polynomial. The green curve is a polynomial of degree 3, allowing the reconstruction of the secret S using four or more points. Interpolation is applied to determine the value of $f(0)$ of the polynomial, corresponding to term a_0 and, by definition, to the secret S. To reconstruct the secret S, a group of at least k

users can determine the coefficients used in the polynomial $f(x)$ during the sharing step by means of Lagrange interpolation:

$$f(x) = \sum_{i=0}^{k-1} y_i \times \prod_{u=0, i \neq u}^{k-1} \frac{x - x_u}{x_i - x_u} \mod p \qquad [8.3]$$

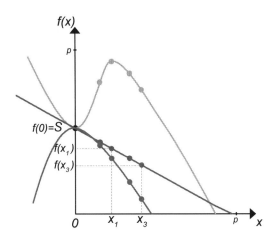

Figure 8.2. *Example of Shamir's method with parameters (2, n) in red, (3, n) in blue and (4, n) in green (Shamir 1979)*

8.2.1.2. *Blakley's method*

The very same year, Blakley proposed a secret sharing method using hyperplanar geometry (Blakley 1979). The secret S is defined as a point in a k-dimensional space such that $S = (x_0, x_1, \ldots, x_{k-1})$. Each user is supplied with a hyperplane of dimension k, such that point S is present in all of the distributed hyperplanes. In formal terms, a hyperplane of dimension k noted H is defined by equation [8.4]:

$$b = \sum_{i=0}^{k-1} a_i \times x_i \qquad [8.4]$$

where a_i with $i \in [\![0 \; ; \; k [\![$ is the ith coefficient of the hyperplane of dimension k defined by the set $\mathbf{a} = \{a_i\}$ and b is the coefficient.

Using hyperplanar geometry, the secret point is the point of intersection of any group of k or more hyperplanes. Figure 8.3 shows the intersection of hyperplanes at a single point for $k = 2$ (see Figure 8.3(a)) and for $k = 3$ (see Figure 8.3(b)), respectively. The distributed shares are thus hyperplanes of dimension k, and more precisely the coefficients of the equation representing the hyperplane $H_j = (\{a_{j,i}\}, b_j)$ with $j \in [\![0 \; ; \; n[\![$.

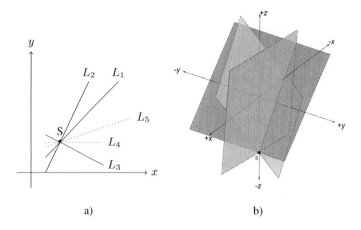

a)   b)

Figure 8.3. *Examples of Blakley's method with parameters a) (2, n) and b) (3, n) (Blakley 1979)*

8.2.2. *Hierarchical aspects*

For some applications, it may be necessary to define a hierarchy of users to provide higher control over access to secret content. For example, in a bank with a safe, it is natural to expect that access to the safe will require the presence of bank employees, some of whom are members of management. Imagine a scenario where three employees, including one manager, or alternatively two managers, must be present in order to open the safe. This example illustrates the use of hierarchical approaches to build an access control structure that varies according to case-specific requirements. In this context, the definition of secret sharing must be extended, adjusting the secret reconstruction process according to the users present. This hierarchical aspect, which we touched on briefly in section 8.1, was first introduced by Simmons (1988).

A hierarchical secret sharing method is defined by several parameters noted $(L, \mathbf{k}, \mathbf{n})$, where L is the number of levels in the hierarchy, $\mathbf{k} = \{k_\ell\}$ is the minimum number of users per level for reconstruction $\ell \in [\![0 \; ; \; L[\![$ and $\mathbf{n} = \{n_\ell\}$ is the maximum number of possible users per level. This approach was developed in response to a need to limit secret access to an authorized set of users. Users belong to groups defined as a function of their position, role or level in the hierarchy:

$$
\begin{cases}
u \in U \\
\mathbb{L}(u) = \ell, \text{ where } \ell \in [\![0\ ;\ L[\![\\
u \in U_{\mathbb{L}(u)} \\
U_{\mathbb{L}(u)} \subseteq U \\
U = \bigcup_{\ell=0}^{L-1} U_\ell
\end{cases}
\tag{8.5}
$$

where u is a user belonging to a group of authorized users U and the user group of level $\mathbb{L}(u)$, noted $U_{\mathbb{L}(u)}$.

In the literature, hierarchy defines how users and groups organize the secret access structure together. Hierarchical secret sharing methods correspond to the implementation of these hierarchies in the context of secret sharing approaches. Different types of hierarchies may be defined, based on their uses and objectives (Simmons 1988).

8.2.2.1. *Compartmented hierarchical secret sharing*

The first category, presented by Simmons (1988), corresponds to compartmented hierarchical secret sharing, or CHSS, schemes. This category corresponds to an access structure with several user groups, where a consensus must be reached within each user group in order to reconstruct the secret. In the case of compartmentalized hierarchical sharing methods, user groups are defined as follows:

$$
\begin{cases}
u \in U \\
\mathbb{L}(u) = \ell, \text{ or } \ell \in [\![0\ ;\ L[\![\\
u \in U_{\mathbb{L}(u)} \\
\forall \ell, \ell' \in [\![0\ ;\ L[\![,\ \ell \neq \ell' \iff U_\ell \cap U_{\ell'} = \emptyset
\end{cases}
\tag{8.6}
$$

Each user u belongs to a group U_ℓ, where $\ell = \mathbb{L}(u)$. The different groups of users are distinct from one another. In a compartmented hierarchy, each group U_ℓ must attain a certain threshold assigned to the group in order to reconstruct the secret. As the groups are distinct from one another, users in a group U_ℓ will not count toward the threshold of a group $U_{\ell'}$. For this reason, if one or more thresholds k_ℓ are not attained in a group U_ℓ, the secret will not be revealed. Figure 8.4 shows an example of a CHSS method with parameters $L = 4$, $\mathbf{k} = (k_0 = 2, k_1 = 3, k_2 = 2, k_3 = 4)$ and $\mathbf{n} = (n_0, n_1, n_2, n_3)$. These parameters indicate that four disjunct user groups must each reach a consensus in order to reconstruct the secret. In this particular case, the

CHSS method requires two users from set U_0, three from set U_1, two from set U_2 and four from set U_3.

U_ℓ	k_ℓ
U_0	2
U_1	3
U_2	2
U_3	4

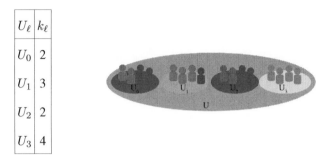

Figure 8.4. *Example of a compartmented hierarchical secret sharing method with parameters L = 4, K = (k_0 = 2, k_1 = 3, k_2 = 2, k_3 = 4) and N = (n_0, n_1, n_2, n_3)*

The most naive implementation of a CHSS method consists of applying a secret sharing method sequentially. First, the secret S is shared, using the parameters $(k = L, n = L)$, in order to generate L shares $(s_0, s_1, \ldots, s_{L-1})$. Next, each of these L shares is shared again between the members of the same group U_ℓ with parameters (k_ℓ, n_ℓ), as shown in Figure 8.5.

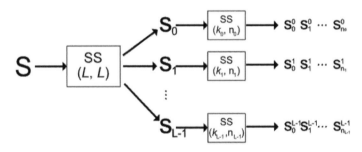

Figure 8.5. *Possible compartmented hierarchical secret sharing process*

8.2.2.2. *Multi-level hierarchical secret sharing*

A second category is made up of multi-level hierarchical secret sharing methods, with an access structure in which users are grouped by access level. Following Simmons' proposals (Simmons 1988), the level defines the position of users in the hierarchy and their capacity to reconstruct the secret with fewer users. Unlike compartmented hierarchical sharing methods, in which users are split into disjoint groups, multilevel hierarchical sharing methods use nested groups:

$$\begin{cases} u \in U \\ \mathbb{L}(u) = \ell, \text{ where } \ell \in [\![0\;;\;L[\![\\ u \in U_{\mathbb{L}(u)} \\ \forall \ell, \ell' \in [\![0\;;\;L[\![, \ell < \ell' \iff U_\ell \subseteq U_{\ell'} \end{cases} \qquad [8.7]$$

One specificity of multilevel hierarchical sharing methods is that different levels are arranged in an order, such that:

$$\forall \ell, \ell' \in [\![0\;;\;L[\![, \ell < \ell' \iff k_\ell < k_{\ell'} \qquad [8.8]$$

The highest level is labeled 0 and the lowest level is $(L-1)$. During reconstruction, the method must verify whether the threshold for level ℓ has been reached (beginning with $l = 0$) with the presence of at least k_ℓ users belonging to the group U_ℓ. If the number of users is sufficient at level ℓ, then the secret will be reconstructed directly based on this set of users. Otherwise, users from level ℓ will be considered as users at level $(\ell + 1)$, and can thus count toward the threshold $k_{\ell+1}$.

Figure 8.6 shows a multilevel hierarchy. Users at the highest level can reconstruct the secret more rapidly. For example, in group U_0, fewer users are needed to reconstruct the secret than for groups U_1, U_2 or U_3. However, this only works with users on the same level (or higher levels), that is, belonging to the same group. Thus, if the number of users in U_0 present at the point of reconstruction is below the threshold k_0, then the secret remains protected. Nevertheless, they can participate in reconstruction in association with users of a lower level.

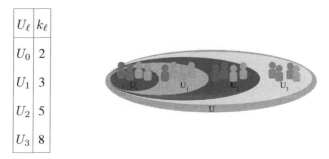

U_ℓ	k_ℓ
U_0	2
U_1	3
U_2	5
U_3	8

Figure 8.6. *Example of a multilevel hierarchical secret sharing method with parameters L = 4, k = (k_0 = 2, k_1 = 3, k_2 = 5, k_3 = 8) and n = (n_0, n_1, n_2, n_3)*

8.2.2.3. *Tassa's method*

The article by Tassa (2007) proposed a hierarchical secret sharing method that combines the two types of hierarchies presented in sections 8.2.2.1 and 8.2.2.2, using Shamir's secret sharing method (Shamir 1979). The purpose of this new type of hierarchy is to allow reconstruction when enough users at all levels of the hierarchy participate, that is, with a minimum number of users per level. The particularity of this approach lies in the fact that higher level users participate in the consensus of the lower levels. Tassa's proposed method is based on a polynomial of degree $(k_{L-1} - 1)$ (see equation [8.2]), and the secret S is hidden in coefficient a_0 of the selected polynomial (Tassa 2007). Tassa's method then transmits the information pair $(u_{\ell,i}, g_\ell(u_{\ell,i}))$ to the ith user belonging to level $\ell \in [\![0 ; L[\![$, where $i \in [\![0 ; n_\ell[\![$, $\mathbb{L}(u_{\ell,i} = \ell)$ is the level of user $u_{\ell,i}$ and g_ℓ is the Tassa polynomial associated with level ℓ. The Tassa polynomial g_ℓ associated with level ℓ is the Shamir polynomial f derived $k_{\ell-1}$ times and noted $f^{k_{\ell-1}}$:

$$g_\ell(u) = f^{k_{\ell-1}}(u) = \frac{d^{k_{\ell-1}} f}{du^{k_{\ell-1}}}(u) \qquad [8.9]$$

with $k_{-1} = 0$.

For example, for three hierarchical levels with thresholds $\mathbf{k} = (k_0, k_1, k_2)$, reconstruction of the secret requires the presence of at least k_0 level 0 users, k_1 level 1 users and k_2 level 2 users. The polynomials used for each level of the hierarchy are given as:

$$\begin{cases} \forall u \in U \\ f(u) = \sum_{i=0}^{k_2-1} a_i \times u^i \\ \mathbb{L}(u) = 0 \Rightarrow g_0(u) = f^{k-1}(u) \\ \mathbb{L}(u) = 1 \Rightarrow g_1(u) = f^{k_0}(u) \\ \mathbb{L}(u) = 2 \Rightarrow g_2(u) = f^{k_1}(u) \end{cases} \qquad [8.10]$$

Taking $\mathbf{k} = (2, 3, 4)$ for the thresholds k_0, k_1 and k_2 and replacing the variables by their values, we obtain the following polynomials:

$$\begin{cases} \forall u \in U \\ f(u) = a_0 + a_1 \times u + a_2 \times u^2 + a_3 \times u^3 \\ g_0(u) = f^{k(-1)}(u) = f^0(u) = f(u) \\ g_1(u) = f^{k_0}(u) = f^2(u) = \frac{d^2 f}{du^{shares2}}(u) = 2 \times a_2 + 6 \times a_3 \times u \\ g_2(u) = f^{k_1}(u) = f^3(u) = \frac{d^3 f}{du^3}(u) = 6 \times a_3 \end{cases} \qquad [8.11]$$

The polynomial g_0 used for the highest level, level 0, is equal to the Shamir polynomial f of degree $(k_{L-1} - 1)$ without derivation, while the polynomial g_1 for users of level 1 is equal to f derived twice, following equation [8.9], since $k_0 = 2$. The polynomial used for level 2 users is equal to f derived three times, following equation [8.9], since $k_1 = 3$.

Figure 8.7. *List of groups with the capacity to reconstruct the shared secret using Tassa's method (Tassa 2007) with parameters L = 3 and k = (2, 3, 4)*

Figure 8.7 shows the list of groups with the ability to reconstruct the secret in Tassa's method (Tassa 2007), with thresholds $\mathbf{k} = (k_0 = 2, k_1 = 3, k_2 = 4)$. In Tassa's proposed hierarchy, users of level 0, 1 and 2 are required to reconstruct the secret. However, as we can see from Figure 8.7, users of level 0 can act as users of levels 1 or 2 for reconstruction purposes. The final group of users shown in Figure 8.7 represents the minimal configuration needed to reconstruct the secret, with two level 0 users, one level 1 user and one level 2 users. Although the hierarchy requires two level 0 users, three level 1 users and four level 2 users, this configuration is possible because the level 0 users also count toward the level 1 and level 2 groups. By adjusting the number of users per level, the presence of certain users may be made compulsory in order to reconstruct the secret. Reconstruction is carried out using a Hermite–Birkhoff interpolation (Schoenberg 1966). A Hermite–Birkhoff interpolation is a means of identifying the unique solution to a linear system formed by a reduced set of users, valid for reconstruction purposes. Formally, when a hierarchical secret sharing method is used in the way defined by Tassa (2007), a matrix relationship is obtained for each group of users authorized to reconstruct the secret, such that:

$$X = \begin{bmatrix} 1 & u_{i_0} & u_{i_0}^2 & u_{i_0}^3 \\ 1 & u_{i_1} & u_{i_1}^2 & u_{i_1}^3 \\ 0 & 0 & 2 & 6u_{i_2} \\ 0 & 0 & 0 & 6 \end{bmatrix} A^T = \begin{bmatrix} a_0 \\ a_1 \\ a_2 \\ a_3 \end{bmatrix} \qquad [8.12]$$

$$X \times A^T = b \Rightarrow X \times A^T = \begin{bmatrix} g_0(u_{i_0}) \\ g_0(u_{i_1}) \\ g_1(u_{i_2}) \\ g_2(u_{i_3}) \end{bmatrix} \qquad [8.13]$$

where i_0, i_1, i_2 and $i_3 \in [\![0\ ;\ |\mathbf{n}|[\![$ with $|\mathbf{n}| = |\bigcup\limits_{\ell=0}^{L-1} U_\ell| = \sum\limits_{\ell=0}^{L-1} n_\ell$ as the number of users (across all groups) participating in secret sharing u_{i_0}, u_{i_1} as two level 0 users, u_{i_2} as a level 1 user and u_{i_3} as a level 2 user. A is the polynomial coefficient vector, X is the matrix of polynomials calculated (without coefficients) and derived (or non-derived) for each user belonging to the reconstruction group, and b is the result of the polynomials for each user.

The user group $(u_{i_0}, u_{i_1}, u_{i_2}, u_{i_3})$ is a group with the capacity to reconstruct the secret according to Tassa's method (Tassa 2007).

By solving the linear system $X \times A^T = b$, we can deduce the set of coefficients A used in the polynomials.

8.2.2.4. *Belenkiy's method*

Belenkiy's hierarchical secret sharing method builds on Tassa's approach (Tassa 2007) to create a new, less restrictive multilevel hierarchy (Belenkiy 2008). In this hierarchy, the secret can be reconstructed when the number of users ℓ reaches the associated threshold value k_ℓ. To create this hierarchy, Belenkiy suggested hiding the secret in the final coefficient of the Shamir polynomial a_{k-1} instead of in a_0 (see equation [8.2]) (Belenkiy 2008). Furthermore, since higher level users receive derivatives of the Shamir polynomial, they can begin reconstructing the secret once the threshold for their level has been reached. If the corresponding threshold k_ℓ is not reached, then users at level ℓ can participate in reconstruction for the next level $(\ell + 1)$ with the corresponding threshold $k_{(\ell+1)}$. Let h_ℓ be the Belenkiy polynomial used to distribute shares to users of level ℓ. Thus, taking the same example as before with parameters $\mathbf{k} = (k_0 = 2, k_1 = 3, k_2 = 4)$, a polynomial of degree 3 will be used (since $k_{L-1} = 4$). The value of coefficient $a_{(k_{L-1}-1)} = a_3$ is assigned to that of the secret, and for each level ℓ, the polynomial is derived ($k_{L-1} - k_\ell$) times:

$$\begin{cases} \forall u \in \mathbb{U} \\ \mathbb{L}(u) = \ell \in [\![0\ ;\ L[\![\\ \Delta = k_{L-1} - k_\ell \\ h_\ell(u) = f^\Delta(u) = \frac{d^\Delta f}{du^\Delta}(u) \end{cases} \qquad [8.14]$$

In this case, a group of k_ℓ users, where ℓ is the level of the attained threshold, will be able to reconstruct the final coefficient $a_{(k_{L-1}-1)}$ containing the secret, as shown in Figure 8.8.

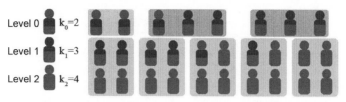

Figure 8.8. *List of groups with the capacity to reconstruct the shared secret using Belenkiy's method with parameters L = 3 and k = (2, 3, 4) (Belenkiy 2008)*

Figure 8.8 shows the set of user groups with the capacity to reconstruct the secret according to Belenkiy's method for three hierarchical levels, and with thresholds $\mathbf{k} = (k_0 = 2, k_1 = 3, k_2 = 4)$ (Belenkiy 2008). Users in level U_0 can reconstruct the secret if at least two members are present, whereas a minimum of three users of level U_1, or four users of level U_2, will be required to reconstruct the secret according to Belenkiy's hierarchy (Belenkiy 2008). As we can see from Figure 8.8, a user of level 0 will not be able to reconstruct the secret alone, but can join users of level 1 or 2 to participate in reconstruction at this level. The final group shown in Figure 8.8 represents the minimal configuration, with four level 2 users who have the ability to reconstruct the secret.

Using the multi-level approach, higher level users can reconstruct the secret faster, or at least help reconstruct the secret with lower level users. As in the case of Tassa's method, Belenkiy's method relies on a Hermite–Bikhoff interpolation to reconstruct the secret. Taking the same example as in Figure 8.8, the level 0 users (u_{i_0} and $u_{i_1} \in U_0$) can reconstruct the secret through their information pair ($u_{i_0}, h_0(u_{i_0})$) and ($u_{i_1}, h_0(u_{i_1})$), according to the following matrix relationship:

$$X = \begin{bmatrix} 2 & 6u_{i_0} \\ 2 & 6u_{i_1} \end{bmatrix}, A^T = \begin{bmatrix} a_2 \\ a_3 \end{bmatrix} \qquad [8.15]$$

$$X \times A^T = b \Rightarrow X \times A^T = \begin{bmatrix} h_0(u_{i_0}) \\ h_0(u_{i_1}) \end{bmatrix} \qquad [8.16]$$

Solving the linear system $X \times A^T = b$ gives a single possible solution for coefficients a_2 and a_3, where a_3 contains the value of the secret.

8.3. Secret image sharing

As we saw in section 8.2, the concept of secret sharing was initially developed for the management of secret cryptographic keys (Blakley 1979; Shamir 1979). Naor and Shamir (1994) proposed an adaption of the concept of secret sharing for the domain of 2D imaging. The authors provided the first definition of visual secret sharing, where the secret is the content of an image. The secret image sharing principle is presented in section 8.3.1. Section 8.3.2 provides a description of visual cryptography, one of the earliest approaches to visual secret sharing. In section 8.3.3, we present secret image sharing methods based on polynomial approaches, ensuring that the reconstructed secret image will be of the best possible quality. Finally, in section 8.3.4, we present the main properties of secret image sharing methods.

8.3.1. *Principle*

Just like secret sharing methods, secret image sharing methods can be split into two parts: sharing and reconstruction. As we can see from Figure 8.9, the input for the method consists of a secret image and parameters k and n, where k is the minimum number of shares required to reconstruct the secret image and n is the number of shares to generate. The particularity of secret image sharing lies in the fact that the shares themselves are images; as Figure 8.9 shows, the output of the sharing step consists of four shares (s_1, s_2, s_3 and s_4) to be distributed to each of the users. The secret image I can then be reconstructed if at least three of these shares are present.

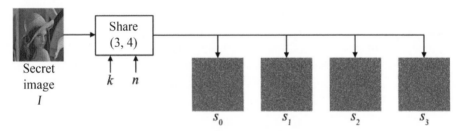

Figure 8.9. *Secret image sharing with four shares*

Essentially, the secret image I is split into several blocks that are then shared and reassembled to create output images s_i, with $i \in [\![0 \; ; \; n[\![$. This block-based treatment is used to eliminate the spatial correlation between pixels. The reconstruction process takes these image shares as input, reconstructing the original image or its visual content.

Figure 8.10 shows the reconstruction of the secret image from Figure 8.9. The contents of the secret image $\hat{I}$ can be constructed using any three of the four shares generated by the sharing process. As the authors of *Visual Cryptography and Secret Image Sharing* (Cimato and Yang 2011) indicate, there are two categories of visual sharing methods: visual cryptography, as proposed by Naor and Shamir (1994), and secret image sharing, proposed by Thien and Lin (2002).

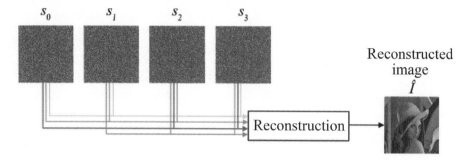

Figure 8.10. *Reconstruction of a secret image*

8.3.2. *Visual cryptography*

The visual security approach proposed by Naor and Shamir (1994) consists of obtaining secret visual content by superimposing two shares. In this method, originally intended for binary (black and white) images, shares are constructed using random binary pixel repetitions, as shown in Figure 8.11.

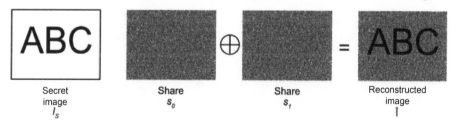

Figure 8.11. *Visual cryptography, where ⊕ corresponds to the XOR binary operator*

Naor and Shamir's method consists of creating two shares (Naor and Shamir 1994). The method preserves the black pixels in the secret image, while leaving the color of the blank pixels random. The secret is then reconstructed by performing the *XOR* operation between the two shares, and the content is uniquely recognizable by the human visual system (HVS). The low complexity of this approach makes it very helpful in cases where a short response time is required. The visual cryptography approach has been studied in considerable detail, notably in terms of varying the different thresholds k and n in order to solve the contrast problem presented by Naor and Shamir (1996). Cimato and Yang (2011) cite three different groups of visual cryptography approaches: XOR-based visual cryptography, random grid visual cryptography and probabilistic visual cryptography. XOR-based visual cryptography corresponds to the approach proposed by Naor and Shamir (1994, 1996). However, XOR-based visual cryptography approaches tend to have a significant drawback in terms of the increase in share size. In order to increase the minimum number of shares required or to generate, each pixel in the secret image will be represented by a block of pixels in each share of size m. Thus, the larger the number of shares to generate or the higher the reconstruction threshold, the larger the size of the shares. Random grids and probabilistic visual cryptography approaches aim to address the shares expansion problem. Kafri and Keren (1987) defined random grids in the form of pixel matrices. Each pixel is either transparent or opaque, and the choice between the two is determined randomly. This has the effect of eliminating the spatial correlation between the pixels. When two or more grids are superimposed, the secret areas appear according to the difference in light transmission of the secret image; thus, the visual secret is recognizable by the HVS. Recently, (Shyu 2013) proposed a generalization of random grid cryptosystem methods for visual secret sharing. Probabilistic visual cryptography addresses the share expansion problems present in the previous methods and provides security for the secret image (Yang *et al.* 2004; Cimato *et al.* 2006). Weir and Yan (2010) developed a comprehensive state of the art of the different visual cryptography techniques in 2010.

8.3.3. *Secret image sharing (polynomial-based)*

In the state of the art, a distinction can be made between visual cryptography methods, where the decoding step is almost instantaneous, and those where reconstruction is more complex. These methods are more costly in terms of time and resources, but provide a better quality reconstruction of the secret image. Furthermore, they are more regularly suitable for use with grayscale or color images than binary images. Thien and Lin (2002) proposed a direct application of Shamir's method to blocks of pixels in a secret image. The method is defined on grayscale (or RGB) images where the pixel value of each color channel varies between 0 and 255. First, in order for the Shamir method to work, a finite field defined by the prime q is used, such that:

$$|\mathbb{F}_q| = q = 251 \tag{8.17}$$

The secret image is then processed so that all of the pixel values fall into the interval between 0 and 250. The value of 251 is assigned to q, as this is the largest prime integer that can be represented by a single byte. Next, instead of using only the a_0 term of equation [8.2], all of the coefficients are used as coefficients of the polynomial to store pixel intensity values. Thus, more or less pixels are used by the polynomial depending on the value of k. The image is then divided into blocks of k pixels that provide the values of the coefficients of the polynomial. The values generated by the polynomials are distributed within each share as pixel values. Share size is therefore divided by $\frac{1}{k}$ with respect to the secret image. This size reduction reduces the storage requirement and enables faster transmission over networks.

8.3.4. *Properties*

Visual secret sharing methods possess a number of interesting properties, in terms of reconstruction quality (Thien and Lin 2002; Yang *et al.* 2007), reduction or expansion of share size (Thien and Lin 2002; Wang and Su 2006), the storage of multiple secret images (Tsai *et al.* 2002; Yan *et al.* 2015), hidden data insertion (Yang *et al.* 2007) or progressive secret reconstruction (Wang and Shyu 2007).

8.3.4.1. *Lossless reconstruction*

The cryptographic methods used in these approaches mean that finite bodies are sometimes required to ensure security. Most methods use a finite body (see equation [8.17]) for grayscale or RGB images. However, the possible values of the pixels in the secret image range between 0 and 255, meaning that information may be lost; the secret image is pre-processed so that the pixel values are between 0 and 250. Most methods involve lossy reconstruction of the secret image (Thien and Lin 2002, 2003; Lin and Tsai 2004; Lin *et al.* 2009; Tsai and Chen 2013). In response to this issue, Yang *et al.* (2007) proposed the use of Galois bodies to avoid truncating pixel values. Galois bodies redefine arithmetic operations so that calculations remain within the body. This notably means, in our context, that non-prime numbers can be used to define them, as long as the selected numbers can be decomposed into primes. Thus, a Galois body can be used for pixel values such that

$$GF(256) = GF(2^8) \tag{8.18}$$

This Galois body is widely used in cryptography and for error codes, as it allows bytes to be manipulated easily.

8.3.4.2. *Reduction or expansion of share size*

Thien and Lin (2002) were the first to propose reducing the size of shares by taking advantage of the form of the chosen polynomials. Using the remaining coefficients of the selected polynomial to generate the pixel value of the shares, pixels are then processed by blocks of k pixels in the secret image. Each block of pixels in the secret image corresponds to a pixel in the shares. The authors were thus able to reduce share size to only $\frac{1}{k}$ of the size of the secret image. More recently, Chen *et al.* (2016) presented findings on share size reduction for other general access structures.

8.3.4.3. *Data hiding*

Since the images shared with users look like white noise, it is easy for a controller to detect suspicious images in a network in the context of covert communication and block their transmission (Kahn 1996). In order to transfer shares over networks in a less suspicious manner, Thien and Lin (2003) took advantage of their share size reduction strategy to hide their shares in host images. These images are known as *meaningful shadows*, where the *shadows* are images, distributed to users, that look like any other image. Many other authors have worked on developing discreet share insertion methods (Lin and Tsai 2004; Yang *et al.* 2004, 2007). The secret image is processed so that all pixel values are between 0 and 250.

8.4. 3D object sharing

The upsurge in applications using 3D data, such as 3D scanning, creation and printing, over the last decade means that 3D objects have become important financial assets for their owners. The intellectual property of creators must be preserved, and the massive use of distributed storage solutions has accentuated the need to protect this content. The principle of secret 3D object sharing is described in section 8.4.1. In section 8.4.2, we present methods for secret 3D object sharing based on binary shares, while in section 8.4.3, we describe secret 3D object sharing methods in which the shares take the form of 3D objects.

8.4.1. *Principle*

Just like secret image sharing, 3D object sharing makes use of known secret sharing methods (Blakley 1979; Shamir 1979). The state of the art on 3D object sharing is still very limited (Elsheh and Hamza 2010, 2011; Anbarasi and Mala 2015; Tsai 2016; Lee *et al.* 2017; Beugnon *et al.* 2019b). Secret sharing methods are mainly used to protect 3D content, but also to reduce the cost of storing and transmitting shares. Another case of use is to simplify the transfer of 3D objects, and in the context of streaming multiple 3D objects (Lee *et al.* 2017). The 3D object sharing methods also have a sharing step and a reconstruction step. However, we can distinguish two main categories of sharing, namely methods not preserving the format of 3D objects and providing binary shares (Elsheh and Hamza 2010, 2011; Anbarasi and Mala 2015) as output, and methods providing 3D objects as shares (Tsai 2016; Lee *et al.* 2017; Beugnon *et al.* 2019b).

8.4.2. *Methods without format preservation*

The first 3D object sharing methods focus on applying secret sharing methods directly to 3D data, for both geometry and connectivity information (Elsheh and Hamza 2010, 2011; Anbarasi and Mala 2015).

8.4.2.1. *Elsheh and Hamza's first method*

Elsheh and Hamza (2010) proposed a first approach to protecting the position of vertices and their connectivity based on Blakley's method (Blakley 1979). The authors proposed a partition with a threshold k equal to 3. The coordinates are directly interpreted as elements of a finite field determined by a prime number q large enough to represent the coordinates. For each vertex, two coefficients a_i and b_i are then randomly generated, where $i \in [\![0 \; ; \; n[\![$ and n is the number of shares to generate. The coefficient c_i is determined using the equation:

$$z = a_i \times x + b_i \times y + c_i \tag{8.19}$$

such that x, y, z are the coordinates of the vertex being shared.

The same process can be carried out for connectivity, with each triangular facet of the 3D mesh being represented by a triplet of vertex indices (v_u, v_w, v_t) such that $u, w, t \in [\![0 \; ; \; V[\![$, where V is the number of vertices.

8.4.2.2. *Elsheh and Hamza's second method*

Elsheh and Hamza then proposed a second approach based on Shamir's method (Shamir 1979), using the same approach that Thien and Lin (2002) applied to 3D images: the method produces shares which are smaller than the secret image (Elsheh and Hamza 2011). As in their first method (Elsheh and Hamza 2010), the authors proposed applying the secret sharing method, with $k = 3$, to the data directly, modifying the finite body using a prime number greater than the number of vertices. The drawback to this method is that the number of vertices in the 3D object is increased to ensure that the vertex indices are valid. Furthermore, as in Thien and Lin's approach (Thien and Lin 2002), the method does not select a block of k pixels, but rather k coordinates or indices. The size of the shares is thus reduced to $\frac{1}{3}$ that of the secret 3D object. Finally, Elsheh and Hamza showed that an additional compression step could be applied to the generated shares, using the entropic compression method introduced by Huffman (1952) or that included in the ZLIB program (Deutsch and Gailly 1996).

8.4.3. *Methods with format preservation*

Tsai (2016) and Lee *et al.* (2017) recently proposed the use of hidden data to replicate the approach proposed by Thien and Lin (2003) by hiding the shares in host images. Contrary to previous methods, the minimum threshold for reconstructing a secret 3D object k is no longer fixed at 3. In order to insert shares into host 3D objects via data hiding techniques, the data to insert must be compressed, and the host objects must be dense enough to offer sufficient capacity. Resampling and surface subdivision methods are used to increase the natural share storage capacity of the host 3D object.

8.4.3.1. *Tsai's method*

In Tsai's method, only the geometry of the secret 3D object is retained; the object is pre-compressed using space division and quantization methods (Tsai 2016). The compressed data are then shared using Shamir's method (Shamir 1979) and inserted into 3D objects using a data hiding technique, which is sufficiently robust to modifications.

8.4.3.2. *Lee* et al.*'s method*

The method developed by Lee *et al.* (2017) does not aim to ensure the security of 3D objects, but to enable more cost-effective transmission in order to display a set of n 3D objects in a 3D streaming context. Their method consists of sharing several 3D objects of low quality, with the aim of displaying the n 3D objects as soon as k shares are downloaded in high quality. Thus, the shares are inserted into the high-quality 3D objects, specifically in the Reed-Solomon (Reed and Solomon 1960) codes, making it possible to reconstruct the whole set of n 3D objects in low quality. The original 3D objects are decimated to a certain level and then compressed using ZLIB (Deutsch and Gailly 1996). The compressed data is then processed and transformed into Reed-Solomon codes (Reed and Solomon 1960), which can be assimilated to shares according to Shamir's method (Shamir 1979).

8.4.3.3. *Beugnon* et al.*'s method*

In 2019, Beugnon *et al.* (2019b) proposed the first selective sharing approach for secret 3D objects which preserves the 3D format. Drawing on their earlier work on selective 3D encryption (Beugnon *et al.* 2018), the authors developed a method that selects a portion of the bits of the floating point representation used to represent the coordinates of vertices according to a degradation level. The latter deduces a sequence of bits to be selected and shared in order to build new 3D objects, called shared 3D objects, which are distributed to each user. These shared 3D objects may be assimilated to low-quality versions of the secret 3D object. This approach preserves the size of the original 3D object within the shared 3D objects, enabling independent reconstruction of the vertices. The authors used both Blakley and Shamir's secret sharing methods (Blakley (1979) and Shamir (1979)), described in their article (Beugnon *et al.* 2019a), in presenting their secret sharing approach. The bits representing the coordinates within the shared 3D objects, which form the output for the method, contain the result of sharing by replacing selected bits with bits extracted from shares generated using sharing methods. The bits selected by the degradation level have an effect on the visual security level of the shared 3D objects, which may be totally confidential or recognizable, but protected against illegal use. Once k shared 3D objects are combined, a high quality, lossless version of the original 3D object can be reconstructed.

Figure 8.12 shows an application of Beugnon *et al.*'s approach (Beugnon *et al.* 2019b) using Shamir's method (Shamir 1979) to a 3D object noted $\mathcal{M}$, representing a shoe (mesh provided by the Stratégies company[1]), with parameters $(k, n) = (3, 4)$ (see Figure 8.12(a)). The 3D objects shown in Figure 8.12(b-e) are the four shared images generated by the sharing process. These 3D objects have the same number of vertices as the original 3D object; their geometry is degraded, but they remain usable within a 3D environment. Figures 8.12(f) and (g) show that identical versions of the original, secret 3D object can be reconstructed from any group of three or more shared 3D objects. Figure 8.12(h) shows a reconstruction created using only two shared 3D objects, rather than three; in this case, the reconstruction is no less degraded than the shared 3D objects.

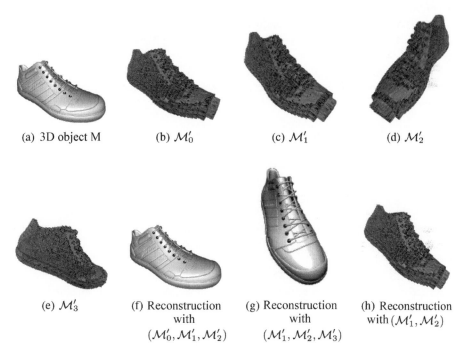

(a) 3D object M   (b) $\mathcal{M}_0'$ (c) $\mathcal{M}_1'$ (d) $\mathcal{M}_2'$

(e) $\mathcal{M}_3'$ (f) Reconstruction   (g) Reconstruction   (h) Reconstruction
                              with   with   with $(\mathcal{M}_1', \mathcal{M}_2')$
                         $(\mathcal{M}_0', \mathcal{M}_1', \mathcal{M}_2')$ $(\mathcal{M}_1', \mathcal{M}_2', \mathcal{M}_3')$

Figure 8.12. *Results of the sharing and reconstruction process for a 3D object $\mathcal{M}$ with parameters $(k, n) = (3, 4)$, using the approach defined by Beugnon et al. (2019b) and Shamir's method (Shamir 1979)*

---

1 Available at: https://www.romans-cad.com/.

8.5. Applications for social media

Social networks are immensely popular, with over two billion active users worldwide. The rapid development of these networks has raised many questions regarding image protection. Notably, multi-party privacy conflicts can arise when a photo is published by its owner. This is because the privacy settings applied to an image are those specified by the owner, and the people in the picture are not involved in the process. For example, say a person, Alice, takes a photo with her group of friends and posts it on her personal page. Her entire network has access to this photo, according to the privacy settings that Alice has defined. Her friends who are present in the photo are not involved in the publication process: they are not consulted and their agreement is not required in order to publish the photo, despite the fact that it contains their personal information. This is a major problem, and effective solutions are needed to manage these multi-party privacy conflicts. In this section, we aim to address this problem by describing a hybrid photo sharing method for social networks (Beugnon *et al.* 2019c).

Consider an image showing a group of n users. First, the regions of interest (ROI) R_j, with $j \in [\![1; n]\!]$, corresponding to each participant are identified using a face detection algorithm. The coordinates of these regions are then used to determine the parts of the image to protect using secret image sharing techniques. Note that the rest of the image, considered as the background, remains in the clear (public content).

Belenkiy's hierarchical secret sharing method, applied to images, is used to protect the n RIs. This approach, based on Tassa's hierarchy (Tassa 2007), is disjunctive and multilevel, as described in section 8.2.2.4. To avoid data loss, secret sharing is carried out in the Galois field $GF(2^8)$, as proposed by Yang *et al.* (2015). An identifier x_j, with $j \in [\![1; n]\!]$, is assigned to the j-th participant, and the value x_0 is assigned to the public server:

$$\begin{cases} x_j \in GF(2^8) \\ x_j \neq 0 \\ \forall j, \ell \in [\![0; n]\!], j \neq \ell \Leftrightarrow x_j \neq x_\ell \end{cases} \qquad [8.20]$$

The n participants define a confidence level within their group, selecting a threshold k such that $1 \leq k \leq n$, indicating the minimum number of users needed to reconstruct all of the RIs, that is, the entire image in the clear domain. Figure 8.13 gives an overview of the encoding phase.

Each RI R_j is shared using $n + 1$ protected RIs R_j^ℓ, with $\ell \in [\![0; n]\!]$. Each share S_ℓ, with $\ell \in [\![0; n]\!]$, is the same size as the original image; S_0 is the public share, consisting of all of the shared pixels (level 2) in the n RIs $\{R_j^0\}_{j \in [\![1;n]\!]}$, along with the pixels in the original image which lie outside of the RI. The other shares $\{S_\ell\}_{\ell \neq 0}$ contain the shared pixels (level 2) in the RI R_j^j corresponding to the user ID x_j, the shared pixels (level $k+1$) in the other $n-1$ RIs $\{R_j^\ell\}_{j \in [\![1;n]\!]}$, $\ell \neq j$, and the background pixels from the original image.

Shares are obtained by treating each RGB component of each RI R_j, with $j \in [\![1;n]\!]$, in isolation. For each component, the pixels coded on 8 bits, read sequentially, are considered as secret values s to share ($s \in GF(2^8)$). To share each secret value s, a sequence of random values $a_0, a_1, \cdot, a_{k-1}$ is generated and a_k takes the value s. These values are then used to define a polynomial of order k:

$$f(x) = \sum_{i=0}^{k} a_i x^i \qquad\qquad [8.21]$$

The shared value corresponding to s in R_j is then calculated in the following way, as a function of the polynomial:

– the hierarchical level for the public share S_0 is assigned a threshold of 2, so that R_j can be reconstructed if the user with ID x_j gives their consent. The shared value is equal to $f^{(k+1-2)}(x_0) = f^{(k-1)}(x_0)$, where $f^{(k-1)}$ is the derivative of order $(k-1)$ of f shares; note that this shared value is also used in the reconstruction of R_j even if the user with ID x_j does not give their consent, as long as at least k users are involved in reconstruction;

– the hierarchical level for a user with ID x_j is also assigned a threshold of 2. Users must be able to reconstruct their own RI easily, using only the public share S_0. The shared value is equal to $f^{(k+1-2)}(x_j) = f^{(k-1)}(x_j)$, where $f^{(k-1)}$ is the derivative of order $(k-1)$ of $f(.)$;

– the hierarchical level for users with ID x_ℓ, with $\ell \neq j$ and $\ell \neq 0$, is assigned a threshold of $k+1$. Thus, each shared value is equal to $f^{(k+1-(k+1))}(x_\ell) = f(x_\ell)$. In this case, k participants must give their consent to permit a full reconstruction of the secret image, using the public share and their own shares.

There are two possible scenarios for the decoding phase, as shown in Figure 8.14. If the number of users k' is below the confidence level determined by the group k, then the k' shares $\{S_\ell\}$, where $\ell \in [\![1;n]\!]$, and the pubic share S_0 are used to reconstruct k' RIs $\{R_j\}$, corresponding to the k' participants in the clear domain. Each secret value s of each R_j can be reconstructed using the Lagrange interpolation method. The user with ID x_j and the public server (ID x_0) have an equation with two unknown coefficients a_{k-1} and $a_k = s$. The value of s can be obtained by solving the linear system formed by these two equations. Note that the $n - k'$ RIs of users not participating in the reconstruction process remain protected.

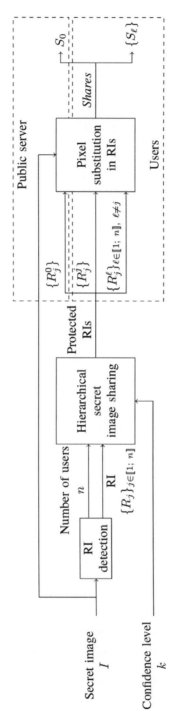

Figure 8.13. *General overview of the encoding phase*

If the number of participants k' is equal to (or greater than) the confidence level k, then the $n - k'$ RIs corresponding to users not involved in the reconstruction are also reconstructed. Each of the $k' \geq k$ participants has an equation with $k + 1$ unknown coefficients $a_0, \ldots, a_k$, where $a_k = s$, enabling them to reconstruct the secret value s. Furthermore, the public server has an equation with two unknown coefficients a_{k-1} and $a_k = s$. This means that the number of equations is sufficient to solve the system, and the value of s_ℓ can be found. The image obtained after reconstructing the n RIs $\{R_j\}$, where $j \in [\![1; n]\!]$, is exactly the same as the original, since enough users have accepted its publication (according to the level of confidence defined by the group).

A full example of the hierarchical secret image sharing method applied to a social network context is shown in Figure 8.15. The chosen parameters are $k = 5$ and $n = 8$. In this case, the RI detection process identified eight users ($n = 8$), and the original image can be reconstructed with the consent of at least five of these users ($k = 5$). Figure 8.15a shows the RIs identified using a face detection algorithm. Following the approach described above, a public share, S_0 share, is published on the social network, as shown in Figure 8.15b. Each user of ID x_j, with $j \in [\![1; n]\!]$, receives their own personal share S_j in which all RIs are protected. Note that by using this share alongside the public share S_0, each user is able to reconstruct their own RI R_j, as shown in Figure 8.15c. This shows the partial reconstruction obtained by combining share S_2, corresponding to the user ID x_2, with the public share S_0. The RI R_2 is thus reconstructed in the clear, while all other RIs remain protected. As long as the number of users involved in the reconstruction k' is below the confidence level k defined by the user group, full reconstruction of the original image is impossible. In Figure 8.15d, $k' = 3$ shares S_1, S_2 and S_4 (corresponding to x_1, x_2 and x_4) are combined, together with the public share S_0. In this case, only the background of the image and RIs R_1, R_2 and R_4, corresponding to the users involved, are clearly visible. The privacy of users who are not involved in this reconstruction is protected, and their faces are not visible. On the other hand, when $k' \geq k$ or more shares are combined, for example when $k' = 5$, as shown in Figure 8.15e, then the original image can be reconstructed in full. The k' shares S_1, S_3, S_5, S_7 and S_8, corresponding to participant IDs x_1, x_3, x_5, x_7 and x_8, are recombined, one by one, with the public share S_0 to reveal the contents of RIs R_1, R_3, R_5, R_7 and R_8. Additionally, the $n - k' = 3$ remaining RIs R_2, R_4 and R_6 are reconstructed using the k' shares and the public share to decode the image, using the hierarchical secret image sharing process. This results in a full and perfect reconstruction of the original image.

Table 8.1 shows the average results obtained for the PSNR, Shannon entropy and SSIM statistical measures, based on the generated shares S_ℓ, for each protected RI R_j^ℓ. We see that the PSNR value is less than 10 dB, the SSIM is close to 0, and the entropy is very close to the maximum value of 8 bits/pixel. These results indicate that the content of the RIs is protected in each share.

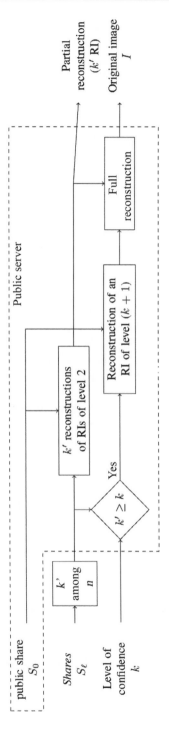

Figure 8.14. *General overview of the decoding phase*

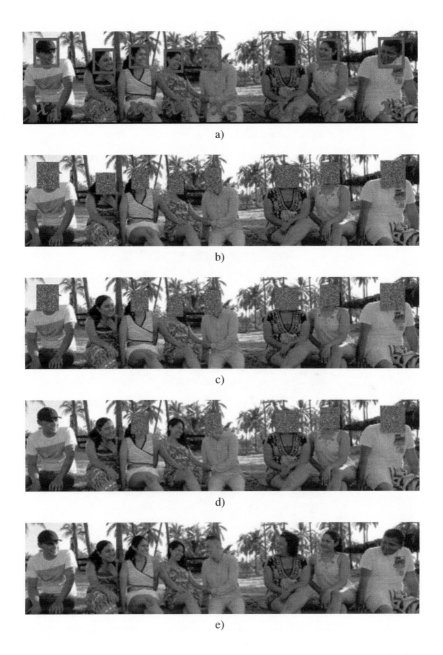

a)

b)

c)

d)

e)

Figure 8.15. *Illustration of the hierarchical secret image sharing method in a social networking context, with parameters k = 5, n = 8*

COMMENT ON FIGURE 8.15.– *(a) original image after detection of the RIs corresponding to the eight users (faces, in red); (b) public share S_0 published on social networks; (c) partial reconstruction of the image using share S_2 corresopnding to user ID x_2 and the public share S_0, (d) partial reconstruction of the image obtained by combining the shares of $k' = 3$ users (S_1, S_2 and S_4, corresponding to x_1, x_2 and x_4) and the public share S_0; (e) perfect reconstruction of the original image, obtained by combining the shares of at least $k' = 5$ users (S_1, S_3, S_5, S_7 and S_8, corresponding to x_1, x_3, x_5, x_7 and x_8) and the public share S_0.*

Figure 8.16 shows the histograms of the pixels in RI R_1 in the original image I and in its protected form R_1^0 within share S_0. The distribution of pixels in the protected RI R_1^0 is almost uniform, indicating that the hierarchical secret image sharing method preserves the visual confidentiality of pixel values in each generated share.

	PSNR (dB)	SSIM	Entropy (bpp)
I	∞	1.0	7.489
R_1^ℓ	7.463	0.0083	7.925
R_2^ℓ	7.569	0.0070	7.945
R_3^ℓ	8.044	0.0076	7.941
R_4^ℓ	8.029	0.0018	7.935
R_5^ℓ	9.445	0.0104	7.944
R_6^ℓ	7.665	0.0073	7.949
R_7^ℓ	8.380	0.0072	7.943
R_8^ℓ	7.956	0.0078	7.956
Mean	8.069	0.0072	7.942

Table 8.1. *Statistical measures obtained from shares S_ℓ for each protected RI (from Figure 8.15)*

The results presented here demonstrate the effectiveness of the hierarchical secret image sharing method in real-life situations and security contexts. This approach can also be extended to more traditional multi-party privacy cases, where all users must give their consent for partial reconstruction. In this case, the confidence level is simply set at $k = n$ during the sharing phase.

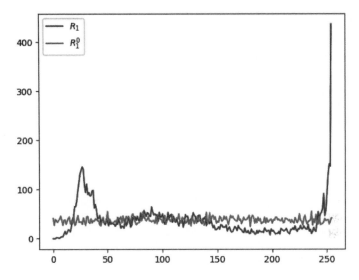

Figure 8.16. *Histogram of pixels in RI R_1*
in the clear domain and of its protected version R_1^0

8.6. Conclusion

In this chapter, we presented and discussed the notion of secret sharing. The concept, developed in the late 1970s by Blakley (1979) and Shamir (1979), has its origins in methods designed for secret cryptographic key management; its scope was extended to new areas of security in the 1990s. In light of developments in encryption techniques, secret sharing methods began to be adapted for multimedia data, notably 2D images, from 1994 (Naor and Shamir 1994). The authors of this paper established a definition of visual secret sharing, considering the secret to be the contents of an image. A new wave of work on protecting and sharing secret images was launched in 2002, with the adaptation of Shamir's method (Shamir 1979) to enable image format preservation (Thien and Lin 2002). Finally, secret sharing began to be adapted for 3D objects in the 2010s (Elsheh and Hamza 2010) to meet the growing security needs resulting from the massive use of distributed storage solutions.

In the approach described in section 8.5, we showed how secret image sharing techniques can be used to manage multi-party privacy conflicts (Beugnon *et al.* 2019c). Using a hierarchical method for sharing secret regions of interest within an image, a photograph representing several people may be disseminated, but without the subjects' identity being revealed without their consent. Individuals are identified using a face detection and recognition algorithm, and users define a trust threshold k, determining the minimum number of users who must provide consent in order for the image to be displayed in full on the social network. If this threshold is not crossed, then only consenting subjects will be shown. Following the detection phase, the method determines specific regions of interest for each identified person; these are then shared using Belenkiy's method, protecting the pixels in question (Belenkiy 2008). Each user receives a share which may be used to reconstruct the region of interest corresponding to their face. Our experimental results highlight the feasibility of this method and its potential for application within a social network context as a tool for managing multi-party privacy conflicts. Note that the regions of interest correspond to a box around the area corresponding to a face. Future developments may focus on only selecting the pixels corresponding to the face of the detected person, or on improving rendering by applying selective encryption at the pixel level in the regions of interest, rather than creating a noise-type effect. Different levels of confidentiality (transparent or sufficient) may thus be applied to different regions of interest, depending on users' needs. Another promising area of investigation is the development of secret image sharing methods that are robust to lossy compression, notably in relation to the JPEG standard (Wallace 1992): most image sharing platforms and social networks now apply JPEG compression to transmitted images.

As we saw in section 8.4, Beugnon *et al.* (2019b) have proposed a selective secret 3D object sharing method, in which each user receives a shared 3D object representing a low-quality version of the secret 3D object, corresponding to a chosen degradation level. This method preserves the input format by using shares which are, themselves, 3D objects, and allows the degradation level to be controlled. A secret sharing method, based on either Blakley (1979) or Shamir (1979), is applied to a sequence of selected bits within the coordinates of the vertices of the secret 3D object. The shared 3D objects generated in this way are then distributed to users. These objects are low-quality versions of the original, created as a function of the desired level of degradation. A high-quality, lossless version of the secret 3D object can be reconstructed when a subset of k out of n users combine their shares. To date, this is the only method that has been developed for selective sharing of secret 3D objects. Further work in this area may concern new functionalities, such as progressive reconstruction, whereby the quality of the reconstruction varies according to the number of contributing users. It may also be interesting to include hierarchical functionalities, establishing different access rights for the 3D objects, so that reconstruction may be carried out more quickly by users with the highest authorization level. In this case, each user would receive a shared 3D object with a particular level in the hierarchy and according to a chosen degradation level. Higher level users could thus reconstruct a better-quality version of the secret 3D object than their counterparts.

8.7. References

Anbarasi, L.J. and Mala, G.A. (2015). Verifiable multi secret sharing scheme for 3D models. *International Arab Journal of Information Technology*, 12(6), 708–713.

Beimel, A. (2011). Secret-sharing schemes: A survey. In *International Conference on Coding and Cryptology*. IWCC, Qingdao.

Belenkiy, M. (2008). Disjunctive multi-level secret sharing. *IACR Cryptology ePrint Archive*, Citeseer, 18, 1–14.

Benaloh, J.C. (1986). Secret sharing homomorphisms: Keeping shares of a secret secret (extended abstract). In *Advances in Cryptology – CRYPTO' 86*, Odlyzko, A.M. (ed.). Springer, Berlin/Heidelberg.

Beugnon, S., Puech, W., Pedeboy, J. (2018). From visual confidentiality to transparent format-compliant selective encryption of 3D objects. In *International Conference on Multimedia & Expo Workshops*. IEEE, San Diego.

Beugnon, S., Puech, W., Pedeboy, J. (2019a). A format-compliant selective secret 3D object sharing scheme based on Shamir's scheme. In *International Conference on Acoustics, Speech and Signal Processing*. IEEE, Brighton.

Beugnon, S., Puech, W., Pedeboy, J.-P. (2019b). Format-compliant selective secret 3D object sharing scheme. *IEEE Transactions on Multimedia*, 21(9), 2171–2183.

Beugnon, S., Puteaux, P., Puech, W. (2019c). Privacy protection for social media based on a hierarchical secret image sharing scheme. In *International Conference on Image Processing*. IEEE, Taipei.

Blakley, G.R. (1979). Safeguarding cryptographic keys. *Proceedings of the National Computer Conference*, 48, 313–317.

Brickell, E.F. (1989). Some ideal secret sharing schemes. In *Advances in Cryptology – EUROCRYPT '89*, Quisquater, J., Vandewalle, J. (eds). Springer, Berlin/Heidelberg.

Brickell, E.F. and Davenport, D.M. (1991). On the classification of ideal secret sharing schemes. *Journal of Cryptology*, 4(2), 123–134.

Brickell, E.F. and Stinson, D.R. (1992). Some improved bounds on the information rate of perfect secret sharing schemes. *Journal of Cryptology*, 5(3), 153–166.

Chen, Y., Chen, L., Shyu, S.J. (2016). Secret image sharing with smaller shadow sizes for general access structures. *Multimedia Tools and Applications*, 75(21), 13913–13929.

Chor, B., Goldwasser, S., Micali, S., Awerbuch, B. (1985). Verifiable secret sharing and achieving simultaneity in the presence of faults (extended abstract). In *26th Annual Symposium on Foundations of Computer Science*. IEEE, Portland.

Cimato, S. and Yang, C.-N. (2011). *Visual Cryptography and Secret Image Sharing*. CRC Press, Boca Raton.

Cimato, S., Prisco, R.D., Santis, A.D. (2006). Probabilistic visual cryptography schemes. *The Computer Journal*, 49(1), 97–107.

Deutsch, P. and Gailly, J.-L. (1996). Zlib compressed data format specification version 3.3. Report, IETF.

Elsheh, E. and Hamza, A.B. (2010). Robust approaches to 3D object secret sharing. *Image Analysis and Recognition*, 326–335.

Elsheh, E. and Hamza, A.B. (2011). Secret sharing approaches for 3D object encryption. *Expert Systems with Applications*, 38(11), 13906–13911.

Farràs, O., Martí-Farré, J., Padró, C. (2012). Ideal multipartite secret sharing schemes. *Journal of Cryptology*, 25(3), 434–463.

Harn, L. and Lin, C. (2009). Detection and identification of cheaters in (t, n) secret sharing scheme. *Designs, Codes and Cryptography*, 52(1), 15–24.

Huffman, D.A. (1952). A method for the construction of minimum-redundancy codes. *Proceedings of the IRE*, 40(9), 1098–1101.

Ito, M., Saito, A., Nishizeki, T. (1989). Secret sharing scheme realizing general access structure. *Electronics and Communications in Japan (Part III: Fundamental Electronic Science)*, 72(9), 56–64.

Kafri, O. and Keren, E. (1987). Encryption of pictures and shapes by random grids. *Optics Letters,*, 12(6), 377–379.

Kahn, D. (1996). *The Codebreakers: The Comprehensive History of Secret Communication from Ancient Times to the Internet*. Simon and Schuster, New York.

Krawczyk, H. (1993). Secret sharing made short. In *Advances in Cryptology – CRYPTO '93*, Stinson, D.R. (ed.). Springer, Berlin/Heidelberg.

Lee, S.-S., Huang, Y.-J., Lin, J.-C. (2017). Protection of 3D models using cross recovery. *Multimedia Tools and Applications*, 76(1), 243–264.

Lin, C. and Tsai, W. (2004). Secret image sharing with steganography and authentication. *Journal of Systems and Software*, 73(3), 405–414.

Lin, C., Harn, L., Ye, D. (2009). Ideal perfect multilevel threshold secret sharing scheme. In *Fifth International Conference on Information Assurance and Security*. IEEE, Xi'an.

Naor, M. and Shamir, A. (1994). Visual cryptography. In *Workshop on the Theory and Application of Cryptographic Techniques*. EUROCRYPT, Pérouse.

Naor, M. and Shamir, A. (1996). Visual cryptography II: Improving the contrast via the cover base. In *International Workshop on Security Protocols*. Springer, Cambridge.

Nojoumian, M. and Stinson, D.R. (2015). Sequential secret sharing as a new hierarchical access structure. *Journal of Internet Services and Information Security*, Innovative Information Science and Technology Research Group, 5(2), 24–32.

Reed, I.S. and Solomon, G. (1960). Polynomial codes over certain finite fields. *Journal of the Society for Industrial and Applied Mathematics*, 8(2), 300–304.

Schoenberg, I.J. (1966). On Hermite-Birkhoff interpolation. *Journal of Mathematical Analysis and Applications*, 16(3), 538–543.

Shamir, A. (1979). How to share a secret. *Communications of the ACM*, 22(11), 612–613.

Shyu, S.J. (2013). Visual cryptograms of random grids for general access structures. *IEEE Transactions on Circuits and Systems for Video Technology*, 23(3), 414–424.

Simmons, G.J. (1988). How to (really) share a secret. In *Advances in Cryptology – CRYPTO' 88*, Goldwasser, S. (ed.). Springer, New York.

Tassa, T. (2004). Hierarchical threshold secret sharing. In *Theory of Cryptography Conference*. TCC, Cambridge.

Tassa, T. (2007). Hierarchical threshold secret sharing. *Journal of Cryptology*, 20(2), 237–264.

Thien, C. and Lin, J. (2002). Secret image sharing. *Computers & Graphics*, 26(5), 765–770.

Thien, C. and Lin, J. (2003). An image-sharing method with user-friendly shadow images. *IEEE Transactions on Circuits and Systems for Video Technology*, 13(12), 1161–1169.

Tsai, Y.-Y. (2016). A secret 3d model sharing scheme with reversible data hiding based on space subdivision. *3D Research*, 7(1), 1.

Tsai, M. and Chen, C. (2013). A study on secret image sharing. In *6th International Workshop on Image Media Quality and its Applications*, IMQA, Tokyo.

Tsai, C., Chang, C., Chen, T. (2002). Sharing multiple secrets in digital images. *Journal of Systems and Software*, 64(2), 163–170.

Wallace, G.K. (1992). The JPEG still picture compression standard. *IEEE Transactions on Consumer Electronics*, 38(1), XVIII–XXXIV.

Wang, R.-Z. and Shyu, S.-J. (2007). Scalable secret image sharing. *Signal Processing: Image Communication*, 22(4), 363–373.

Wang, R.-Z. and Su, C.-H. (2006). Secret image sharing with smaller shadow images. *Pattern Recognition Letters*, 27(6), 551–555.

Weir, J. and Yan, W. (2010). A comprehensive study of visual cryptography. *Transactions on Data Hiding and Multimedia Security*, 5, 70–105.

Yan, X., Wang, S., Niu, X., Yang, C.-N. (2015). Random grid-based visual secret sharing with multiple decryptions. *Journal of Visual Communication and Image Representation*, 26, 94–104.

Yang, C.-C., Chang, T.-Y., Hwang, M.-S. (2004). A (t, n) multi-secret sharing scheme. *Applied Mathematics and Computation*, 151(2), 483–490.

Yang, C.-N., Chen, T.-S., Yu, K.H., Wang, C.-C. (2007). Improvements of image sharing with steganography and authentication. *Journal of Systems and Software*, 80(7), 1070–1076.

Yang, C.-N., Li, P., Wu, C., Cai, S. (2015). Reducing shadow size in essential secret image sharing by conjunctive hierarchical approach. *Signal Processing: Image Communication*, 31, 1–9.

Zhao, J., Zhang, J., Zhao, R. (2007). A practical verifiable multi-secret sharing scheme. *Computer Standards & Interfaces*, 29(1), 138–141.

List of Authors

Gildas AVOINE
INSA Rennes
Univ Rennes
IRISA
CNRS
France

Cyril BERGERON
Thales SIX GTS France
Gennevilliers
France

Sébastien BEUGNON
LIRMM
Université de Montpellier
CNRS
France

Sébastien CANARD
Orange Labs
Applied Crypto Group
Caen
France

Sergiu CARPOV
Inpher
Lausanne
Switzerland

Christophe CHARRIER
GREYC
Normandy University
University of Caen
ENSICAEN
CNRS
France

Olivier DÉFORGES
IETR
INSA Rennes
Univ Rennes
France

Caroline FONTAINE
LMF
ENS Paris-Saclay
University of Paris-Saclay
CNRS
Gif-sur-Yvette
France

Thierry FOURNEL
LaHC
University of Lyon
University of Saint-Étienne
CNRS
France

Petra GOMEZ-KRÄMER
L3i
La Rochelle University
France

Wassim HAMIDOUCHE
IETR
INSA Rennes
Univ Rennes
France

Vincent ITIER
CRIStAL
University of Lille
CNRS
IMT Lille Douai
France

Amine NAIT-ALI
LISSI
University of Paris-Est
Créteil Val de Marne
France

William PUECH
LIRMM
Université de Montpellier
CNRS
France

Pauline PUTEAUX
LIRMM
Université de Montpellier
CNRS
France

Cédric RICHARD
CNRS GdR ISIS
Côte d'Azur Observatory
University of Côte d'Azur
Nice
France

Christophe ROSENBERGER
GREYC
Normandy University
University of Caen
ENSICAEN
CNRS
France

Renaud SIRDEY
CEA, LIST
University of Paris-Saclay
Gif-sur-Yvette
France

Iuliia TKACHENKO
LIRIS
Université Lumière Lyon 2
CNRS
France

Alain TREMEAU
LaHC
University of Lyon
University of Saint-Étienne
CNRS
France

Index

3D object, 259, 276

A, B

attack, 10–12, 14, 15, 22, 47, 50, 52,
   60, 68, 73, 74, 91, 98, 100, 105,
   108, 111, 113, 138, 140, 149, 150,
   155, 165, 177, 190, 191, 259
AVC (Advanced Video Coding), 113,
   130, 131, 137, 141, 143–145
biometrics, 1
   hidden, 12, 13

C

capacity, 3, 12, 24, 50, 66, 68, 71,
   110, 136, 181, 192, 195, 219, 221,
   234, 239, 269, 271
cloud, 23, 24, 91, 113, 114, 196, 197,
   215, 219, 220
code, 33–36, 41, 42, 44, 45, 47, 49,
   50, 71, 92, 108, 235, 275, 278
   bar, 42
      two-level, 44
      watermarked, 47

copy-sensitive graphical code, 33,
   41
copy detection, 35, 42, 43,
compression, 12, 66, 68, 73, 74, 91, 92,
   94, 105–108, 110, 114–116, 123,
   129, 130, 134, 135, 201, 202, 216
computation techniques using
   encrypted data, 196
confidentiality, 92, 99, 113, 114, 129,
   165, 173, 178, 193, 200, 215, 220
convolutional neural networks, 50,
   78, 80
counterfeit, 11, 31, 50, 52
crypto-compression, 91, 106–108,
   110, 113, 114, 116, 123, 129
cryptography, 91, 96, 98, 129, 131,
   176, 178, 216, 272, 273
   visual, 216, 272–274

D

data aging, 24
DCT (discrete cosine transform), 43,
   93, 95, 106, 109, 113, 121, 135,
   202

Printed and bound by CPI Group (UK) Ltd, Croydon, CR0 4YY

28/10/2024

14581339-0001